PSYCHOLOGY,

OR,

ELEMENTS

OF A

NEW SYSTEM OF MENTAL PHILOSOPHY,

ON THE BASIS OF

CONSCIOUSNESS AND COMMON SENSE.

DESIGNED FOR COLLEGES AND ACADEMIES.

BY S. S. SCHMUCKER, D.D.,

PROFESSOR OF CHRISTIAN THEOLOGY IN THE THEOLOGICAL SEMINARY, GETTYSBURG.

SECOND EDITION, MUCH ENLARGED.

NEW YORK:
HARPER & BROTHERS, PUBLISHERS,
329 & 331 PEARL STREET,
FRANKLIN SQUARE.
1855.

PREFACE.

As the following publication proposes a system of mental philosophy in some degree new, a few words in regard to its origin may be due alike to the writer and the reader. In general, it owes its existence to the author's desire to promote the cause of truth and science. That cause he regards as identified with the happiness of his fellow-men and the glory of his God. At an early age, he was deeply impressed with the conviction, which no reflecting mind can fail to feel, that mental philosophy is properly the basis of all science, and that a correct acquaintance with the properties and operations of the mind, would not only facilitate our progress in the study of every department of truth, but, what to him was a matter of supreme importance, would also enable us to acquire a more correct view of the moral condition of the soul, and shed abundant light on some of the practical doctrines of Revelation. This latter consideration is mentioned here, because it was really the writer's principal motive for pursuing this subject, although he has by no means mingled religion with metaphysics in the following treatise; on the contrary, his investigations of the one were conducted altogether independently of the other. About sixteen years ago, having been called to take charge of a theological seminary, he felt it a duty to devote particular attention to his instructions in this department, and formed a resolution, which has doubtless had some influence on this system. He had considerable acquaintance with the patriarchs of British metaphysics, Locke, Reid, Stewart, and Brown, as well as with some few German authors; but neither of them seemed to present an entirely natural and satisfactory exhibition of his own mental phenomena. He then resolved to study exclusively his own mind, and for ten years he read no book on this subject. During this period, he spent much of his time in the examination of his own mental phenomena, and having travelled over the whole ground, and employed the leisure of several additional years to review and mature his views, he now presents to the public the following outline of a system, as in all its parts the result of original, analytic induction. That he regards it as a more natural, faithful, and intelligible exhibition of the operations of his own mind than is contained in any other work which he has seen, he will not dissemble. Since the features of his own system have been settled, the writer has looked at various other works, and found much that is valuable, especially in the recent publications of his own countrymen, Professors Upham, Day, Tappan, and others, yet nothing which seemed to invalidate his system, or render dubious the propriety of its publication.

As this work is designed, not only for intelligent popular readers, but also for use in colleges and academies, the author has abridged his manuscript, and made it sufficiently brief to leave ample room for the explanatory observations of the professors and teachers, as well as written exercises of the students. For an experience of more than twenty years in teaching has convinced him, that the most successful method of imparting a thorough knowledge of such subjects, is to combine with a brief text-book the explanations and illustrations of the instructer, and, at the same time, to require the student to exercise his pen in preparing either essays on the most prominent topics, or an analysis, or a regular compend of the whole.

After frequent solicitation from those who heard the author's lectures, and from some other gentlemen of high literary and scientific rank who examined the manuscript, this work is at length submitted to the public, with an earnest solicitude that it may subserve the cause of truth and human happiness. The author does not flatter himself that his views on all the topics discussed, have reached entire accuracy; he will thankfully receive and carefully weigh any suggestions which may be made, especially if presented in the spirit of benevolence or of literary comity. If the map of the human mind here presented is found to be more faithful and intelligible than those heretofore in use, if it tends to make perspicuous a subject hitherto proverbially abstruse and obscure, it will doubtless find friends, and the author will rejoice in the assurance that he has not toiled in vain. Of the salutary influence of the principles and results attained, on the grand interests of fundamental Christianity, he entertains no doubt.

The influence of the views here presented on logic, rhetoric, and a number of related sciences and topics, will be evident to the scientific scholar. Perhaps at a future day some of these relations may be prosecuted by the author, if his health and numerous other duties will permit. With these remarks the work is now commended to the blessing of God, and the favour of the friends of true philosophy and religion.

S. S. Schmucker.

Theological Seminary,
Gettysburg, Pennsylvania.

SECOND EDITION.

In preparing for the press this enlarged edition of his Mental Philosophy, the author faithfully availed himself of the suggestions of the principal reviews of the work which have met his eye. Among these, that in the American Biblical Repository, by the distinguished President of Pennsylvania College, exhibited the greatest familiarity with the subject and with the work, and presented the most numerous suggestions for its enlargement. To that gentleman, as well as to the reviewers in the Methodist Quarterly Review, and the New World, and others, the author takes pleasure thus publicly to acknowledge his obligations. In all cases he has carefully weighed their suggestions, and, in most instances, been led to make some farther illustrations or additions, which, he trusts, will contribute to the value of the work. He has been happy to find in these writers but little dissent from his general system. The principal topics on which he has made additions, amounting in all to about one third of the whole work, are the following: the classification of the different objects or entities in the universe ; the subject of mnemonics, or the art of improving and aiding the memory ; the processes of perception and sensation through the bodily organs, and the different theories for their explanation ; the different classes of feeling, especially the intellectual and moral emotions ; the nature of analytic reasoning, and laws of human belief ; imagination ; and the operations of conscience.

The work is again commended to the blessing of God and the favour of the public.

May, 1843.

CONTENTS.

INTRODUCTION.

PART I.

COGNITIVE IDEAS.

CHAPTER I.

CHAPTER II.

CHAPTER III.

PART II.

OF SENTIENT IDEAS.

CHAPTER I.

CHAPTER II.

CHAPTER III.

PART III.

ACTIVE OPERATIONS.

CHAPTER I.

INTELLECTUAL PHILOSOPHY

INTRODUCTION.

It has long been a subject of remark, that while the science of mathematics, which discusses the properties and relations of space and number, is accompanied by the most conclusive evidence, and bears conviction with it at every step of its progress, the philosophy of the mind still remains enveloped in comparative darkness and uncertainty, after the intellect of ages has been expended in its investigation. The question arises, Are not both similar in their nature, and alike susceptible of demonstrative discussion? It seems evident, that they are not precisely alike, and yet much of the obscurity enveloping mental science, doubtless arises from the unphilosophical manner, in which its investigations have been conducted, and the inappropriate style in which the result of them has generally been recorded. The superior force of mathematical reasoning, arises from three sources. *First*, from an intrinsic difference in the nature of the subjects discussed. *Secondly*, from the more rigidly analytic method of investigation, pursued in the mathematics. And, *thirdly*, from a less elegant, indeed, but more precise and perspicuous method of conveying to others the knowledge we have acquired.

B

A distinguished and popular writer* of the present day, alleges the difficulty of ascertaining with precision the operations of other minds, as a prominent cause of the uncertainty of mental science. But this appears to us to be an erroneous view. All minds are, in healthy subjects, constituted essentially alike; and as every student of this science has access to the phenomena of his own mind, he can draw from this source abundant materials for the examination of any and of every aspect of the subject. We have, moreover, the candid testimony of a multitude of writers on these topics, each presenting the details of his own mind; so that this science need not labour under obscurity for want of the experience of different and independent witnesses. The testimony of consciousness in regard to our individual mental operations separately considered, seems also to be distinct and satisfactory. And the testimony of others concerning the clearness of their consciousness, coincides with our own experience. But when we attempt to trace the unknown cause of these operations which lies behind them; or to determine and systematize their relations to each other, which are often diversified and obscure, we encounter difficulties on every side. And these difficulties encumber the investigation of our own mental phenomena, as well as those of others.

It is indeed true, that in morbid mental action, the operations of different minds are very diverse, and the careful collation of these diversified phases

* Dr. Abercrombie on the Intellectual Powers, p. 15, 16, Harpers' ed.

of mental obliquity, is interesting to the student of mental science and essential to the physician; but the true intellectual system must be deduced from the phenomena of mind in its ordinary, its healthy condition. We return therefore to the position, that the causes of superior lucidness awarded to mathematical science are chiefly three.

The first of these causes, namely the intrinsic difference between the subjects discussed in these sciences, is derived from the Author of our being. We are so constituted that the properties and especially the relations of space and number, are more clearly apprehended by us than those of mind. Yet this difference is not so great as might, at first view, be supposed. Much of it arises from the fact, that from our earliest years we are engaged every hour in perceiving and judging of space and number, while the phenomena of the mind are seldom thought of until we reach the years of maturity, and then generally at short periods as subjects of theoretical study. Our perceptions of the former are therefore improved in an incalculably higher degree than our views of the latter.

The second source of superior clearness has been stated to be a more rigidly analytic method of investigation. This has led to greater improvements in these sciences, and hence the evidence attending their discussion is also greater. The fact that a better method of philosophizing has usually been pursued in the mathematical sciences is not altogether adventitious. We believe it to be chiefly owing to the peculiar nature of the properties and relations of space and number, and to the fixed and simple nature of mathematical language, which consists chiefly of a few figures and signs, and a small number of well-defined words, while it wholly rejects the flowers of rhetoric.

The same method of inductive investigation is the only one, by which real progress can be made in mental science, or in any other department of human knowledge. It will appear more clearly in the sequel, that all those of our ideas which are *knowledge*, are mental representatives of entities; i. e., of things, and their relations, existing in nature; and can be obtained, originally, in no other way than by the careful examination of entities themselves. Hence, however knowledge already acquired may afterward be combined and arranged, the only accurate method of obtaining its original elements is by patient successive examinations of those entities of which we wish to obtain a knowledge. After such a careful examination of all the facts in the case has been made, and we have thus obtained accurate mental representatives of them all; then, and not until then, can we with certainty decide, whether or not any supposed property or law belongs to them all. That method of philosophizing, therefore, which affirms a general law after the examination of a few facts, must forever be insecure, and tend to obstruct the progress of any science.

The third source of the superior lucidness of mathematical discussions, is the simple, literal, concise style, in which they are recorded for the instruction of others, and the specific numeric notation of every item of knowledge obtained. It will hereafter appear more clearly, we trust, that one of the most prolific sources of error in human knowledge, is the use of language which does not express our ideas with entire, specific exactness. But mathematical language, consisting of a few figures, letters, and signs, and a small stock of well-defined words, the same idea is almost universally designated by one and the same term. No attempt is made to avoid the repetition of the same word in the same sentence, however often the same idea may recur; and the man would expose himself to ridicule, who should attempt to imbody the demonstrations of Euclid in profuse and florid language. Hence arises a degree of perspicuity of style never attained and rarely aimed at in the discussions of any other science. Nor is the precise separation of each item of knowledge from every other, and its numerical notation unimportant. It enables the reader to know exactly how far an author has succeeded in establishing the positions assumed, and of which of them the evidence is inconclusive. Thus, those positions, the demonstration of which appears conclusive to all, become a common stock of knowledge. On these others can build, assuming them as correct, and can then direct their attention to positions yet doubtful.

The same inflexible precision of style and the distinct separation of the items of our knowledge would doubtless tend in a high degree to advance the science of mental philosophy; and ought, so far as the different nature of the subjects will admit, certainly to be introduced. Yet, if even equal precision could be attained, the style of discussion in Mental Philosophy would still be far more copious and diversified, because the subjects of which it treats are incalculably more numerous and difficult.

The question here arises, What is the exact nature of the demonstration and proof in mathematics, and what in mental science? If a writer wishes to produce conviction, which of his ideas relating to the subject under discussion, should he exhibit to his readers in the language just recommended, and what active operation of mind must he perform?—Geometry discusses the properties and relations of space. Demonstration in this science sometimes consists in bringing the several diagrams or figures, between which any relation is affirmed, or in supposing them to be brought into such local contiguity as will enable the eye to perceive the relation at a glance. Such is the nature, e. g., of the demonstration of the theorem of Euclid known as Prop. IV. of Book I., viz.: If two triangles have two sides, and the included angle of the one equal to two sides and the included angle of the other, they must be identical or equal in all respects. For it virtually consists in supposing one of the two figures to be placed upon the other, and then conducting the eye through the successive survey of its several parts; and it is found that in this survey the mind intuitively perceives the coincidence of each. Sometimes the demonstration consists in reducing the diagram into such other elementary figures by additional lines, &c., as are intuitively discovered by the eye to possess the property in question, and which exemplify some of those self-evident cases termed axioms. Axioms in Geometry consist of generic affirmations of certain facts or properties of space which are intuitively perceived to be true in individual and specific familiar cases. E. g., the axiom—things equal to the same thing are equal to one another—is first learned from the observations of early life. We perceive in the familiar objects around us which we touch, see, and handle, that if any two of them are equal or like to a third, they are also, in the same respects, like each other. The observation is extended from one case to another, until, finding no exceptions to it, we set it down as a universal maxim, and confidently employ it as one of the instruments of reasoning. This is the case with other axioms. In arithmetic the same observation is intuitively made in reference to small numbers, and gradually extended to large ones, in regard to which the mind could not intuitively see its truth, but, after the preliminary process, confidently and safely assumes it.

When small numbers are added together, the mind can intuitively perceive the truth of the sum total. Thus, that $2+3=5$, every one can perceive to be true. But when large numbers, extending to many figures, are added, the mind cannot see the truth of the sum total by comparing the entire numbers. We are certain of its accuracy only by successively going through the addition of each figure, and knowing that this operation has been accurately performed. So, also, when the multiplica tion or division of small numbers is performed, the mind intuitively perceives the accuracy of the operation; but in large numbers our perception is indistinct. Our confidence in these cases rests on our assurance of the accuracy of the rule or mode of operation, which assurance is acquired in the case of small numbers. The same is the case with the arithmetical proportions, *e. gr.*, 1 : 3 : : 2 : 6, &c.

The ocess of reasoning in mental science is entirely different. The items of proof and the subjects of discussion are all mental phenomena, of which each individual must judge for himself by the testimony of his own consciousness. The art of understanding the subject well, and of writing upon it lucidly and conclusively, consists in the habit of carefully studying the operations of our own minds, and of clothing the result of our observations in such perspicuous and appropriate language, as will most successfully conduct our readers or hearers through the same process on the points in question. Discussions on this subject are successful in producing conviction, just in proportion as they enable the reader to verify the writer's assertions in his own mind. The reader's own consciousness must respond at every step to the truth of the positions advanced; and conviction terminates, as soon as the response is doubtful, or the reader cannot perceive, in the operations of his own mind, the truth of the author's assertions.

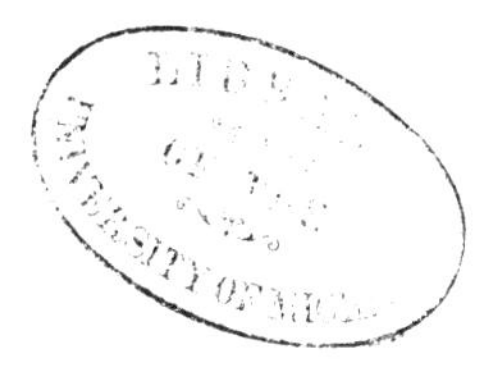

THE SUBJECT MATTER AND DIVISIONS

OF

MENTAL PHILOSOPHY.

Mental Philosophy may be defined to be that science which discusses the properties and operations of the human soul. Other objects, that is, entities, in the universe, are also the subject of investigation; but only in as far as their influence on the phenomena of mind is concerned. Thus, in treating of some of our ideas, we find them to be mental representatives of external objects around us, and we are necessarily led to examine those objects or entities, to ascertain what we may and do know of them, and what is the process by which, through the bodily organs, we obtain this knowledge.

This science was formerly termed *Metaphysics*, a term barbarously derived from the Greek, in which its appropriate primitive metaphusikē (μεταφυσικος, -η, -ον) is not found. It is supposed to have originated from the misapprehension of the inscription on a work, consisting of fourteen books, concerning which it is doubtful whether, at least in their present form, they belong to the productions of Aristotle, among which they are found. It is an ancient, though not perfectly substantiated opinion, that Andronicus of Rhodes, who arranged the works of Aristotle into classes, after he had thus assorted the books on logic, ethics, and physics, placed together several disconnected tracts on different subjects, and endorsed them "meta ta physica" (to be placed or read, *after the works on physics*). Subsequently the discussions contained in those books, were united into a science, which from the above inscription was termed Metaphysics; because it succeeded, or because it went beyond physics.

The term *Anthropology* is used especially in Germany, to designate that science, which discusses the nature of man, as consisting of a body and mind, and especially the influence of the former on the latter. It is sometimes divided into Somatology and Psychology, the former embracing all those bodily peculiarities and circumstances, which are supposed by some writers to exert an influence on the mind. In this department much that is fanciful and ridiculous has been written.

By Psychology is meant everything, that appropriately belongs to the discussion of the nature, structure, and operations of the mind, exclusive of Logic, which is a more extended exhibition of the laws of the mind in one branch of psychology, namely, the *process of reasoning*. It is this latter science which we propose to discuss on the present occasion.

An important preliminary question here arises, What are the proper materials which ought to be embraced in this science? These we maintain are, not so much the supposed faculties, of which we know nothing directly, but the known phenomena of the mind, and all those other known entities or existences, which exert an influence upon these phenomena, or are concerned in their production. The proper basis for a division of mental phenomena is another important aspect of our subject. We suppose it evident that any correct classification of mental operations, must be based on those phenomena of mind, which are known to us, and not on unknown and supposed faculties or essence of the mind. The divisions adopted in the various systems extant are numerous. The first and most generally received in the English philosophical world, is that into about *nine faculties of the mind*. This division was in the main adopted by Dr. Reid, Mr. Stewart, and the other principal metaphysicians in England and America, until the recent introduction of Dr. Brown's system, which has gained many admirers.

We shal' first specify some of these divisions and definitions which have heretofore been received. The mind has usually been divided into the following faculties:

1. The faculty of *perception*, which is regarded as that inherent part of the original constitution of the soul of man, by which he obtains knowledge of external objects, through the instrumentality of his bodily organs.

2. The faculty of *consciousness* is that power of the soul of man by which, according to Dr. Reid, he has "immediate knowledge of all his present thoughts, and purposes, and, in general, of all the present operations of his mind."

3. The faculty of *conception* is that power of the soul of man by which he has knowledge of things not perceived through the instrumentality of his senses; or, according to Stewart, it is "that power which enables the mind to form a notion of an absent object of perception, or of a sensation which it has formerly felt."

4. The faculty of *judgment* is that inherent power of the soul by which we decide that any proposition is true or not true. It is also termed the faculty of *understanding*.

5. *Memory* is that faculty of the soul by which we have a present knowledge of our past mental operations.

6. By the faculty of *reasoning* is commonly meant that inherent power of the soul by which we infer conclusions from premises. "Reasoning," says Dr. Reid, "is the process by which we pass from one judgment to another, which is the consequence of it. In all reasoning, therefore, there must be a proposition inferred, and one or more from which it is inferred."

7. The faculty of *conscience* has by some been considered as that power of the soul, by which we experience either remorse or self-approbation on a review of our conduct; while others regard it "as that internal sense which decides upon the moral character of actions."

8. The faculty of *feeling* is that power of the soul, by which we experience sensations or feelings and emotions.

9. The faculty of *volition* is that power of the

soul by which we choose, determine, resolve, purpose, or will to perform or not to perform any contemplated action, of which we judge ourselves capable.

The general division of these powers adopted by Dr. Reid was into two general classes, viz.: First. INTELLECTUAL POWERS. Secondly. ACTIVE POWERS.

By *intellectual powers* he means those powers by which we perceive objects and conceive of them; and remember, analyze, or combine them, and judge or reason concerning them.

By *active powers* he understands all those powers of the soul which lead to action, or influence the mind to act, such as appetites, passions, affections, &c.

Mr. Stewart, the successor and commentator of Dr. Reid, divides the powers of the mind into three classes. First. *Intellectual.* Secondly. *Active* or *Moral.* And, thirdly, *Social Powers;* which latter belong to man as a member of political society.

The last division, which has obtained much currency in the English philosophical world, is that of Dr. Brown, who divides the powers of the soul into *two classes,* and designates them by the terms EXTERNAL and INTERNAL *affections* or *states of the mind.* This division appears to bear a distinct affinity to the old classification into *sensations* and *reflections,* although Dr. Brown expends not a little labour in refuting that ancient division. The EXTERNAL AFFECTIONS Dr. Brown has subdivided according to the organs of sense which are employed in their production, viz., *Smell*, *Taste*, *Hearing*, *Touch*, and *Sight*. These he denominates the more definite external affections, while he makes another class of a less definite character to embrace hunger and muscular pleasures and pains. The INTERNAL AFFECTIONS he subdivides into two orders. Order I. embraces the *intellectual affections*. Order II., the *emotions*.

Order I. embraces, First. *Simple suggestion*. Secondly. *Relative suggestion*, or feelings of relations. Order II. he divides into, First. *Immediate*. Secondly. *Retrospective*. And, thirdly, *Prospective Emotions*.

In Germany, a different division of the powers or faculties of the mind has, for some time past, been adopted by many writers on psychology. "The greater part of psychologists," says Professor Fischhaber, "have arrived at the conclusion, that the soul of man possesses three principal powers or faculties, viz., the power of sensibility (Gefühlsvermögen), the understanding or intellect including the various operations of what are termed the intellectual powers (Vorstellungsvermögen), and the will (Begehrungs or Willensvermögen)." This division, which is in many respects a very good one, has been substantially adopted by that excellent writer of our own country, Professor Upham, if we may judge from a brief notice of his recent work which we have seen. He, however, very properly changes the order of these faculties, placing the intellect first, which some of the Germans had assigned to the middle; and by the introduction of

Dr. Brown's system of suggestions, and of his own numerous investigations on other important aspects of the subject, he has doubtless prepared a work of high and lasting merit.

After mature deliberation, we are unable to adopt either of these divisions, although each of them contains much that is true and useful; but we propose another which appears to us more simple, more natural, more clear and intelligible, and more accurately conformed to the known phenomena of mind. This is a threefold division, into

I. Cognitive ideas.

II. Sentient ideas.

III. Active operations.

When we strictly contemplate the phenomena of mind, apart from the powers from which they result, we perceive no other differences of a *generic* character between the intrinsic nature of our ideas themselves, than a threefold one. They are all, in their own nature, either *knowledge*, or they are *feeling*, or they are *action*. Let the reader verify the truth of this assertion by an examination of his own mental phenomena, and he will be the better qualified to judge of its accuracy, and to enter into the subsequent discussions. Let him take any one within the wide range of his thoughts, and upon examination it will be found that it is in its nature either *knowledge* of something in the external universe or in the regions of mind, or it is a *feeling* pleasant or painful, or it is an *active process* of some kind or other, in which his mind was engaged.

Thus, when we examine the ideas designated by the terms tree, stone, horse, water, air, electric fluid, mind, deity, &c., we find them to be our *knowledge* of certain objects in creation, whose existence we believe, because we have, in various ways, ascertained some properties of each. Other terms, such as joy, contentment, hope, sorrow, love, friendship, gratitude, hatred, anger, condolence, pity, envy, jealousy, &c., all express, not knowledge, but *feeling* ; that is, a certain *sentient* state of the mind, either pleasant or painful, terminating either on ourselves or on others. While a third class of terms, such as, to examine, to inspect, to arrange, to classify, to speak, to walk, all imply *activity*, and, indeed, are most prominently distinguished from the other by the circumstance of their being in their own nature different species of activity. The only method by which each individual can acquire a correct idea of the difference between these three kinds of ideas or mental phenomena, is by examining the testimony of his own consciousness. These ideas, whether cognitive, sentient, or active, are in their elements simple ideas, and no definition can explain them without the testimony of consciousness.

This triple division is marked out by criteria, which we shall more fully discuss when we enter upon the separate consideration of each individual class of our ideas, when we think it will be clearly seen that all our ideas are resolvable into these three classes, either as leading ideas, or appendages of such as are.

This system differs from the one last mentioned in its essential features.

(*a.*) They differ in the principle on which they are constructed, the former being a division of the supposed faculties or powers of the mind, of which we have no immediate knowledge; while the one we propose is strictly a division of the *operations* of the mind, actually and immediately known to us by consciousness. As we know nothing certainly of the mind except its operations, it seems to be more philosophic and safe to base our divisions on these operations, and in a great measure limit our discussions to them.

This feature of diversity is applicable only in part to the excellent work of Professor Upham, who carefully distinguishes between the faculties of the mind and its operations, or, as he terms them, *states;* yet even he, in his general nomenclature, divides his subject into the states referring to the Intellect, the Sensibilities, and the Will, by which latter terms we understand him to mean not operations of the mind, but powers or faculties. He is thus led, like his predecessors, to class together, under one head, operations which are generally different in themselves, namely, such as are cognitive, with some which are sentient, and others that are active.

(*b.*) These systems differ in the lines of division actually adopted by them, and in the operations of mind severally assigned to each. The first division of the former system embraces all the operations both of our first and third divisions, excepting only a subdivision of our third, namely, the voluntary mode in which our active operations sometimes occur; and that which forms but a subdivision of our third division, constitutes the whole of it in the other system.

(*c.*) It will also be found, upon examination of the contents of their different parts, that the two systems diverge materially from each other.

Our view of the entire mass of the active operations of the mind, as resolvable into five generic active processes, is, if we mistake not, new; nothing resembling it being found, as far as we know, in any other work. In our representation of the will, and its relation to the activity of the soul, and also in regard to the spontaneous portion of our mental activity, our investigations conducted us to some peculiar results. But we prefer to let the learned reader, who is familiar with other systems, judge for himself how far ours differs from those that have preceded it, and what may be its value, either as a whole or in its particular parts. In pursuing our investigations, we have been anxious that they might conduct us along the paths of truth, regardless of the question whether we agreed with our predecessors, or differed from them.

ON THE EXTENT OF THE SEVERAL PARTS OF THIS THREEFOLD DIVISION.

I. *The extent of the* COGNITIVE CLASS OF IDEAS.

This class, we suppose, embraces,

First. What are termed *Perceptions*, which are, by the definition itself, evidently " knowledge of external objects obtained through the instrumentality of our bodily organs."

Secondly. Our acts of *Consciousness.* According to the old definition of consciousness, as being our knowledge of all our present mental operations, the very existence of this operation has been denied, and not without at least partial grounds. May not the whole difficulty of writers on this subject have arisen from their not observing the grand threefold division of all our mental operations on which our system is founded ? Of the first class of our ideas, viz., the *cognitive* class, it may justly be said that they could scarcely be considered as knowledge at all, if we did not know them at the very moment in which they are attained. As to the second class, that of our *feelings*, the case is somewhat diverse. Yet certainly we have a knowledge of them, that is, are conscious of them, and can distinguish our knowledge of the feeling from the feeling itself, the very moment after it occurs. In reference to the third class, it seems, at all times, a matter of great facility, to discriminate between an active operation, which we are performing, and our knowledge of the fact, that we are, at present, engaged in it, and of the nature of the operation itself. It is by consciousness that we have a knowledge of all the operations of our mind. It is, therefore, an extensive source, or rather department, of our knowledge. It embraces our knowledge of all the so-called internal states of the mind.

Thirdly. Our *conceptions* also manifestly belong to the cognitive class of ideas. It cannot fail to be perceived, that every conception which we have, is a conception of something, is knowledge. It has indeed been maintained, that our conceptions are "knowledge, not obtained through our bodily organs." This, so far as their original elements are concerned, we are compelled to regard as erroneous. Our system leads us to a different opinion; yet, as this subject will meet us at a future stage of our discussions, we shall not now enter on it. Conceptions are evidently knowledge of relations, abstract truths, &c., and thus belong to the cognitive class of our ideas. Thus our idea of virtue is termed a conception; and when carefully analyzed, we find it to be a cognitive idea of the relation of agreement, between certain actions and the law of God, or standard of right. Again, we are said to "conceive" the meaning of general propositions. Our idea of the proposition: virtue is productive of happiness, is termed a conception. When examined, this idea is a *cognition* of the fact learned by experience or observation, that actions of a given kind are productive of happiness. The cases in which this truth is witnessed, are all individual, but by a mental process of frequent occurrence, hereafter to be explained, which we term Modification, we omit the individual actions, or subjects of the proposition, and employ the general term, virtue, embracing them all. Of this general term virtue we affirm the predicate of the proposition, affirm the relation of causation, our idea of which is cognitive, and was learned from individual cases.

Fourthly. It embraces our *judgments:* for what are they but a knowledge of the relations between propositions?

Fifthly. It embraces our *recollections.* These are nothing else than retrospective knowledge, as will easily be perceived by all.

Sixthly. It embraces the results of reasoning, such as belief, &c. The process of reasoning is itself an active operation, and belongs to our third class; but the result of the process is a distinct thing. It is conviction of the truth or falsity of some alleged truth, it is belief. This belief, or conviction, is evidently cognitive, it forms an item in our stock of knowledge.

Seventhly. It embraces the dictates or decisions of conscience, which are nothing else than the results of our judgment concerning the propriety or impropriety of our own conduct. As acts, or rather the results of judgment, are evidently cognitive, the dictates of conscience are in part also of the same nature. Yet there is also obviously something active about the dictates of conscience. They contain not only a cognition of duty, but also an impulse to obey it. This impulse is active, and will be discussed in the third general division of our subject, when we treat of our first Constitutional Inclination.

II. *On the extent of* SENTIENT IDEAS.

Some objection might, at first view, be made to the use of the term ideas, as expressive of this second class of mental phenomena, our feelings. We therefore request the reader to recollect that, throughout this work, we employ the word *idea*, not in its ancient Platonic sense, to signify the supposed external and immaterial forms of things ; nor with the Peripatetics, to designate certain forms, phantasms, or sensible species emanating from all external things, and serving as the object of perception to the mind; but we use it in its *popular* sense, sanctioned by the usage of the present age, to signify any and every mental operation or phenomenon of which we are capable, and purely and exclusively the *mental* act. "In popular use," says the distinguished American lexicographer Webster, "*idea* signifies notion, conception, thought, opinion, and even purpose or intention." In like manner, when, in the sequel, we speak of the mind's reflecting on any particular idea, we again disclaim the belief of any images or species of objects, and mean simply the past operations of the mind itself.

This class embraces what are usually termed, first, *Sensations;* secondly, *Emotions;* thirdly, *Affections;* fourthly, *Passions*, to a certain extent.

Sensations have been regarded as the feelings which are connected with the perceptions of external objects. They are simply pleasant or painful, and evidently they are sentient in their nature. The term sensation, in our language, as well as the corresponding word, *sensus*, of the Romans, and *αἴσθημα* of the Greeks, is used with considerable latitude, as designating both the cognitive and sentient result of the action of our bodily organs ; that is, as indicating both the perception of external objects obtained through the senses, and the feelings attending them. In the classification here proposed, we employ the term in the latter, which must doubtless be admitted to be its most appropriate signification. The perceptions of external objects obtained through this source, are discussed in the cognitive department of our work, because they are obviously knowledge. Sensations have also sometimes been defined "as states of mind immediately successive to a change in some organ of sense, or, at least, to a bodily change of some kind ;" but this definition is also applicable to perceptions.

By *Emotions* are indicated feelings consequent on other mental operations than present perceptions of external objects ; yet this distinction is not uniformly observed by the best writers. On the contrary, the term emotion is often used for a complex operation of the mind, in which, though feeling of a particular species preponderates, a cognitive element is also clearly included, as will, we think, appear when the emotions are particularly discussed. Emotions may justly be considered as subsequent to our intellections, and prior to the desires and other active processes connected with them, or with the intellections to which they succeed.

Affections is a term applied to emotions of a pleasant character.

Passions also are regarded as emotions, but of a painful kind. Yet as all emotions are feelings of some kind or other, it is evident that they all belong to the second class of ideas according to our division, except in as far as passions fall within the department of our periodical appetites, in which case they are active in their nature, and are discussed in the third part of this work. Our own division of the feelings is different, as will be seen in the second part of this work, where other definitions of them are also given.

III. *On the extent of* ACTIVE OPERATIONS.

This class embraces what are usually denominated,

First, *Volitions*, in which is comprehended the whole extent as well as every variety of the direct action of the will.

Secondly, those operations of the mind termed *processes* of reasoning, but not their results; for the results of reasoning are knowledge, or conviction, or belief, and therefore they belong to cognitive ideas.

Thirdly, the *act* of memorizing, and not its results; that is, the process of mental effort, by which we impress upon our memory the contents of any portion of a book or manuscript, or of a discourse which we have heard. But the impression itself thus made upon the mind is cognitive.

Fourthly. The *intellectual act* of communicating our thoughts to others, either orally or by letter.

Fifthly. Some other active processes, the nature of which will hereafter be more fully explained.

When we term the third class of mental operations active, we do not wish to convey the idea, that the soul itself, in acquiring either knowledge or feeling, is in a state of entire passivity; for there is, doubtless, activity in the soul during all its operations. But, it must be remembered, we are here classifying and characterizing the *ideas* or *operations* of the mind, and not the *powers* of the mind itself. Our division is a classification, not of the activity of the soul itself, but of the *results* of its agency. The soul is often voluntary and active in seeking the excitement of feeling; yet the feeling itself, thus excited, seems to be in its own nature merely sentient. It is in itself simply pleasure or pain. Thus also the act of acquiring knowledge by inspection is active, and often even voluntary; but the ideas acquired, the knowledge obtained, is not active; but consists simply of mental representatives of entities, and is best characterized by the term *cognitive*. These ideas are simply knowledge and nothing more.

As all the ideas or operations of the mind thus resolve themselves into three classes, viz., Cognitive, Sentient, and Active, the entire science is most aptly divided into three general parts, one of which is devoted to each of these classes of mental operations.

PART I.

COGNITIVE IDEAS.

It is evident, even on a superficial survey of those ideas which are knowledge, that at least some of them, especially such as relate to material objects around us, are mental representatives of things, or subsistencies, or entities, which exist without the mind. Thus, no one can doubt, when reflecting on his idea of an orange, that the fruit, of which the idea in question is the representative, had a real existence; for he has often handled, tasted, and eaten it. In short, when we carefully examine our cognitive ideas, and the source whence we derive them, we find that they are acquired through the medium of certain parts of our body, called organs of sense; and from the operations and powers of mind, of which all men are possessed. We see, also, that our mind, which perceives, and the organs, through which it perceives, are not in themselves sufficient to furnish us with these ideas. It is farther necessary, that the organs of sense be brought into a particular relation to certain external objects. This relation is either that of actual contact, as in the case of touch and taste, or, it consists in bringing the organ into the direction of the object, with nothing intervening which prevents the rays of light from being reflected from that object to the eye;

or it consists in a relation of proximity to the object, so that the vibrations of the air may be conveyed to the ear, as in sound. We, therefore, here clearly perceive three distinct things: *first*, the external entity, or object, of which our cognitive ideas are the mental representatives or knowledge; *secondly*, the knowledge itself, or the representatives, or ideas, which we have of external objects; and, *thirdly*, the organic process, by which we obtain our ideas, or knowledge. The discussion of each of these three things will therefore appropriately form a subdivision of this part of our subject.

CHAPTER I.

OF OBJECTIVE ENTITIES AS SUBJECTS OF OUR KNOWLEDGE.

BEFORE entering on the discussions of this chapter, we premise an explanatory remark relative to our use of the word entity. This term, long since naturalized in our language, we use with more than ordinary frequency, because its signification is more generic than that assigned by usage to the words more commonly employed, such as thing, substance, &c. The latter are ordinarily restricted, in the popular mind, to material objects, and present some difficulty, as they excite in the mind the impression of inaptitude when applied to some other subjects of our knowledge. In the progress of our discussions, we need a term of such latitude of import as to be applicable to any and every reality in nature. Such is the term entity, in the caption of this chapter, which signifies anything that has existence, and, therefore, answers our purpose.

But we proceed with the discussion of the peculiar topic of this chapter. It is indeed true, that in all our reflections on the properties of objects around us, it is not the objects themselves, but only our ideas or mental representatives of the properties of those objects, which are the immediate subjects of observation to the reflecting mind. But it may be asked, What evidence have we that anything beyond our ideas has a real existence ? How do we know, that such a thing as even the material universe does actually exist ? To this we reply, that if we were deprived of the power of bodily action, and capable of performing no other mental act than that of reflection, and what we, in the sequel, term the process of *Inspection*, it might indeed be impossible for us to establish the objectivity of external objects, that is, their real existence, out of, and independently of the percipient mind. But, when we can take a supposed object or entity, such as an apple, into our hands, and perceive that it has weight; when we feel its shape or relation to space ; when we take a knife and cut it in pieces, and eat it, we constitutionally judge it to be different from our idea of an apple, in which idea, we cannot perceive either weight, or shape, or divisibility, or capability of being eaten. Moreover, all these operations may be performed with closed eyes upon an apple which we never saw, and of which identical apple, therefore, we never had and can never acquire any farther idea than is obtained by touch and taste. In short, whenever we are using our bodily organs in touching, tasting, seeing, hearing, or smelling any object, then the external object itself, either directly, or mediately, and not our idea of it, is the subject of the operation. But as soon as we reflect on some idea, formerly obtained through our bodily organs, this idea, and not the entity itself, is the subject of the operation. During this reflection, we neither do nor can use the bodily organ; for if that organ be employed, and the attention of the soul be directed to it, the act of reflection immediately terminates. We therefore, through the instrumentality of our senses, perceive in external entities properties entirely different from those of an idea; and we also judge that the entity or substratum to which they belong is a different one; we judge that the external entities are possessed of real objectivity, that is, have an actual existence out of our minds. As to the accuracy of this judgment, it would be equal folly either to question it, or to attempt its confirmation by fine-spun trains of abstruse ratiocination. All mankind constitutionally believe the well-ascertained testimony of their senses. Not even the veriest skeptic can bring himself to doubt it in the affairs of practical life. Who ever heard of one that would walk into a fire which chanced to be in his way, believing that what appeared to be a burning pile, was only an idea of his mind? Or who among these doubting philosophers did not instantly forget his sophistical reasonings, and step aside, when he saw a serpent, or any other dangerous object in his path? In like manner, all men, by a similar necessity of their mental structure, judge that combinations of properties which are entirely different from each other, appertain to different substrata or subjects. Can any person, when contemplating the properties of a stone which he has in his hand, believe them to be parts or properties of a feather, that happens to be lying on it? Neither can any man, while true to the dictates of common sense, believe them to be mere ideas or properties of his own mind, or of that of another.

The universe, as known to us, consists of nothing else than infinitely various *combinations* of properties and their relations. We may select any object we please, throughout the whole range of the universe, and this remark will be found to hold good. Examine a tree, a stone, a flower, a gas, a mind, and it will be perceived that all the knowledge we possess of them is knowledge of their properties and relations. Thus of any particular stone, we know its colour, its shape, its gravity, its divisibility, &c.; but what the stone is, beyond its properties, we know not. We may analyze it, and reduce it to its constituent simple substances, but, in this respect, nothing is gained by the process; for each individual element is, like the compound, known to us only by its properties. Of gases also our knowledge is a knowledge of mere properties. Take, for example, our atmosphere, which is composed of two gases, oxygen and nitrogen, or, as the older chemists termed it, azote. We do not see it, but we feel its resistance when walking against a strong current of air, or, as it is termed, wind. We observe its solidity, for we see that water is excluded by it from any confined vessel or receiver. So, also, we learn its elasticity, its ability to support combustion, and various other properties ; but what either nitrogen or oxygen is, beyond these properties, we know not. And so of mind also ; we know its properties or phenomena, its capacity for knowledge, for feeling, for active operations, and its susceptibility of being influenced through bodily organs ; but what the mind is, beyond these susceptibilities or properties and phenomena, no man can tell.

Again ; *every such combination of properties, as found in nature, is individual ;* that is, it is in some respects different from all others. No two stones, or two trees, or any other two objects, are exactly alike, in regard to all their properties, and to every particle of matter contained in them.

Still, many combinations have the greater part of their properties in common, and differ only in the residue. Thus, many animals resemble each other in having four legs, others in having two ; some by eating flesh, and others grain or grass ; some by bringing forth their young alive, and others by incubation. In the vegetable kingdom, some plants have their stamens and pistils visible, others not, they being too small to be observed by the naked eye. In the former of these classes, termed phenogamous, the different plants differ in the number of their stamens, from one to ten. And thus, by their various points of agreement in stamens, pistils, &c., they are arranged in botany.

Finally; the various gradations of similarity in all different entities form a just basis for their classification. On such a classification is human language founded. No language has a specific name for every separate object, for every individual tree, or stone, or leaf, or flower.

Human language ordinarily has words merely to express,

First, our ideas of each property of entities, such as black, white, soft, hard, heavy, &c.; but there is not a separate name for these properties as found in different objects or entities. No matter what be the entity in question, there is ordinarily but one name for one property, no matter how many entities possess it in common.

Secondly, words to express our aggregate idea of each species of combinations, as stone, tree, bird, fish, &c.

Thirdly, words for our ideas of some other classifications and abstractions still more generic, such as quadrupeds, bipeds, graminivorous, carnivorous, viviparous, oviparous, &c.

Fourthly, to express our ideas of the relations of the different objects or entities in nature, such as similarity or diversity of colour or shape in two balls, contiguity or distance between two objects, as to place, or time, &c.

On the different degrees of similarity observable in the various combinations of properties found in nature, that is, on the different degrees of similarity in the objects around us in the world, different classifications have been based. Sometimes, all things .are spoken of as divisible into matter and mind. This division is good so far as it goes; but, as we shall see in the sequel, is not sufficiently precise. Such entities as can be chemically analyzed, have also been reduced to their elementary substances, and arranged according to them. Yet as chemical analysis cannot reach all objects in nature, such as mind, &c., this classification must omit some entities of which we have mental representatives, would omit some of the subjects of our cognitive ideas. However accurate and adequate this division may be for the purposes of physical science, we need another more comprehensive, for the more general purposes of mental philosophy, in which every object in nature, of which we have any knowledge, however slight or limited that knowledge may be, claims some attention, and is entitled to a place.

In all our reflections on absent entities, and our attempts to classify them, our *ideas* of their properties, and not the properties themselves, are the subjects of our attention. We spend our whole life in acquiring mental representatives of the different entities or objects in the universe; but as only a small portion of them can at any time be present before us, we cannot classify these objects themselves in any other way than by comparing and arranging the ideas of them thus obtained.

In endeavouring to make a classification of all known existences or entities, by examining our cognitive ideas, we must be careful to make thorough work. We must summon before us the whole mass of our knowledge, the entire aggregate of all our cognitive ideas in every department of science, physical, intellectual, and moral. We must, as it were, assemble our ideas of the heavens, and the earth, and all the different objects known to be in them: not only of those objects of which we have personal knowledge, but also of all others, whatever be the means by which we become acquainted with them. Our ideas of God, of angels, of devils, of space, of time, of number, of virtue, of vice, of similarity, of diversity, of analogy, of fitness, of causation, and of every species of agency, mechanical, instinctive, and voluntary or moral, must all be taken into account. We may review the contents of the most extensive libraries, including discussions on every conceivable subject in the wide range of human knowledge, and every idea we meet, which is of a *cognitive* character, which is in its nature knowledge, must be embraced in our classification.

Numerous and complicated as this immense mass of ideas would at first view appear to be, on a closer examination they will all be found to resolve themselves into three generic classes; they are either ideas of *substantive objects*, of objects to which a combination of properties appertains; or they are ideas of these individual *properties* themselves; or, thirdly, they are ideas of *relations* which exist between several such substantive objects or entities as wholes, or between the properties belonging to them.

After we have removed from our view the latter two classes of ideas, namely, those which are mere individual properties, and those which are relations; and inquire into what general classes may those substantive entities or objects be reduced, to which these properties and relations belong, we arrive at something like the following list of objects:

Solids; Liquids; Gases; the Ethereal or *Incoercible fluids*, such as *Light, Caloric, Electric Fluid, Magnetic Principle; Mind; Spirit; Glorified Bodies; Deity;* together with *Time, Space*, and *Number*, which are peculiar in their nature. The precise number of these classes is not at all material to our system; it can be increased or diminished as the future investigations of science may dictate. This division we do not propose for the purposes of the physical sciences; but of metaphysical: not as adapted to sciences whose discussions are confined to material objects; but to mental philosophy, which requires an enumeration of all the objects in existence, of which we have any, even the slightest knowledge, of which we possess any cognitive ideas whatever.

Having thus obtained an enumeration of the objects in existence, of which we have some knowledge, some cognitive ideas, that is, an enumeration of the objects to which the combinations of properties belong, which are found coexisting in nature, let us examine more closely these individual properties, that we may more accurately determine their nature.

Of *solid* bodies we find the properties to be such as length, breadth, divisibility, colour, vis inertiæ, gravity, solidity, &c. In regard to other properties, such as malleability, solubility, &c., solids may be subdivided into different classes. No one of these properties is ever found existing alone. There are always several of them found together, and these coexisting properties we constitutionally attribute to one object, as the properties of such object. Thus, with our bodily organs, we perceive a combination of properties, rotundity of shape, solidity, colour, &c., and to the object to which we judge these properties to appertain, we give the name ball. But we know nothing about the ball itself, beyond its various properties.

Liquid substances, such as water, milk, &c., possess many of the properties of solids, excepting always solidity itself. They exhibit very little resistance to the touch, yet enough to inform us of their presence by that organ alone, independently of colour. They cannot be accumulated, unless they are confined by some vessel, nor be made to retain any particular shape, except that of the vessel in which they are contained.

Gases, or aeriform fluids, are in most cases invisible; but their existence is learned from other senses, such as touch and smell. No man can doubt the reality of the atmosphere, when he feels the impulse of a strong wind, and attempts to walk against it; or when he witnesses the effects of a hurricane, overturning houses and prostrating the loftiest oaks of the forest.

Of the existence of *light*, we are convinced by the testimony of sight, by the different impression made on this organ by light, and its absence, darkness. In the same way we learn the other properties of light, its different colours, its qualities of reflection, refraction, its motion, &c.

Caloric is, indeed, invisible, but its properties, and, consequently, its reality, we learn from the sense of touch, and from the various visible effects which it produces on other bodies.

Thus also the *Electric Principle*, which probably stands connected with some common basis of light, caloric, and magnetism, is also invisible; but its existence is demonstrated by the interesting and important phenomena which it produces. Of these phenomena we have certain knowledge by our senses, and cannot doubt whether they belong to some cause, or object, by which they are produced.

The principle or fluid of *Magnetism* is likewise not visible to human eyes, but its existence is admitted, as the cause or agent, to which we must ascribe a distinct class of phenomena, well ascertained by the testimony of our senses.

Of *Mind* we learn the existence in various ways. We are conscious of the operations of our own minds. We know, too, that our bodies are to a certain degree under the control of our minds; and that certain definite actions of our bodies are consequent on the purposes of our minds to perform them. Now, as we perceive, in the bodies of all other persons, actions of the same character, actions as evidently and systematically adapted to intelligent ends, as those which in ourselves we know to result from the volitions of our minds; we reasonably infer, that in others, also, there is a mind connected with the body. This inference is the more irresistible, as we cannot perceive in matter, under any circumstances, any properties which bear the slightest resemblance to an approximation to the nature or powers of mind. On the contrary, all that we know of the one, is different from all we know of the other. Nor is it only in the case of man that we infer the existence of mind from the actions of the body. In the case of all animals, we infer the existence and the grade of intellect possessed by them, from the various degrees of intelligence, design, and forecast, inferable from their bodily actions.

The properties of mind are knowledge, feeling, and action; or cognition, sensibility, and activity, together with susceptibility of influence from bodily organs. Every mental operation is either knowledge, feeling, or action; but no simple operation consists of several or all these properties together.

It has been customary to consider the phenomena of mind, as generally different from the phenomena of other entities, in their relation to our minds as subjects of knowledge. This habit we are compelled to regard as incorrect. We know generically just as much about one entity as about another, that is, we know certain properties of each, and these properties are the subjects of our ideas about them respectively. This much also we know about mind, and more we do not know of anything else, even of the grossest forms of solid matter. It is, therefore, erroneous to assert, that we know less of the essence of mind, than of the essence of other entities. With regard to solids, liquids, gases, &c., we know no more about their essence than about that of mind; neither do we know less, because the substratum, or essence, of all the things or entities in existence, is unknown to us. Our knowledge of each, regards only its properties or operations. But in all other entities except mind, men generally agree in admitting that there must be a substratum, to which these properties belong. Some, indeed, attempt a different explanation, by referring the aggregation of these properties into one whole, to a supposed plastic power of the mind (πλαϛικος, πλασσειν, to form, to fashion, to make). But we perceive no advantage in this representation, over the old common-sense view, which has prevailed among British metaphysicians, of a constitutional judgment; and the ideas attached to the phrase "plastic power," are entirely too loose and indefinite for metaphysical purposes. We regard it, therefore, as an intuitive judgment of the mind, that wherever we observe properties, or operations, they belong to a subject or agent. All languages distinguish mind from its properties, as clearly as they do solids and other entities from their properties. The structure of the human mind seems to require us to suppose the existence of such a substratum; as is evident from the fact, that all languages are constructed on this principle or supposition. As the Author of our nature gave us this mental structure, it is probable that such substrata do belong to all entities. Indeed, what are these properties, but properties of the entity itself? What are they but those aspects of the substratum, which, by virtue of our organization, are within the reach of our knowledge? The known properties of any object, such as copper, lead, silver, gold, are the several aspects, in which these metals are perceptible to us, with our present organization. In a different state, with more organs or senses than we now possess, we might perceive additional properties of these metals; but those properties perceived by us, prove that the subject, or substratum, to which they belong, is actually known to us, as far as these properties extend. Hence, as there is no difference in this respect between mind and other entities, we are compelled to regard the views of Hume and others, who regard the mind as merely a bundle of ideas, and of Brown, who considers all ideas as the mind itself in certain states,* as unphilosophical in themselves, independently of their tendency to foster a skeptical or infidel disposition. The habit of regarding the phenomena of mind as generically different from those of other entities, has probably arisen in part from the old imperfect division of all entities into matter and mind, into material and immaterial, and from the maxim thence inferred, that mind is indivisible. But the different properties, operations, and powers of the mind, which are the subjects of all the ideas we possess of this entity, are as distinct from each

* See some excellent observations on the fallacy of Brown's view, in the Biblical Repertory of Princeton, for 1830, p. 186.

other in their nature, as are the different properties of solids and liquids. Hence, it is evidently unphilosophic to assert, that the unknown, ulterior something, supposed to belong to mind, as the substratum of its phenomena or properties, is or is not possessed of indivisibility.

Of *Spirits*, that is, disimbodied minds, or minds that have never been associated with bodies, our only certain knowledge is derived from revelation; although tradition and analogy may afford some probable arguments in favour of their existence. The cardinal known distinction between mind and spirit, is the connexion of the former with a body as the organ of its action, and its susceptibility of being influenced by the body in various ways. To this class of entities belong the spirits of departed saints, whose bodies shall slumber in the grave till the resurrection, as also the angels, archangels, and devils; in short, all created spirits, of which we have any knowledge, or which may exist, unknown to us, in the boundless empire of Jehovah.

To *Glorified Bodies* we assign a separate class, because, although we know only that little about them which the Scriptures teach us, the Apostle Paul evidently represents them as different from all other objects, as "spiritual" bodies (*σωματα πνευματικα*), "celestial bodies," and "incorruptible," which predicates necessarily imply an entity radically different from ordinary matter.

The *Divine Being*, though a spirit, differs from all other spirits, as the Creator from the creature, the Infinite from the finite. The ideas we possess concerning God, are derived partly from the works of Nature, and partly from revelation. Mortal eyes have not seen him, mortal ears have not heard him, but that the reality of his existence may be deduced from evidences of various kinds, establishing his agency and attributes, is admitted by all except the atheist. Our knowledge of the attributes and existence of God, so far as it is derived from nature, consists of ideas of virtues, which we observed in good men, separated by a mental process from every imperfection, with which they are mingled in human beings, and elevated to the highest conceivable degree. We thus acquire our ideas of the incomparable excellences of the Divine Being. Perceiving, in the structure and operations of the universe, the evidences of these incomparable attributes, we constitutionally judge (know) that they appertain to some *substratum or being;* which being, we in the same constitutional manner judge to exist. We do not affirm, that we actually obtain our knowledge of the Divine character and existence by such a process of reasoning; but suppose, that by this process we can verify and confirm these truths, which are ordinarily taught us by tradition, long before we reach the maturity of mind necessary for such trains of ratiocination.

Our additional knowledge, derived from revelation, concerning the Divine Being, his works, his will, and his moral government, likewise consists of ideas, the constituent elements of which were originally derived from human beings and human institutions. Through the medium of these ideas, and their various and new combinations and applications, together with anthropopathic representations, the most minute and detailed account of the will, the providence, and the moral government of God is represented to us, and we are instructed by precept and example, what the Author of our being would have us to do.

Whether the human mind, if left wholly to itself, would have discovered the existence of God, from the contemplation of the works of Nature, is somewhat uncertain; as it is much easier to perceive the truth, propriety, and excellence of an invention or discovery after it has been made, than to make it. But there is obviously an aptitude in the human mind to see the evidences of the Divine existence and attributes after they have been revealed to us, which is generally done either by tradition, or the written revelation.

That we have some knowledge of *Space*, *Time*, and *Number* will be admitted by all, although the precise nature of these entities has been the subject of much disputation. Into these disputes we shall not here enter; and we therefore, for the present, leave it undetermined, whether these entities are objective, that is, have existence either out of our minds, as independent entities, or as forms of existence of other entities, or as limitations, or necessary forms of our perceptions; or are mere subjective conceptions of the human mind, having no existence out of the mind itself. In regard to space, our ideas of its properties seem to be principally those of length, breadth, divisibility, and capacity. Our ideas of time seem to be referable to duration (or length), augmentability, and divisibility; while the properties of number seem to be its capability to be added, subtracted, multiplied, and divided.

Number comprehends an indefinite series of units. The decimal system of designating and calculating numbers is arbitrary, and seems to have been adopted fortuitously. It is neither based on anything peculiar in the intrinsic nature of numbers themselves, requiring ten figures, and calculation by tens, rather than by any other number; nor is it, by any means, as the ancient Pythagoreans supposed, the most perfect system that could be devised. The dodecadal (duodecimal), having twelve different figures, would be far more convenient; as the number twelve can be divided more frequently without a remainder, and, consequently, calculations by the dodecadal, or duodecimal system, would be far less encumbered by fractions, than when conducted on the decimal plan. The Roman method of quintal calculation, having only five figures, is virtually the same as the decimal. They employed the letters I and V; and then double V thus $^{\mathrm{V}}_{\mathrm{A}}$, forming X; then C (centum) for hundred, M (mille) for thousand, &c.

SECTION II.

Division of these Classes of Entities.

All these classes of entities, when attentively examined, appear to be of two distinct kinds, and may, therefore, with propriety, be referred to two generic classes:

I. *Absolute* (or universal, or subjective).

II. *Concrete* (or individual).

Absolute entities, are those of which we can conceive, without any reference to those of the concrete class. To this class belong *Time*, *Space*, and *Number*. The properties and relations of the absolute entities are, in their very nature, more definite and clear than those of the concrete. They are, moreover, immutable in their character; hence the sciences discussing these entities, such as arithmetic, geometry, and mathematics in general, are more certain, conclusive, and immutable. Accordingly, they are termed "exact sciences," and not without obvious reason. Between the absolute or universal entities time, space, and number, the mind perceives some points of difference; but they are rather specific than general, and all three properly belong to one general class.

Concrete entities are those, of which we cannot conceive, except as existing in the absolute class, or, as being related to it. To this class belong *Solids*, *Liquids*, *Aëriform substances*, and, in short, all the different classes of known entities, except *Time*, *Space*, and *Number*.

SECTION III.

Subdivision of Individual Entities.

All entities of every class may naturally be divided into *substantive*, *adjective*, and *composite*, because all objects perceived by us in nature, are either entire individual objects, or they are one or more properties of such object, or they are relations of some kind or other, perceived to exist between the perceived properties of objects, or performed by one entity or another. As every entire individual object has in reality substantive existence for itself, it may, with propriety, be designated a substantive entity. There is an additional advantage in the adoption of this term, which will appear in the sequel, when we make some application of this subject to the structure of language and universal grammar.

A substantive entity, then, is that in which properties cohere, or coexist; or, we might say, a substantive entity is that to which any number of coexisting properties appertain. Accordingly, every simple substance, or chemical or ential element, separately viewed, as also each aggregate of all these ential or chemical elements found coexisting, is a substantive entity; such as wood, water, tree, horse, &c. These ential elements are known to us only relatively; we know their properties and their relation to time, space, and number, and to each other. In the case of solids and liquids, and such other substances as can be subjected to chemical analysis, the ential elements and chemical elements are the same. But the term chemical, in this application, is not so well adapted to metaphysical purposes, because the usage of our language confines it to a certain portion only of entities, such as solids, liquids, gases, &c. It is not improbable, that all the classes of entities have ential elements, as well as those which chemical analysis can reach; though of course they are very different from them in their nature. Ential element is a more suitable term, and designates the substratum, to which any set of properties, found coexisting in any class of entities, belongs.

The idea which we have of a substantive entity, is the aggregate of our ideas of all those essential, permanent properties, which are found coexisting in the same entity, and, without any one of which, the residue could not be designated by the substantive name, which they collectively bear.

If I am asked what idea I have of a stone, a tree, an apple, or an orange, I must admit that my only knowledge of them is knowledge of the properties which habitually belong to them. I perceive their colour, their solidity, their shape, &c., but what their intrinsic nature or essence is beyond these properties, I know not. Thus also no man ever saw, or tasted, or touched a mind. Yet every one is conscious of his own mental operations, knows the phenomena of his own mind, and constitutionally judges, that the mental operations of which he is conscious, must belong to a mental agent, which agent he calls himself.

Yet our idea of an object, of a substantive entity, does not embrace every property it may chance to possess. Thus, trees and stones may differ in colour, shape, or size, and yet be appropriately designated by the same name. Those properties only are embraced in our ideas of a substantive entity which permanently and invariably belong to every individual object to which the name in question can appropriately be applied. If language furnished a word to designate every particular individual tree and stone, then every property and circumstance belonging to each stone or tree, and necessary to its identity, would properly be represented by such word. But this is not the character of any language on earth. Therefore it is our ideas of only those properties common to all the individual trees or stones of a particular species, which form the ingredients of the collective idea that we attach to a word designating a substantive entity, that is, they are our idea of the substantive entity itself.

An *adjective* entity is any one property of a substantive entity considered individually; as length, breadth, colour, gravity, or any other known property. Human language, in most cases, contains words to designate each individual property of an entity of which we have an idea, and also names or words, by which those properties, which are found coexisting, are collectively designated, not, indeed, as individuals, but as entire species, such as stone, tree, house, &c.

A *composite entity* consists of two or more adjective entities, viewed together, and considered in regard to some relation subsisting between them. Sometimes, several properties of the same entity, constitute a composite entity, between the parts of which some relation is observed. Thus, different parts of a painting may have different colours, and may be viewed in relation to this difference. These relations of entities exert a very important influence on some of the active operations of the mind, and an acquaintance with them, belongs to the most important branches of our knowledge. These relations are not the properties of either part of the composite entity alone; nor have they a separate existence of their own apart from the related entities; but they are relations existing between them, and perceivable by the mind. Still, in this case also, our knowledge is a knowledge of relations which actually exist independently of our minds. Thus, we behold two beautiful, dark, Arabian horses, and perceive a similarity of colour between them. Who can doubt, that this similarity would have existed, whether we had seen it or not? Or whoever imagined, when contemplating the exact adaptation of the wheels of a watch to act upon one another, that this supposed adaptation existed only in his own mind? Our ideas of relations, like our ideas of substantive and adjective entities, do not resemble the entities themselves, but are only the divinely appointed mental representatives of them. Yet, the relation of similarity of colour between two gray horses, is as certainly seen by the eyes, as is the colour of either horse alone, and the constitution of our minds compels us to believe the similarity of colour between them to be real; that is, we just as invariably believe our idea of the perceived similarity to be an idea of an objective truth, of a reality, as we do believe our idea of the colour of each horse individually to be such.

SECTION IV.

Relations of Entities.

I. What are the perceptible relations of *Absolute Entities* to each other?

II. What are the perceptible relations of *Concrete Entities* to each other?

III. What are the perceptible relations between *Concrete* and *Absolute Entities?*

The relations which the human mind is capable of perceiving between entities, both absolute and concrete, are exceedingly numerous, and may be variously divided. The following division may serve as a basis of a comprehensive and accurate classification.

I. *The relations of* ABSOLUTE ENTITIES *to each other.*

(*a.*) Equality, diversity, antecedence, subsequence, &c., of different portions of *Time.*

(*b.*) Equality, difference, progression, or ratio, plurality (plus), minority (minus), &c., of different *Numbers.*

(*c.*) Equality, diversity, contiguity, remoteness, superiority (above), inferiority (below), of different portions of *Space.*

In reference to each of these relations, language embraces a vast multitude of words, expressing them in different methods and different aspects.

II. *The relations of* CONCRETE ENTITIES *to each other.*

(*a.*) Similarity and diversity of any of the different classes of entities, in regard to any one or more of their properties.

(*b.*) Contiguity of any of the concrete entities to each other in regard to Space, Time, or Number.

(*c.*) Fitness, physical, intellectual, and moral. Physical fitness includes the relations which are the basis of beauty, symmetry, taste, &c., in the material world. To this class must be referred the relations of harmony or discord, perceived between different sounds. The relation exists between the atmospheric vibrations themselves, and even in the vibrating chords which produce the undulations of the atmosphere. The reason why discordant vibrations produce unpleasant feelings in us, while those which accord are pleasing, is unknown to us. But these vibrations themselves are well understood, and their chords and discords are the subject of the most obvious mathematical calculation. Intellectual fitness embraces our perceptions of fitness in the operations of the mind, in all the various departments of its agency. Moral fitness embraces all our duties to God, to ourselves, and our fellow-men. They are all fitnesses perceived by the mind to exist objectively between us and God, and our fellow-men. The whole field of moral and religious obligation, of philosophic and Christian ethics, is embraced in this relation. Thus, a dictate of conscience is our knowledge of a composite entity, viz., a law; that is, the expressed will of the lawgiver or his acknowledged representative, and some action of a person under obligation to this law. The relation perceived between them, is that of moral fitness or agreement, or of unfitness or disagreement.

In virtue of our constitutional activity we must act somehow. By inspection we perceive the moral fitness of some actions, viewed in relation to the law, and the unfitness of other actions; and the first Constitutional Inclination of the soul (see part iii. of this work) urges us to that which is morally fit, which is right. This complex operation, when referring to our own actions, constitutes the dictates of conscience. There is, therefore, in the dictates of conscience, something that is impulsive and something that is judicial; both a judgment and an impulse, and also a feeling.

(*d.*) The relation of analogy. This relation is based on past experience. The maxim, "Every effect must have a cause," is an analogous judgment, resulting from experience. Stated at length, it would read thus: Every effect we ever knew had a cause, hence all others probably will have.

(*e.*) Causation, or agency in general. That causation differs from mere antecedence is evident. They can often be distinguished by the following circumstances: 1. The cause also produces such consequents, under other circumstances; whereas the mere antecedent, is, on other occasions, and under other circumstances, not attended by the consequent. 2. By some known, intelligible aptitude in the cause to produce the effect, while this is not found in the mere antecedent. The light and heat of the rising sun, are both antecedents to the melting of the snow on a winter morning. That the heat and not the light, is the *cause* of the effect, is demonstrated by the fact, that caloric without light will produce the same effect; as when snow is brought near to a dark but heated stove or other iron; while light, with little or no caloric, produces no such effect, as is exemplified in the case of a candle borne over the snow. Thus also in the machinery of a watch, there is a perceptible adaptation between the parts to act upon one another, and to produce the effects for which they are designed.

But even this judgment of perceptible adaptation, is the result of former experience in similar cases. And this experience amounts only to a knowledge of the fact. In any new case, not embracing perceptible adaptation on which former experience has instructed us, our belief of the existence of a causative relation is purely the result of present observation, and strong or weak according to the extent and uniformity of that observation. These facts appear clearly to prove, that our confidence in the uniformity of the operations of nature, and of the relation of cause and effect, is not, as has sometimes been affirmed, an original instinctive principle in the mind; but is a general abstract belief or confidence, derived from our experimental observation of individual cases. Experience teaches us, that the world is governed by general laws, or, rather, that God causes the properties of all objects in our world, to act in uniform ways or modes, termed laws of nature. Many of these we learn in youth. To these laws, we refer all the phenomena, for which they will account. If we meet with an event or effect which the known laws do not explain, we look for another law. Thus additional laws are occasionally discovered, and thus our confidence in the uniformity of nature's laws, is acquired without the supposition of any instinctive, or original, or à priori principle or knowledge in the mind. The relation of causation, or agency, is very comprehensive and embraces three different species:

(1.) *Mechanical agency.*

(2.) *Instinctive agency.*

(3.) *Rational or moral agency.*

By *Mechanical agency* we mean all the unintelligent and merely physical changes of inert matter, such as the motions and changes of the heavenly bodies, of solids, liquids, &c. The mechanical changes may be divided into two classes: *First*, the uniform or universal changes, viz., gravitation, attraction, cohesion, repulsion, &c. These are termed laws of nature, by which phrase, however, cannot properly be meant an agent or cause of action; but it is merely a statement of our cognitive idea of a uniform mode of action or of changes observed in entities, of which action or changes God is the agent or cause. *Secondly*, mechanical agency includes contingent changes, such as those actions, motions, or changes which are occasioned by the impulse or influence of other bodies.

The *second* kind of general agency, viz., the *instinctive*, embraces all those actions of irrational animals, which result from what is termed instinct, that is, a propensity prior to experience and independent of instruction; such as the incubation of hens, &c.

The *third* species of agency is *rational* or *moral agency*. To this class belong all those actions of men, either voluntary or spontaneous, which are free, for which we are accountable, and which may be termed moral actions. This class is of the very utmost importance, and embraces in it the entire field of all that diversified agency, which is peculiar to man, as a rational and accountable creature of God.

III. *Relations between* ABSOLUTE *and* CONCRETE *entities.*

(*a.*) In reference to number: addition, multiplication, subtraction, and division of numbers (not of concrete entities). These operations are active relations of agency, performed by the *concrete entity* man, on our ideas of the *absolute entity* number.

(*b.*) In reference to space: mensuration of its parts by the concrete entity man; and fitness or unfitness of any concrete entity to occupy any given portion, or form of it.

(*c.*) In relation to time: calculation of its parts by man; and the relation of fitness or unfitness of a given portion of it to any specified purpose.

The relations of entities may be divided into *transitive* and *intransitive.* The first, or transitive class of relations, embraces the relation of causation or agency in general, mechanical, instinctive, and moral. The second, or intransitive class, embraces the relations of similarity, diversity, contiguity, and, in short, all the other relations excepting those of causation and agency in general.

These two classes may again be subdivided into *absolute* or indicative, and *hypothetical* or subjunctive. These relations are, in human language, most naturally expressed by verbs. Those words expressing transitive relations are in their primitive nature active verbs; those expressing intransitive relations are in their original form neuter verbs, verbs expressing a state of being. Passive verbs appear to be an improvement in language, and are not based on any separate distinction in the relations themselves, but refer simply to the entities between which they exist, and determine whether the speaker was the agent or recipient of the active influence, which they always express. This is beautifully illustrated by the Hebrew verbs in the Kal voice. The radical word throughout expresses the relation of *action;* the appendages prefixed and suffixed only designate the relations of the speakers and others, as the agents or recipients of the action. The same is also true, in a certain degree, of Latin and Greek verbs.

The subdivision of both classes of relations into *retrospective*, *present*, and *prospective*, is obviously natural, and is expressed in language by the past, present, and future tenses of verbs. Each of these is again twofold; the relation is either absolute or hypothetical. In the former case the verb expressing this relation is in the *indicative*, and in the latter case it is in the *subjunctive* mood. The *imperative* mood is the annunciation to an individual, of his relation of obligation to perform a prescribed act; whether this obligation results from his relation to the speaker as authorized to command him, or to some other human being, or to God.

The other parts of speech express ideas, which may probably be reduced to appendages of the above-named three. Thus the *prepositions* "to," "in," &c., express relations of the verb, and are often incorporated with it; as *intro*duce, *in*duct, *post*pone, *sub*ject, &c., &c. *Adverbs* stand for ideas which qualify adjectives or composite entities, that is, adjectives or verbs.

CHAPTER II.

OF OUR COGNITIVE IDEAS, OR MENTAL REPRESENTATIVES OF ENTITIES.

SECTION I.

What is the exact nature of those of our ideas which are knowledge?

In reply to this inquiry, we remark, that it is probably impossible to describe the intrinsic nature of our ideas in any other way than by stating that they belong to the class of entities termed mind; and that every individual knows for himself what his ideas are, by the testimony of his own consciousness. One cardinal feature of the first class of ideas, by which they are clearly distinguished from all others, is, that they are representatives of either the properties or relations of things actually existing. It is, indeed, true of many of our cognitive ideas, that they do not represent actual realities with exactness. Thus those ideas formed by the active process of the mind, hereafter explained under the name of *Modification*, such as abstractions, generalizations, mathematical, moral, and metaphysical axioms, do not correspond exactly to realities, to real entities; yet the elements of which they are composed are all derived from the contemplation of individual realities, and whatever is affirmed in them, however generic it may be, is true of all the objects embraced in their terms: though it does not constitute a specific or distinguishing representative of any one of them. Thus the proposition, "things equal to the same thing are equal to each other," contains a cognitive idea, viz., the relation of sameness between three or more objects. It is true, this general proposition does not affirm this relation of any particular object. Nevertheless, it was originally learned by observing its truth in numberless individual cases, even in our earliest years, and it is in reality true of every object embraced in its terms, that is, it is a correct mental representative of every specific object embraced in its generic terms, so far as the particular relation affirmed is concerned. Thus, if two triangles or circles are equal in capacity to a third triangle or circle, they are equal to each other. The disputed question, whether our ideas are to be considered as something distinct from the mind itself, we feel constrained to answer in the affirmative; while we, of course, must reject the old Peripatetic notion, that these ideas are literal images, resembling the entities, which are the subjects of them.

SECTION II.

What are the criteria by which the cognitive class of ideas is distinguished?

The following criteria may, we think, be clearly perceived, and should be regarded as characteristic:

I. The cognitive ideas have for their objects entities existing out of the mind, that is, things of any and of every description. As we regard the mind as distinct from its operations, it is evident that this language does not exclude from the list of cognitive ideas the knowledge of our own mental operations. In short, our knowledge of mental phenomena of every sort is embraced in this class, whether they be past, present, or prospective; whether they be the operations of our own, or of other minds.

II. The cognitive ideas derive their form and are dependant for their character on the entities themselves which are the subjects of them, which have existence independently of us, and would be what they are if we had not this knowledge of them. We, of course, do not mean, that there exists any literal resemblance between our ideas of entities, and these entities themselves. Thus, our idea of a peach or a pear, does not resemble the object itself, in any one particular. But we mean, that there is a correspondence between the difference subsisting among different objects in nature, and the intellectual representatives of them, which, by the constitution of the mind, these objects produce, when brought within its observation. The same entities, when fairly viewed, always produce the same representatives in the mind of the same person; but it also affords the same idea to all other persons, or rather an idea exactly similar. All men have the same uniform representatives of entities; hence they can converse intelligibly about them. If the same entity afforded to different persons different representatives of itself, men could no more converse intelligibly about it, than if they did not understand the same language. Our idea of an entity, accordingly, is not what we please that it shall be, but is such, as, by the constitution of our minds, is naturally produced by the entity itself, when brought under the observation of the mind. Nor is our knowledge of the relations of entities, what we choose to make it; but what God has made it by our mental structure. Thus, whether a landscape, or any other object, shall appear to us beautiful, or otherwise, does not depend upon our wishes. Beauty, and the reverse, are properties and relations inherent in the objects, to which they belong, and our apperception of them depends on their existence in the object, which is the subject of our observation.

Our knowledge of the truth or falsity of a proposition no more depends upon our previous wishes, if the examination was impartial and faithful, than does the shape of a book, or the colour of an apple, when presented to our eyes. How often are not men called to attend the examination of a friend, who has been charged with some heinous crime, which, if established, would hurl him from the respectable eminence which he occupied in society, and prove him unworthy of the confidence which they had reposed in him, and of the affections of which he had been the subject. These friends protest his innocence, and gladly lend him every aid in obtaining able counsel, and the attendance of every desired witness, to wipe away the odious stain from his character. With intense feeling they enter the halls of justice, anxiously wishing that their friend may succeed in proving himself still worthy of their affections and respect. But, alas! one witness after another is heard, one item of evidence after another is brought to light, until the guilt of their former friend no longer admits of any doubt. They hear the testimony in his favour, they listen to the arguments of his counsel, and find nothing but subterfuge and conjecture; find, indeed, even in the nature of the efforts made to save his character, collateral evidence of his guilt, and are compelled, though with bleeding hearts, to believe that he who stands before them convicted as a criminal, is no longer the upright man, whom they loved and respected as a friend. Here the result of the investigation was the knowledge, that the charge alleged against their friend was true; a knowledge of the relation of probation (proof or evidence), between the facts adduced in the trial and the guilt of their friend. Surely no one would contend that the nature of the result depended on their wishes, or on anything else than the nature of the testimony itself, that is, on the facts, the entities and their relations, of which they acquired knowledge during the trial.

III. The entities which are the subjects of our cognitive ideas, must have an existence previously to our knowledge of them. When we make a volition, the subject of that volition is the intended *future* exertion of some physical or intellectual power, and the subject of the volition has no previous existence. But when we have a knowledge of an apple, a stone, a mind, of space, or number, these cognitive ideas, or knowledge, are mental representatives of entities previously existing; and, according to universal consent, they presuppose such previous existence. Thus, even in a fictitious narration, all the elements, so far as they are cognitive, are made up of ideas of entities which separately had a real existence.

SECTION III.

The nature and sources of ERROR *in our cognitive ideas.*

In order to obtain a correct view of this extremely important subject, it is necessary first to advert to the exact nature and divisions of truth. All truths may be divided into three classes:

I. *Real* or *objective truths*, that is, entities themselves, existing in nature.

II. *Idealistic* or *subjective truths*, that is, correct mental representatives of objective entities, that is, of objects in nature.

III. *Nominal* or *verbal truths*, that is, propositions or sentences, expressing in accurate language, correct ideas of things, correct mental representatives of objective entities.

This division is evidently based on the nature of things, and affords us no small aid in understanding the sources, whence sprung the former philosophical sects of Realists and Nominalists, as well as the modern Idealists.

The rancorous contentions of the former sects,

about the metaphysical question, whether our generic ideas are mere names (nomina rerum, seu flatus vocis) as the Nominalists contended, or *realities* existing in nature, generic archetypes according to which all individual entities are formed, as was maintained by the Realists from the days of Aristotle till the time of Roscellinus, in the eleventh century, were continued through subsequent ages, and rose to such a height, that the blood of several distinguished leaders was shed in the contest. The points of controversy were generally the influence of these metaphysical theories on the various doctrines of the Christian religion. There was scarcely a university in Europe that was not more or less affected by these controversies. Nor can it be said that they were ever decided, although the Realists appear more generally to have been the stronger party. These litigations continued till the sixteenth century, and often exerted an influence on the decisions of ecclesiastical councils.

Philosophers of modern days, especially in Germany, have used the terms Realism and Idealism in a somewhat different sense, as characteristic of their several systems of philosophy.

By *Realism* they designate that system of philosophy, which not only admits the existence of something real or actual, something objective in nature; but also regards this real something as the original material, anterior to the ideal, and out of which the ideal (that is, consciousness, conception, knowledge) was deduced. The principle of this system is "*reale prius, ideale posterius*," the real existed first, the ideal is posterior to it. But to the various modifications of this system, it may justly be objected, that the derivation of the *ideal*, that is, of mental action, from the *real*, that is, from the organization of matter, necessarily results in materialism. There is, moreover, no necessity whatever of deriving either mind from matter, or matter from mind, either the ideal from the real, or the real from the ideal. Both are realities created by God, and it is one of the idle conceits of philosophy, falsely so called, to suppose, that a system, to be complete, must have some one element to start from, out of which everything else can be evolved.

By *Idealism* they designate that system of philosophy which regards "*the real*" (das Reale), that is, the actual or material world, as merely ideal or imaginary, and assumes that there exists nothing in nature corresponding to our ideas of the material world; but that we ourselves confer objectivity on those ideas, that is, conceive the existence of something real as corresponding to our ideas (to the ideal), because by a necessity of our nature we find ourselves possessed of those ideas. This system regards "*the ideal*" (das Ideale) as first, and the real as posterior to it, yea, admits the existence of the real or material universe, only because and as far as, the belief of it is the necessary result of our mental structure. The real (say they) is the mere product of the ideal. But this system is after all not what it boasts to be, a system of pure idealism, for it begins by assuming the "reality" of the "ideal," that is, it assumes the existence of the *mind* which is the subject of the ideal, the mind in which the ideas of the universe are found. To escape from this difficulty, some idealists have supposed, these ideas of the material universe, to be produced in us immediately by God, the infinite mind. Fichte and others suppose the mind itself to be the originator of these ideas, acting by virtue of its original activity, according to certain laws or limitations of its nature, which are incomprehensible to itself (to the ego). This system is termed by German philosophers *Egoistic Idealism.*

The *transcendental* Idealism of *Kant* is, however, materially different from this. He admits or assumes the existence of "the real," that is, of the material world; but maintains that it cannot be *known to us* as it *is in itself* objectively, apart from our views of it, but only as it appears to us through the medium of our senses.

But our present design does not permit us to enlarge on the opinions of these writers; yet we think the view of this subject to which our system naturally leads us, will enable the reader to form a clear conception of the extent to which each system adheres to the truth. The exact truth in the dispute between the ancient Realists and Nominalists, will fully appear in the discussion of the third active process of the mind, *modification*, in the last part of this work; where abstraction or generalization is discussed as a part of that process. The mind doubtless does possess the power of framing general ideas, which, though derived from real objects in nature, do not exactly correspond to any specific one. Yet are these not merely names, as the

Nominalists held, but actual generic conceptions, as the later Conceptualists more correctly maintain.

But we return to the discussion of the nature of truth.

We have said, that all entities in the natural, intellectual, and moral world, and their relations, are realities or truths objectively considered. The word *truth* is indeed not often used precisely in this sense. Most generally it has a reference to our *ideas* of entities, and is therefore used subjectively; but, if we wish to begin at the ultimate ground of our subject, we may be permitted to employ the word in this signification. The objective realities exist out of the mind, and would be what they are if we knew nothing about them. They are the subjects of our knowledge, and the ultimate basis of truth.

Our cognitive idea of each objective reality, or entity, if it accord with the original, that is, if it be what by divine appointment and the constitution of our minds, that entity is designed to give, is an *idealistic truth*, or a truth subjectively considered, and evidently differs from objective truths. Subjective truth is more limited in its extent than the objective, and is of different extent in different minds. There is an immeasurable difference between the extended and diversified knowledge of a Mosheim, a Leibnitz, or a Newton, and the limited stock of ideas found in the mind of an ignorant, unlettered savage; but doubtless the knowledge of the most deservedly celebrated universal scholar, falls short of the entire range of real existences in an inconceivably greater degree.

The manner in which God determined the nature of our representatives of entities, is by the structure of the human mind itself; so that if we have freely and impartially examined an entity with all the light attainable, the idea then formed of it in the mind, is that appointed by God as its representative.

A *nominal* or *verbal truth*, is a sentence or proposition, spoken or written, in which a correct idea of a real entity is expressed by the precise words, which, according to the usage of language, are employed to designate those very ideas.

All error in statements, whether oral or written, must be situated in one of these two latter departments. There may be an error in regard to the entire objective entity. Thus a timid individual, in a dark night, indistinctly beholding a stump before him, may believe it a robber, and so relate his story; but he has made a premature and gratuitous inference from the indistinct testimony of his senses, and thus obtained a false idea of an entity. The error here is evidently in the idealistic department. Though the error in this case concerns the objective entity, it specifically consists in the want of conformity of the subjective idea or mental representative, to the objective or real entity. In short, the error can never lie in the first department, namely, that of real or objective truth. Objective truths, or entities, are and must ever be, just what they are independently of our knowledge of them.

The fact that our mental representatives of them are correct or incorrect, cannot affect them in any degree.

But, if an individual, who has a correct idea of an entity, either inadvertently, or through design, or through ignorance of language, describes his idea in terms which express either more than his precise idea, or something radically different from it, the error will be a nominal or *verbal* one; it will consist in the incorrect selection of words to express the ideas. In addition to these two locations of error in statements, there is another in the hearer or reader. Error may be seated in the incorrect association in the mind of the reader or hearer, between the words which he reads or hears, and his own ideas. Thus, a sentence describing correct ideas in accurate language, might be mistaken by an ignorant person. With these preliminary views, we can find no difficulty in tracing the following sources of error:

SOURCES OF ERROR IN HUMAN KNOWLEDGE.

Involuntary Error embraces,

I. *Incorrect original mental representatives* of entities. These may arise from the following sources: (*a.*) From a hasty, superficial inspection of entities. (*b.*) From forgetfulness of the exact mental representative originally obtained, and a consequent misstatement of it. (*c.*) From listening to one part of a statement, and neglecting to listen to the whole. This remark applies not only to substantive and adjective entities but also to composite. The relations of sameness and contrariety may be easily observed by attentive inspection. But haste and inattention may also lead to error. The relation most difficult to be accurately discerned is that of causation, which is often prematurely admitted, where there was mere sequence.

II. Involuntary error may arise from *incorrect selection of sounds and written words*, to express to others the true mental representative which we really have. Thus we may select a word more or less specific than it ought to be; as, for example, when we charge many with a crime which belongs only to few; or, our expression may convey different circumstances from those which actually exist; we may incautiously denominate that self-interest, which was really gratitude, and that pride, which, in fact, was vanity.

III. Involuntary error may arise from the real imperfection of language, which does not furnish words to express our ideas with precision on all subjects. Thus, in translating a work, and giving an account of foreign countries, we find offices, coins, &c., different from any found in our own country, for which we have no exact name in our tongue. In the New Testament, *denarius* is translated a penny, and *δαιμων*, devil; not because the English words were supposed by the translators exactly to correspond in meaning to the Greek, but because our language furnishes no words of precisely the same meaning. We have no coin exactly corresponding in value to the denarius, and, therefore, no word in popular use to designate it.

IV. Involuntary error may arise from mistakes in judging of the motives of others. We may suppose we perceive the relation of causation, between ambition and certain conduct of an individual, whereas that conduct results from a sense of duty in him.

V. Involuntary errors may arise from unintentional, illogical reasoning, from fallacy either in the major or minor proposition, or in the conclusion. This embraces also premature generalization, in which the conclusion is more general than the extent of our induction justifies. In short, it embraces every species of sophism, which can occur in any form of the syllogism. But it is unnecessary to specify these minutely at this time.

VI. Another source from which involuntary error may arise, is the misapprehension of a correct sentence, through ignorance of language.

SOURCES OF VOLUNTARY ERROR.

I. *Intentional misstatement* of entities, simple or composite; that is, of things or actions, from malice or any other motive. In these cases, men intentionally use words which recall or suggest to others erroneous mental representatives, words which excite in them the idea of some evil property or relation, in connexion with an individual, to whom that property or relation does not belong.

II. Voluntary error may arise from indulgence in the habit of mere high colouring, without directly stating a falsehood.

III. Voluntary error may consist in voluntary ignorance, resulting from the neglect of the means of information within our reach. It is obviously the duty of man to avail himself of all the opportunities appropriately within his reach, to extend the sphere of his knowledge, and to correct any errors which he may have adopted, either innocently or through neglect. Whoever, therefore, remains in error from this cause, may be justly charged with voluntary error, and will doubtless be held responsible for it by the omniscient Judge.

IV. Voluntary error may arise from the indulgence of prejudice in regard to persons or things. So strong, indeed, is the influence of our personal feelings upon us, that every friend of the truth should incessantly be upon his guard, lest he be led captive by it.

V. Voluntary error may result from the indulgence of passion. Passion prompts to speedy and premature action, and thus prevents deliberate investigation, and enlightened, conscientious choice. When error has been detected in our knowledge, or when we have reason even to suspect the accuracy of any of our opinions, it becomes us to institute inquiry and settle the point. The generic method of rectifying any mistaken views, is to pass successively and carefully through the several steps by which, according to the laws of mind, we obtain our information on the point in question. Truth may justly be regarded as that which the constitution of our minds compels us to believe, when its evidences are fairly presented, and impartially weighed. We may assume it as an undeniable position, that the evidences of truth are stronger than those of error, and will, when carefully pondered, produce on a well-balanced mind a conviction precisely as strong as it was designed by the Creator to be, and as it is our duty to entertain.

From the above considerations we see, at a glance, the fallacy of the favourite sentiment of free-thinkers, that man is not responsible for his opinions, that they are what they are by a constitutional necessity of our minds, and lie beyond the sphere of human responsibility.

SECTION IV.

Division of our Cognitive Ideas.

All our cognitive ideas may be divided into *Individual* and *Relative:* and again into *Retrospective*, *Present*, and *Prospective.*

I. Of Individual knowledge. To this class belongs our knowledge of every individual substantive entity in nature, and also of every individual property belonging to any entity. Our *retrospective* knowledge of individual entities is also of the same individual class; as is, in like manner, our *prospective* knowledge of them.

II. Of Relative knowledge. To this class belongs all our knowledge of composite entities, that is, of two or more adjective entities viewed in connexion, in respect to some particular relation between them. Of this kind are our perceptions of all the different relations of sameness or difference in size, colour, shape, local contiguity, &c., of all perceivable objects. They are nothing else than a knowledge of two or more of these adjective entities viewed together, and viewed in reference to some one or more of their relations to each other. Thus, I see before me a father and his son; my perception of each of them alone is individual knowledge; but the father is twice as tall as the son. I view them in connexion, to ascertain their relative magnitude, and my knowledge of this relation of difference is relative knowledge. It is a knowledge of something really existing, not in either of them alone, but in both taken together.

To this class, also, belongs the greater part of our *conceptions*. Many individual, abstract terms, when rightly examined, are nothing else than signs of such composite entities. What do we mean by the terms virtue and vice, more than our knowledge of the relation of agreement or disagreement, between human actions of a certain kind and the law of God, or the structure of the universe. Just as the mind, though it at one view acquires a knowledge of the size, form, and colour of an object, may make either of these items of its knowledge the exclusive subject of reflection, or of other mental operations; so it may, by the process of abstraction, make these items of its knowledge of the characteristics of human actions the subject of reflection, without connecting with them the idea of individual persons. Of this kind, evidently, are our ideas of virtue and vice; and language affords us words to designate these items of knowledge, as well as others.

Geometrical axioms also belong to relative knowledge. Thus the axiom, "Things which are equa. to the same thing, are equal to one another," expresses our knowledge of the relation of sameness in dimensions or number, between three, given entities. The axiom, "When equals are added to equals, the wholes are equal," more definitely stated, would stand thus: If to quantities, dimensions, or numbers already equal to each other, equal additions be made, the results will also be equal: and in this form what does the proposition express but our knowledge of the relation of agreement in quantity, dimension, or number between several entities viewed together as one compound entity under the specified circumstances. Thus we might review all the twelve axioms of Euclid, and would find them all to confirm the statements we have made.

To the same class of relative knowledge belong all the relations (not properties) of numbers in arithmetical calculations. Thus, "twice three are six," when fully stated, means, that the number three twice taken, or counted, bears the relation of equality to the number six.

Metaphysical axioms, when rightly examined, also belong to this class of relative knowledge. Thus, "Every effect must have a cause," or, more fully stated, every effect we ever knew had a cause, hence all other effects most probably have, seems to be nothing else than our knowledge of the relation of analogy, between two or more given substantive or adjective entites, viewed in relation to each other. Self-evident truths consist mainly of relations between entities.

Moral abstract propositions are also resolvable into expressions of our knowledge of some relation or other. Thus the maxim, "Vice is productive of misery," may be regarded as an abstract expression of the relation of causation, subsisting between sinful actions and misery; or it may be changed into the knowledge of the relation of analogy by thus altering the terms: "Vicious actions have, so far as we have been able to observe, always sooner or later produced unhappiness, therefore they, in all probability, will do so also in future."

Dictates of Conscience, or *Moral Judgments*, that is, judgments concerning the morality of actions, concerning their conformity or non-conformity to the law of God, are also relative knowledge. The operations of conscience, when correctly analyzed, consist of three distinct elements, the *judicial*, the *sentient*, and the *impulsive*. The judicial element is cognitive, and consists in a judgment of the mind concerning the relation of our actions to our ideas of the law of God, as being conformed to them, or in violation of them. If the views of men concerning the Divine law were always correct, the decisions of conscience would invariably be accurate as to the moral character of human actions. This judgment concerning the morality of the action always precedes as well the emotion of pleasure or pain, approbation or disapprobation, as the impulsive dictate of obligation, to perform or not to perform the act contemplated. Hence, as the views of the heathen concerning the law of God are very erroneous, they approve of many actions, such as parricide, infanticide, sacrifice of human beings, which are highly sinful, although their *intention* in all these cases may be to do right. And even Paul, so long as he considered Christianity a violation of the law of his God, says, "I verily thought with myself that I ought to do many things contrary to the name of Jesus of Nazareth," although after his judgment of the character of the act was changed, he deeply regretted his conduct.*

Belief of a relation, is also relative knowledge. Belief may be divided into *immediate* and *acquired;* the former embracing what are usually termed constitutional or intuitive judgments, and the latter, acquired or deduced judgments. There is no other difference between immediate and acquired judgments except that the relation subsisting between the two entities is so obvious in the one case, that the mind immediately perceives it to exist; and in the other, that the relation is so indistinct, that other additional related entities, must be examined before the mind perceives it to be true.

Both intuitive and acquired truths may be divided into those relating to our own minds, and those which refer to other entities. To the first class of truths, belong such as these: that the testimony of our senses fairly ascertained, is true—that we exist—that the several operations of our minds may generally be relied on—that we are possessed of personal identity. The second class embraces truths relating to the absolute and to the concrete entities.

* See Part II., Moral Emotions, and Part III., First Constitutional Inclination.

Among them are the truths, that every effect must have a cause—that the laws of nature, i. e., the established modes of the Divine agency, are uniform—metaphysical axioms—moral truths, &c.

All belief, therefore, of whatever degree, whether presumptive, or probable, or certain, differs in degree, but not in kind. And the all-wise Creator has so constituted the mind, that when the evidences of any truth are fully exhibited and impartially weighed, the strength of our belief will be proportionate to the degree of evidence.

Retrospective, Present, and Prospective Knowledge.

Our cognitive ideas may again be divided into retrospective, present, and prospective.

I. *Retrospective knowledge* is our knowledge of all our former cognitive, sentient, and active ideas, and is usually termed recollection or acts of memory. It embraces all our past operations. This species of knowledge may be subdivided into *spontaneous* and *voluntary* retrospective knowledge. By the former, or spontaneous retrospective knowledge, is meant that, which is not produced in the mind by a volition to recall it. By the latter is meant those recollections of former mental operations, which are produced by a voluntary effort to recall them. This effort consists in an active review of related things, times, and places, and sometimes in a review of the letters of the alphabet, in expectation that the sight of the first letter of a word, will recall the whole word, and with it, our knowledge of the thing or entity. The extent of our spontaneous retrospective knowledge and the extent to which, and the facility with which we can voluntarily recall it, depend on the following circumstances.

1. On the natural aptitude of the mind for this exercise; or, in other words, the natural retentiveness of memory. This differs in different persons, but is, among all the powers of the mind, the most susceptible of improvement by practice. Some men appear to have at constant command an intuitive retrospect of the great mass of the former incidents of their life, and of the sciences which they have studied. Doubtless this superior and abundant mass of materials, must necessarily give superior scope and success to those active operations of the mind, which are based on them. It is thus, that men of genius, having the vast experience of former ages, and an extensive acquaintance with the laws, properties, and relations of entities at command, can produce much more accurate specimens of prospective knowledge, and make more able vindications of the positions they assume with regard to any subject.

2. The second ground of difference in the extent and facility of our retrospective knowledge, is found in the different degrees of logical accuracy, with which our knowledge is arranged, on paper or in the mind, according to the different relations themselves which subsist between the entities. It is a well-established fact, that our knowledge of those entities, which are clearly connected by some obvious relation, such as sameness, contrariety, genus,

species, &c., are most easily and most extensively recollected. Hence, one method of facilitating our voluntary recollections of former entities is, habitually to classify our knowledge according to the most obvious relations of the entities themselves, which are the subjects of them, or with some principle or fact, confirmed or illustrated by them. This habit we strongly recommend to the young student. If early formed, and steadily persisted in, it will lead to the gradual and easy accumulation of an amount of useful knowledge, far greater, more various, and more readily at command, than would otherwise be retained. One important method of aiding us in committing a speech, or sermon, or any other composition to memory, is to write it in such a logical manner, according to the objective relations of the subjects themselves.

3. The third ground of difference, is found in the different degrees of frequency, with which the knowledge to be retained was revised by the mind, and the feeling or interest which was felt in it.

Our retrospective knowledge will be increased by the following methods: 1. By thinking frequently of the ideas intended to be recollected. 2. By reviewing those ideas together, which we wish to recollect together; and in the very same order in which we desire to remember them. 3. By connecting them, in the act of memorizing, with some principle or fact, which we will be sure to remember at the intended time. 4. By the habit of studying *subjects* rather than *books*. This is an extremely important habit, which, as it is of constant application, and may be continued through life, exerts a very perceptible influence on intellectual character and attainments. The man who reads through, even the more important works to which he has access, not only vainly expends his time in perusing much that he knew before, but also pursues an intellectual habit not the most profitable. It is not even every good book that deserves to be read through. Far better is it for the student, to keep up merely a general acquaintance with the publications which he deems worthy of his attention, by an examination of their table of contents, and a *tasting* of them on some of the most important topics, so as to form an estimate of the character and strength of the author, and then lay them by for future use; while he devotes the greater part of his time to the systematic study of subjects, examining, on each such subject, all the valuable authors to which he has access, and tracing the subject through all its various ramifications and relations. The selection of these subjects should be influenced by the professional duties of the individual; and, while collateral matters of taste and science should not be excluded, yet the more extensively the choice of subjects coincides with our daily duties, the greater will be the eminence attained. 5. Our retrospective knowledge will be increased by interesting our feelings in the subject, by viewing its relations to some of the constitutional inclinations of the soul, hereafter to be explained.

Scarcely any bounds can be affixed to the degree of improvement which the retentive powers have sometimes attained. Kepler, the celebrated German mathematician, could repeat the whole of Virgil's Æneid, and even specify the first and last lines on every page of the copy which he used. Henry de Mesmes could repeat the whole of Homer; and of the celebrated Pascal it was said, that he very rarely forgot anything which he had ever known. Cyrus, we are told, knew the name of every soldier in his army; and Themistocles could call by name the twenty thousand inhabitants of Athens. Even admitting that these accounts must be received, as we suppose they must, with some qualification, they are remarkable and most interesting examples of mnemonic power. These were instances of persons in health, who exhibited these extraordinary powers through life. But there are other facts, which shed a new light on the retrospective power of the soul, and seem to prove that persons of the most ordinary talents, yea, that the soul of every man naturally possesses equal and even greater mnemonic powers, which are now confined by the organs of the body, but will be fully developed in the eternal world. Different diseases have called forth temporary exhibitions of this superior power of memory. "A case occurred at St. Thomas Hospital, of a man who was in a state of stupor in consequence of an injury of the head. On his partial recovery, he spoke a language which nobody in the hospital understood, but which was soon ascertained to be Welsh. It was then discovered that he had been thirty years absent from Wales, and, before the accident, had entirely forgotten his native language. On his complete recovery, he entirely forgot his

Welsh again, and recovered the English language. A lady, mentioned by Dr. Pritchard, when in a state of delirium, spoke a language which nobody about her understood, but which also was discovered to be Welsh. None of her friends could form any conception of the manner in which she had become acquainted with that language; but, after much inquiry, it was discovered, that in her childhood she had a nurse, a native of a district on the coast of Brittany, the dialect of which is closely analogous to the Welsh. The lady had, at that time, learned a good deal of this dialect, but had entirely forgotten it for many years before this attack of fever."* But the most interesting case with which we have met, is that mentioned by Coleridge, of a young woman in Germany, some time before 1798. Though she could neither read nor write, yet, when labouring under a nervous fever, she uttered numerous sentences in Latin, Greek, and Hebrew. Her case excited great attention, and was, for a season, regarded as inexplicable. At length it was discovered that, in early life, she had lived in the family of a learned Protestant minister, who was in the habit of walking up and down the passage of his house, into which the kitchen door opened, and reading aloud his favourite authors in these languages. And it was also found, that the passages which she recited corresponded with these authors. In these cases it is evident that the impression made upon the memory, though the persons had not the power to recall them in health, were, nevertheless, not lost, but still remained engraven, as it were, on the tablets of the

* Abercrombie on the Intellectual Powers, p. 123

soul, and disease wrought such a change in the bodily organs, or exerted such a stimulus upon the brain, that the soul had more free scope for action. Why, then, may we not indulge the amazing, the appalling, yet highly probable conjecture, that *thought is indestructible* in its nature, that every individual idea we have ever had, though now forgotten by us, is indelibly impressed upon the soul, is, as it were, locked up in its inner recesses, and at the great day of eternity will stand in full view before us, will be recollected as vividly as the occurrences of yesterday? It seems, indeed, highly probable, that such an increased recollection will bring the whole agency of our present life into close connexion with the eternal world, and that, in the providence of God, this whole accumulated mass of our thoughts will be the basis of our future retribution, will be the occasion, or will give some peculiarity to the circumstances of the happiness of the righteous and misery of the wicked.

Various attempts have been made, both in ancient and modern times, to aid the energies of this important power of the soul by artificial contrivances, not one of which has commanded the permanent approbation of the wise and judicious. Some empyrics recommended sundry medicinal prescriptions, which are, however, all eventually injurious to both body and mind. Others invented different artificial systems of mnemonics, some of which appear in a few instances to afford an advantage; but all of which are eventually of little or no benefit, and some of them positively injurious to the real improvement of the mind. The credit of having invented the first system of this kind is attributed to Simonides, the poet and philosopher of Ceos, an island in the Ægean Sea, who lived B.C. about 557. On one occasion, as Cicero informs us,* while dining in company with some of his friends, he was called out of the house, but, on coming out, found no one. Just as he was about to return, the house or hall suddenly fell and crushed his friends to death. When the rubbish had been removed, they were found so much disfigured, that they could not be recognised; but Simonides could distinguish them all, because he recollected the place in which each one had reclined around the table. By this incident he was led to reflect, that order, or a proper disposition of the objects to be recollected, affords the greatest aid to memory, and that those who desire to cultivate this talent should select certain places, and picture upon their minds the things which they wish to recollect, and arrange them into these places. Thus the order of the places would enable them to recollect the order of the things, and the pictures or images of these things would point out the things themselves. The same principle of associating our ideas with certain symbols, or images, or hieroglyphics, and arranging these in various ways, seems also to be the basis of the principal systems of mnemonics of modern times.

Different methods have likewise been invented to facilitate the recollection of dates and figures generally. The most popular is, perhaps, that of Feinagle, who framed the following table, which is first to be committed to memory with much accuracy.

* Cicero, De Oratore, lib. ii., § 86, p. 197.

The number in question is then to be expressed by the letters of this key table, taken either from the consonants or vowels, as may seem most suitable, and annexed to the end of the word to which the figures refer.

a	e	i	o	u	au	oi	ei	ou	y
1	2	3	4	5	6	7	8	9	0
b	d	t	f	l	s	p	k	n	z

Thus, to recollect the date B.C. 46, when Julius Cæsar obtained supreme command at Rome, take the letters o(=4) and s(=6), and put them in place of the last letters of his name. We then have Juli*os*, which is easily recollected, and cannot fail to indicate the date 46, unless the alphabet is forgotten. After all, the best general rule, in addition to those given above, is daily practice continued for years, and not entirely omitted even in after life. Quintilian remarks, "Si quis unam maximamque a me artem memoriæ quærat, exercitatio est et labor. Multa ediscere, multa cogitare, et si fieri potest, quotidie, potentissimum est."

We conclude our observations on memory by adding the excellent practical directions to teachers and younger pupils, compiled from Dr. Niemeyer.* 1. We should begin at a very early age to teach our pupils to retain and to repeat what they have heard. Their internal organs thus acquire a certain degree of firmness, and their frequent exercise forms a habit. 2. They should be taught to retain signs, espe-

* *Grundsätze der Erziehung und des Unterrichts*, vol. i., p. 124. On this subject see also an excellent work by Professor Smith, *Education: its History and Practice*, p. 214.

cially words, as well as things. That which is naturally most easy for them, requires less practice; that which is more difficult, should receive the more attention. 3. If they retain words with facility, even without understanding their import, they should be exercised the more faithfully in recollecting ideas and things, both individually, and in their several relations. Otherwise the memory will be cultivated at the expense of the judgment. Thus the pupil should be called on to repeat the *substance* of a discourse which he has heard; or, after he has read one page of a book, let him close the volume, and repeat to you the train of ideas contained on it; or let him trace the thread of a discourse backward to its first idea. As a remarkable instance of the proficiency attainable by this kind of training, we would mention the case of the late Reverend Uhlhorn, pastor of the German Lutheran Church in Baltimore, and one of the most finished scholars that have crossed the Atlantic, who, after twice or thrice perusing any hymn of six or eight verses, was able to repeat it backward, word for word, from end to beginning. 4. If, on the contrary, the pupil finds it easy to retain and repeat a multitude of ideas, concerning that which he has heard, or seen, or read, but cannot preserve their particular order or connexion, or repeat particular expressions; this also requires special attention. For it is, on many accounts, advantageous to be able to retain names, numbers, and passages out of letters or books, and to repeat them verbatim. A number of words should, therefore, daily be assigned, but only such whose meaning the pupil understands, to be committed in a given time, and that number should be gradually increased. Subsequently, select passages from different authors may be assigned, and the interest of the pupils kept up by the matter of the extracts committed, as well as by emulation among the scholars, and explanations of the importance of the exercise. 5. Let not a day pass without some exercise of memory for all the pupils. 6. Let those of defective memory not be discouraged by harshness; but let various methods be employed for their encouragement, by calling to aid the principles of association. Associations of time and place will assist their recollection. Generic ideas will recall the specific one embraced in them, &c.

II. *Present knowledge* embraces the testimony of *consciousness*, by which is meant that knowledge which we have of all our present mental operations of every class. Of course, if the lines of division be strictly adhered to, that portion of our knowledge which can correctly be called present, is comparatively small; for the moment after any act of present cognition is past, it belongs to the retrospective department.

Still, even when circumscribed by these narrow limits, consciousness embraces all the operations of our minds, at the precise time of their performance such as our perceptions, our sensations, our emotions, our passions, our judgments in general, our acts of conscience, and, in short, all our mental operations. So soon, however, as any mental operation of which we are conscious is past, it becomes, as it were, the property of memory, and falls into the retrospective department. Consciousness is an important source of new ideas to us. By it we acquire all our knowledge of the inner man, oı the powers, properties, and relations of our own minds, of that thinking, conscious subject myself. It is by consciousness that we obtain our knowledge of those mental operations expressed by the words thinking, believing, doubting, reflecting, &c.

The term consciousness is strictly confined to the operations and processes which take place in the mind itself, and cannot with propriety be applied to any material object, or, indeed, to any other entity whatever except the phenomena of our own minds. We cannot be said to be conscious of the existence of the earth, or planets, or mountains, or trees, or even of our own bodies. We are conscious of certain perceptions and sensations which these external objects produce in the mind, when they are at the time acting on us through our bodily organs, but not of these entities themselves. Every act of consciousness also, by a constitutional judgment of our mind, implies the existence of a conscious being, of *myself*, from whom it proceeds.

III. *Prospective knowledge.* By this we mean all our knowledge of the probable future existence of entities and their relations. That God has actually bestowed on us some knowledge of futurity, is evident from an examination of our ideas themselves, and even from the structure of human language. Every individual instance in which we use the future tense of a verb, is an exemplification of our remark. The vast sphere of human expectations, of hopes and fears, is distinctly embraced within the limits of prospective knowledge. Indeed, calculations and expectations of a prospective nature enter into all human pursuits and occupations. Without them, all business would be at a stand, the principal motive to human action would be destroyed, and the world itself would cease to be what it is. But here the question arises, Is our prospective knowledge also a knowledge of entities, and their relations really existing? To this we reply, that in part it is; and we suppose the following to be a correct view of this subject:

The subject of our prospective knowledge, objectively considered, seems always to be a composite entity, viz., a present entity and another supposed, future entity of some given character, as existing at some future time more or less distant. The relation between these two, observed by the mind, is that of fitness, or analogy, or causation, &c. Thus our prospective knowledge or belief of the probable future existence of the material world, and of all existing classes of entities and their relations, is nothing else than a knowledge of the relation of fitness or causation, as existing between present entities and the same entities as existing at a future time. Thus, also, we behold a drunkard, fast hastening to the grave, and believe that he may yet live six months, but not six years. In both instances, the subject of our belief, is a composite entity. We observe, in one case, the relation of fitness between the entity, a drunkard, now existing with materially injured health, and his being still alive six months hence; but we also perceive the relation of unfitness, between his present state, and his existence six years hence. Or we might say, we see between his present conduct and his death before six years, the relation of probable causation. We see that intemperance will cause his death in less than the specified time. Our prospective knowledge of future human actions, under given circumstances, is nothing else than a prospective knowledge of the relation of suitableness, or causation, between a given character of an individual, and a particular course of probable conduct. Of the many relations, perceivable between the different classes of entities, a few only seem to serve as bases of our prospective knowledge; viz., *fitness*, by which we mean suitableness, reasonableness, or accordance with the nature of the entity, *analogy*, *causation*, and *revelation*. Analogy, causation, and revelation may be regarded as the arches of the bridge, over which we pass from the present to a knowledge of the future. The relation of fitness is general in its nature, and seems to embrace analogy and causation; yet there are cases in which the mind cannot clearly determine how far the antecedent is really the cause of the consequent, or whether it be merely the antecedent. The revelation, which God has given us, is another totally distinct basis of prospective knowledge. In many items of prospective knowledge derived from this source, we can now clearly perceive also the relation of fitness and causation, since that knowledge has been communicated to us; although we were totally unable, à priori, to discover it. Our belief in a

Divine revelation is a knowledge of a composite entity, viz., the Divine character, as known to us, and certain superhuman actions, termed miracles, of some kind or other. The relation perceived between them, is that of suitableness or exclusive causation; that is, causation which creatures could not exert.

Our prospective knowledge of the future operations and states of all inanimate entities, would be as certain as our present and retrospective knowledge of them, if we possessed a present, omniscient acquaintance with all their properties; and if their circumstances and relations were not changed by the voluntary agency of animated beings, and if we knew that the Divine Being would not withdraw or change these properties. Or, in other words, in a world purely mechanical, in which no voluntary agency was mingled, an omniscient present knowledge, would necessarily imply an omniscient prospective knowledge to beings, endowed like ourselves, with the ability to perceive these relations. In such a world, the prospective knowledge of any creature constituted like man, however limited it might be, would probably be of equal extent with his present knowledge. Yet in our world, the operations of inanimate nature are constantly influenced by the agency of animate beings, rational and irrational; and therefore our prospective knowledge, even of the inanimate world, is, in many cases, very uncertain. Our prospective knowledge of the future conduct of animate beings, especially those of the higher class, must, for obvious reasons, be still more indistinct and uncertain, on account of the voluntary agency possessed by man. Yet here also, whatever prospective knowledge we do possess, is strictly a knowledge of composite entities. Thus, the late sagacious politician Talleyrand had a prospective knowledge of the French Revolution, of 1830, some time at least before it occurred. What else was this knowledge, than a knowledge of the relation of causation between the arbitrary measures of the French king and his cabinet, and a revolution, that is, resistance to these measures on the part of the discontented French people ? In short, every individual has a certain sphere of intellectual vision all around him, which, like the torch of the benighted traveller, enables him safely to steer his course through the circumstances and pursuits of life.

This subject is one of great interest to every reflecting mind. The principles above detailed, seem to present a definite and intelligible view of all our knowledge of futurity. It is nothing else than a knowledge of composite entities, one part of which is present, and the other future. In the *present* part we see the relation of fitness, of causation, of analogy to the supposed future part. On our knowledge of these relations in present entities, depends our power of prospection. All our knowledge of futurity, which is so important in human life, and is the basis of all our plans and enterprises, may be reduced to the simple view, that it is a knowledge of the relations of causation, analogy, and revelation, seen by us in some existing entity, or learned from the inspired volume. On this prospective knowledge, the politician bases his calculations, the man of business and the Christian their arrangements for future operations. We know almost with certainty, that the physical universe, the properties and tendencies of material things, will continue: and it is probable, that the other circumstances of our situation will, in the main, remain unchanged. Thus, we have a highly probable foreknowledge of the future continuance of nine tenths of the circumstances and prospects of our situation. We also know, that the changes which may occur will be limited by the powers of the different agents, and the laws of nature. Hence, the possible changes cannot materially affect our prospects, or alter the propriety and wisdom of our course, and the principles of our action. Relying on all these circumstances, we pursue our course of business, secular or sacred, with confidence and delight.

CHAPTER III.

ORGANIC PROCESS BY WHICH WE OBTAIN OUR IDEAS

The entire human body, considered as an organ for the influence of entities, may be viewed in a twofold light, as a general organ, and as a collection of several organs. The effects produced in the mind through the bodily organs are a knowledge of the shape, colour, odour, flavour, and sound of entities, together with feelings more or less pleasant or unpleasant, attending the operation of each organ. These organs, it need scarcely be observed, are not themselves the percipient agents; but the mere unintelligent instrumentality, through which, by divine appointment, the soul acts. The inverted image of any object within the sphere of vision, is made on the retina of an ox's eye, after it has been taken from the head of the slaughtered animal; but, of course, the eye has no vision. The eyes of animals are mere instruments, like the telescope of the astronomer. Although it is indispensable to the perception of those celestial bodies, which are beyond the reach of the naked eye, yet no one could for a moment imagine that the telescope itself had a perception of these objects. Philosophically speaking, it is, therefore, not the eye which sees, but the soul.

We might divide the results of the soul's action through bodily organs, into those produced through the medium of every part of the surface of the body, such as shape; and, secondly, those for which only particular parts of the body, such as the eye, the ear, the nose, serve as organs, viz., colour, odour, sound, &c. I have knowledge of the sun by my eye, of music by my ear, of the flavour of an orange by my palate, of the odour of a flower by my olfactory organs, of the solidity of a ball by my hand, or some other part of my body which touches it. And, in each instance, this knowledge is more or less pleasant or unpleasant, or, in other words, is accompanied by some degree of feeling, which is in a greater or less degree either pleasing or the reverse.

In all cases, the influence of entities is exerted by the actual contact of the organ; nor does any "operatio in distans," so far as we know, take place. Thus, in taste, the palate and tongue are touched by the article tasted; in hearing, the tympanum of the ear is struck by the vibrations of the atmosphere; in smelling, the olfactory nerves are touched by the particles emanating from the odoriferous body; as is proved by the fact, that the most fragrant rose or shrub, if placed under a glass cylinder, cannot be smelled. In vision, the eyes are touched by the rays of light, proceeding from the object which is seen, either by reflection, or refraction, or repulsion, as the case may be. We are, therefore, under no necessity of having recourse to the exploded theory of animal spirits, or nervous fluid, or of intervening cerebral vibrations, in order to form a connexion between the mind and the object of its perception. And, in all these cases, the nerves of sensation and of motion, which are imbodied in the organ of sense, or constitute a part of it, are connected with the brain, of which they are all branches, and which is the ultimate and principal physical organ, through which the mind acts and is acted upon, in its connexion with the material world. Whether the brain is one general organ, or, as phrenologists contend, consists of a collection of individual organs, each corresponding to a separate faculty of the mind, has been much disputed. But from the harmony of universal science in all its ramifications, we may confidently predict, that the results of Phrenology, when brought to a satisfactory degree of certainty, will not conflict with the true system of Psychology.

The mental resnlts, both cognitive and sentient, of our sensorial action through these organs, are, in general, termed, in popular language, *Sensations.* Thus, we speak of the sensations of sight, of smell, of touch, of taste, &c., meaning principally those cognitions which we derive through these organs, and which are more specifically termed perceptions. This vague use of the term we derive from the Romans, who employ in the same general manner both *sentio* and *sensus*, from which our word sensation is ultimately derived. Yet, as this term is, in common language, more generally used as expressive of *feelings*, and as the related terms, sensibility, sensitive, and sentient, are employed exclusively with a similar reference, a laudable desire of rigid precision, and consistency in metaphysical phraseology, would dictate the constant discrimination between those results of our organic action which are cognitive and those that are sentient, and the employment of the term perceptions, rather than sensations, to designate the former.

The *eye*, or organ of vision, is an instrument constructed with the most perfect accuracy, in accordance with the ascertained principles of optics. The most perfect optical instruments fall far short of it in accuracy and excellence. Indeed, a more striking and intelligible exhibition of the knowledge and wisdom of the Creator, cannot be imagined. The ball of the eye itself is a species of camera obscura. Its exterior consists of two membraneous coverings, the outer one called *sclerotica* (σκληροτι-κης, hard), on account of its superior firmness, and the inner, *choroid* (χοροειδής, like a skin), from its cuticular appearance. Within this inner coat, and expanded over its surface, is the optic nerve, which receives the rays of light, and on which they form an image of the external object, which reflects them to the eye. In the front part of the eye, which is exposed to view, is the *cornea*, so called because, when dried, it has nearly the consistence of very fine horn. It is transparent, and projects from the eyeball, like the segment of a smaller sphere. Back of the centre of the cornea, is a small opening in the choroid, termed the pupil, through which the rays of light enter. And in the rear of this, are the aqueous humour, then the crystalline lens of a dense texture, both nearly of the same size with the cornea, and, lastly, the vitreous or glassy humour, which fills the remaining cavity of the eye. These several pellucid humours collect the rays of light into a focus on the retina.

The eye affords us the knowledge of colour, local direction, and expansion. When I open my eyes, I behold the different objects within the range of my vision, and instantly derive not only the idea of colour, but also of direction or location in space, of every one of them, as I successively direct my attention to each. And, by the improvement resulting from practice, I also become able to judge of the shape and distance of objects through the instrumentality of the eye. All objects of vision occupy relative positions in space, and a perception of this position is one of the primary and original items of knowledge derived through the visual organ. By touch and locomotion, we may obtain similar knowledge, even if divested of sight. Yet the process is more tardy, and can be applied only to such objects as we can personally reach.

Vision is performed through the medium of light, or, more properly speaking, light is the object of vision. It consists of rays of different colours and of different degrees of refrangibility. When we permit a portion of light to pass through a prism, its different colours are separated, in consequence of the shape of that instrument, by which the rays are refracted in different degrees out of a right line. We thus perceive the regular series of colours from red to violet.

The superficial texture of all visible objects may be reduced to precisely as many varieties as are found in colour. Each of the textures reflects, or, according to a different theory, repels the light, in a manner somewhat different from every other, and reflects or repels a surface of rays equal to its own bulk. These rays light upon the lens of the eye, and are converged with the peculiarity of every different texture to the retina; and thus, by divine constitution, we have the knowledge of different colours. So that the rays of light, coming from the objects in different degrees of spissitude, and in the particular state of reflection or repulsion corresponding to the particular texture of the objects, are as much, and in the same sense, the cause of our knowledge of colour, as the particles emitted by the rose and touching our nostrils, are of smell, or the peach touching the palate and tongue, is of taste.

In vision we see nothing, originally, but colour and location, or direction and extension. Distance is not the direct object of vision, because children will stretch out their little hands to catch the moon, until experience teaches them the futility of the attempt; and a person cured of congenital blindness, by an operation for the cataract, will for some time hold out his hand and feel his way, lest he strike against the stove or table at the other end of the room. That we do form some original judgment of extension and peripheral shape by the eye, seems very clear. For, it can be demonstrated that the images formed on the retina, vary and correspond to the different outline and extension of the objects which they represent. Now, as the mind has a correspondent and different idea for every cognoscible diversity of objects, it must have one for this also. It is doubtless true, as Mr. Locke and others have maintained, that a blind man, who had learned by touch the difference of shape between a cube and a sphere, could not, on being restored to sight, discover by his eye, which was cubical? and which was spherical. But this fact does not, we think, prove that we obtain no idea of extension and shape by the eye. It only establishes the position, that the man suddenly restored to sight, could not at once decide which of the two different outlines of which he had an idea by sight, corresponds to the one, to his ideas of which, as obtained by touch, he had given the name either of cube or sphere. Both sight and touch give us distinct and definite ideas of the peripheral shape of objects, but we cannot tell which one of the properties learned by one sense, corresponds to a given property learned by the other sense, until we have ascertained the fact by the conjoined action of both. It must also be remembered that the association between words and our ideas of objects is arbitrary, and is formed only by practice or usage. The blind man has long been accustomed to associate the ideas of touch, which he acquires from those objects, with the words cube and sphere; but when his first vision also gives him the ideas of these objects appropriate to sight, there is no association existing between these ideas and the words cube and sphere. If, therefore, he be asked, which of the two is the figure which he had been accustomed to call either cube or sphere, he could not tell. He could only reply that they appear evidently different; but the association of these new ideas with sounds or names is yet to be formed. As yet, neither of these names will recall or designate his newly-acquired ideas, and he can no more tell which is the cube, and which the sphere, than if you were to ask him in Greek, which is the *κυρος* and which the *σφᾶιρα*. He has not yet learned the correspondence of the ideas themselves, much less of the terms which usage has employed to designate them.

That the eye does not originally give us any knowledge of shape, excepting the mere outline, or extension, is evident; because a well-executed painting will deceive even an adult; and all effort to represent the shape of objects in portraits or other paintings, is based upon this fact, and demonstrative of it. Many of our readers may recollect, that on entering Peale's Museum in Philadelphia, at one end of the long hall, they saw at the other a flight of stairs, and an aged gentleman just in the act of ascending, but, as if attracted by the noise of their entrance, looking back at them, full in the face. On nearer approach, however, the deception was discovered, and the whole proved to be a most successful effort of the artist's pencil, a lasting monument of the high eminence attained by Mr. Peale, in his favourite pursuit. In short, the entity which is the object of our knowledge in vision, is not the external person or thing said to be seen, but is merely the rays of light. No man has ever literally seen his nearest friend, his father or mother, his brother or sister. He has seen the light reflected from them on the retina of his eye, and nothing more. What we see is nothing else than those rays of light which actually enter into the pupil of the eye; and it is experience which teaches us, that there are external objects corresponding to them, from which they proceed. It is the different textures or affinities, corresponding to these different colours seen by us, of which we thus acquire a knowledge.

For the idea of *apparent* and *relative*, but not of *actual size*, we are also indebted to the eye. The image formed on the retina is large or small according to the magnitude and distance of the objects. Thus the apparent magnitude of objects varies, but their real size is of course unchanged. When we first perceive a vessel at sea in the distant horizon, it appears very small; but as it approaches us, its magnitude seems to increase, until it has attained its natural size in proximity; yet the actual size of the vessel was of course unchanged. Of objects equidistant from the eye, vision will give us a correct idea of the relative magnitude. Thus, as we know that the balloon and the basket attached to it are nearly equidistant from us, however far or near they may be, we can form an accurate judgment of the relative size of each, so long as both are visible to us. After we know the distance of any objects, practice enables us to judge of their actual size, by sight. Yet this is, originally, the combined result of touch and vision. Experience teaches us to judge of the diminution which distance makes, in the apparent magnitude of objects; and optical science explains the causes on which these appearances depend. We are so accustomed to see objects diminish in size as they recede from us, that daily observation confers considerable accuracy on our practical judgment; and thus, by a rapid process, we learn to judge of the actual magnitude of all objects, whose distance we know. We form an estimate of the diminution, which the known distance would make in the apparent size of an object, and thus judge of its actual magnitude. The idea, which the mind acquires of the images formed on the retina by different objects, does of course not resemble that image in any known property; yet, for each image, the mind obtains a definite idea, both as to colour, peripheral shape or outline, and size. It is on this principle, that in the science of perspective, we indicate on canvass the increased distance of a known object, by a diminution of its size. And, when we view an object through a spy-glass, and judge it to be brought nearer to us, this effect is produced in accordance with the same principles, the only change being that the lenses of the instrument make the rays of light fall on the retina in a more dilated or expanded form, thus actually making on it a larger image.

When objects are near at hand, or in the vicinity of others of whose distance we have some idea, we can form a judgment from the degree of inclination on the axis of vision and the angles formed with surrounding objects. For this purpose, the Creator has kindly given us two eyes, while for all other purposes one would suffice, as the action of each is separate and independent.

The degree of distinctness with which objects are seen by us also leads us to form some judgment of their distance; as we know that near objects always appear more clearly visible than those afar off. For this cause, objects seen through a mist are judged to be more distant than they really are. The standard by which we judge is the degree of clearness in an ordinary atmosphere, and then our judgment is correct; but when we apply the same standard to the appearance of objects seen through a mist, it is calculated to mislead us.

When a strange object is in the vicinity of another of known size, we can judge of the size of the former by its apparent relative size, even when the distance of both is unknown. On this principle, painters show the size of a house by locating a man, or horse, or fence in its vicinity. As the size of these latter objects varies but little, it forms a standard by which to judge the magnitude of the others.

It is an interesting fact, that objects appear to us in their natural position, while it can be proved that their image formed on the retina is inverted. Nor has any solution been given of this phenomenon, other than that it is the appointed law of the mind. And of similar inexplicable nature is the fact, that though we see objects with two eyes, they appear to a person of sound organs as single; while to persons who are affected with a disease in one eye, which prevents it from being acted on precisely like the other, objects are seen double, that is, images somewhat different are made on the retina of the two eyes, and ideas somewhat different are thus excited in the mind by the same object.

In addition to the perceptions obtained through vision, the eye is also, at the same time, one of the media through which pleasing *feelings* are excited in the mind by external objects. It is through this organ that the pleasant feelings excited by the beauties of a landscape, that is, by the varieties and combinations of its colours, are produced in the mind. In short, this is the organ through which a benevolent God designed to confer, and actually does bestow upon us, a large portion of the incidental happiness belonging to our pilgrimage on earth. Even the light of the returning day is calculated itself to inspire the mind with pleasure; and whithersoever we direct our steps, objects meet the eye calculated to afford us delight. The vegetable kingdom presents to us the flowers of the field and garden, in their numberless varieties and shades of colour transcending the array of Solomon in all his glory: the grain fields, waving like the ocean before the passing breeze; and the trees of the forest bending majestically before the still more powerful storm, are all calculated to excite feelings of the most interesting and pleasing nature. The mineral and animal kingdoms, in like manner, abound in objects calculated to delight the observer. Yea, so susceptible are we of pleasure from this source, that there is need of caution, lest we take so much delight in the creature as to overlook the Creator, by whom all these objects were made, and to whom they are all designed to conduct us. Who among my readers has not seen some naturalist to whom the words of nature's favourite, Pollok, would apply?

> "One made acquaintanceship with plants and flowers,
> And happy grew in telling all their names;
> One classed the quadrupeds; a third the fowls;
> Another found in minerals his joy:
> And I have seen a man, a worthy man,
> In happy mood conversing with a fly;
> And as he, through his glass, made by himself,
> Beheld its wondrous eye and plumage fine,
> From leaping scarce he kept, for perfect joy."

But in regard to vision, and to perception through any of the senses, the *attention* of the mind is necessary to the perfection of the process. The rays of light may be reflected from an object to the eye, and form an image on the retina; but we have no recollection of a perception, unless our attention be directed to the object. The rays of light are at all times as fully reflected to the eye from all other objects within the entire field of vision before us, as from that one to which our attention is at any given time directed; and yet we recollect only the one which has attracted our attention. In short, there are hundreds of images formed on the retina at all times; but it is a law of the soul that, although we have an indefinite simultaneous vision of several objects before us, we take cognizance only of one at a time; and of our perceptions of that one alone do we retain any recollection.

As to the question which has so much puzzled philosophers of all ages and nations, how this perception is effected through the organs; what, for example, is the connexion between the image on the retina and the perception of the soul; our reply is, that it is the constituted order of things, as appointed by God, and inexplicable to us. The image on the retina is as indispensable a link in the chain of instrumentality as the presence of light, and its passage through the lens of the eye; but we can no more comprehend the connexion of the intelligent percipient action of the soul with the last link of instrumental organism, than with the first. In this, as in a thousand other instances, the facts are known and understood, but the mode of their occurrence, or the causal relation between them, is beyond our comprehension.

The *ear*, or organ of hearing, is likewise a complicated and very delicate member, whose structure is not as easily illustrated as that of the eye. Like the latter organ, it is placed in an elevated part of the body, so as to have a more extended sphere of sensorial action. The external ear is expanded, so as to receive a large surface of vibrations of the air, which it conveys to the point of entrance. Thence a tube, termed the auditory passage (meatus auditorius), conducts the vibrations to the tympanum or drum, which is an expanded nerve analogous to the retina of the eye. From the tympanum, these vibrations are communicated, by the means of four little bones, to the water contained in the cavities of the labyrinth. By means of this water, they are conveyed to the auditory nerve, and finally to the brain. In order that the drum of the ear may act more freely, there is a communication, termed the Eustachian tube, extending from the drum to the back part of the mouth, freely admitting the air. Still, hearing may take place, though less perfectly, when the drum has been perforated, as is proved in the case of those persons who can, by taking smoke into their mouth, express it through one or both their ears, and yet are not deaf. In some cases, also, where suppuration had destroyed the continuity of the chain of little bones, the sense of hearing was not destroyed. The principal medium for the conveyance of these vibrations is the air; yet any other body possessing some elasticity, whether it be solid, liquid, or aeriform, which forms a connexion between the sounding body and the ear, may become the medium of sound. Thus our American Indians apply their ears to the ground, to discover the approach of their enemies, whom they could not yet hear through the air. Yet, in a vacuum, sound cannot be communicated, that is, these vibrations cannot be propagated to the ear except by some intervening body. The susceptibility of the auditory organs is different in different persons, but no one can hear the vibrations of a cord which vibrates less than about thirty-two times in a second. The whole range of distinguishable sounds forms upward of nine octaves.

Sound is therefore an idea of the mind, caused by the vibrations of some stricken object, which vibrations are communicated through the air, or some other elastic medium, to the ear. When we hear the discharge of a distant cannon, the noise is not at the cannon, but in our minds. The discharge of the cannon causes a tremendous agitation in the atmosphere around it, which is extended, like the undulations of a pond when a stone is thrown into it, until they reach the ears of all animals within their circumference, and produce in every one of them the idea of sound.

The number of sounds which we can distinguish is very great, both as to variety of tone and strength of utterance, amounting to many thousands. The mind also perceives a number of relations between sounds, and it is the discussion of these sounds and their relations, as well as the calculation of the causes, nature, and number of the vibrations, by which they are produced, which constitute the theoretical science of music. These vibrations are actions of sounding bodies or entities, and our perceptions of them, and of the relations between them, are cognitive ideas. The relations of concord and discord are the coincidence or confusion of the vibrations of the sounding instrument. Thus, those different strings of a piano, which, owing to their length, thickness, weight, and tension, vibrate in the same time, are said to be in unison. If one string vibrates in exactly double the time of another, every alternate vibration of the one will coincide with the vibrations of the other, and form the concord of an octave.

The ear is the medium not only of our knowledge of the vibrations of the atmosphere called sound, but also of the feeling of pleasure or pain, which the different combinations of these sounds, either harmonious or discordant, are intrinsically calculated to produce. When we listen to a piece of music, we find no difficulty in distinguishing between the different notes, that is, the different vibrations of the air, of which we obtain a knowledge through the ear, and the pleasant or unpleasant feelings excited by these vibrations or notes. Nor can we for a moment hesitate in believing, that the difference in the feelings excited by the harmonious or discordant combinations of sound, arises from a difference in the notes themselves, considered as simple entities, or from the relation of concord or discord subsisting between them. These notes, or rather the ideas of them, are the subjects of mathematical calculations in the science of music. But who ever heard of a writer on this subject, speaking of a chord or discord of feeling, that is, a chord of pleasure or a discord of pain ? Or who ever heard a musician speak of an octave of pleasure or pain ? Common sense, and the structure of the mind, have led men to distinguish between these things, and to acknowledge our perception of each note individually, and of the relations existing between them, as entirely different from the feelings, pleasant or unpleasant, excited by them. Although the ear originally affords us only ideas of sound, yet, by practice, we learn to judge of many other things by this organ. There is but little doubt, that an impression somewhat different is made on the tympanum, not only by the different degrees of force with which the undulating atmosphere touches it, but also by the fact of its striking that organ in a direct or oblique manner. Of this difference we have a distinct idea by the ear alone ; yet, by that exclusively, we could never know that the difference in the loudness of the sound resulted either from the degree of force with which the atmosphere is agitated by the sonorous body, or from its proximity or distance from our ear : nor that the difference in our idea, produced by the directness or obliquity with which the undulations of air strike the ear, was indicative of the local direction of the sounding body whence they proceeded. It is by the combined use of sight, touch, and locomotion, that the distance and direction of the sonorous body are originally learned, and practice then enables us to judge of these circumstances by the ear alone. Yea, we even go farther, and apply these results to objects which could not be reached by touch. It is thus that, having learned the velocity of sound, we judge of the distance of clouds, by the length of time intervening between the flash of lightning in them and our hearing the thunder. An interval of half a minute, we know, proves the cloud to be about six and a half miles distant. Children hear persons addressing them, and at the same time see whether they are in front, at their side, or in their rear; and thus early learn to associate the peculiar sounds produced by persons speaking from different directions, with that direction itself. What this peculiarity about any sound is, it is not easy to describe; yet every person is familiar with it from experience. Nay, so obviously do we thus judge of direction by the ear, that if the vibrations proceeding from a sounding body fall on some smooth and solid surface, and are reflected to our ear, thus causing what is termed an echo, we judge the cause of that echo to be in the direction not of the original sounding body, but of that smooth and solid surface which reflected them. In the same indirect manner, the loudness of a sound becomes an index of the distance of the object whence it proceeds. By the combined use of different organs, we become familiar with the ordinary loudness of any customary sound at a given distance, and also learn to distinguish and recognise these different sounds, such as those produced by different musical instruments, by the voice of man, and other animals, &c.; and these data being known by experience, we can form a judgment by the ear alone, of the distance of the sounding body. By these results of experience, a kind of practical commutation of the senses takes place, and in the daily occurrences of life, though many objects are within the reach of only one organ, we at once acquire an amount of knowledge of them, which originally belongs to several. In the first volume of the Manchester Philosophical Memoirs is contained the following statement concerning a blind man in that city, quoted by Professor Upham: "I had an opportunity of repeatedly observing the peculiar manner in which he arranged his ideas, and obtained his information. Whenever he was introduced into company, I remarked that he continued some time silent. The sound directed him to judge of the dimensions of the room, and the different voices, of the number of persons that were present. His distinction in these respects was very accurate, and his memory so retentive, that he was seldom mistaken. I have known him instantly to recognise a person on first hearing him, though more than two years had elapsed since the time of their last meeting. He determined pretty nearly the stature of those he was conversing with by the direction of their voices; and he made tolerable conjectures respecting their tempers and dispositions by the manner in which they conducted their conversation."

The organ of *touch* is the whole body, wherever nerves extend, either over its surface, or through its interior. It has been a subject of dispute, whether the nerves of the hand have naturally greater acuteness of sensibility than those of the other parts of the body. As the acuteness or strength of all our local organs is confessedly much increased by practice, and, as in the case of this general organ, those parts of it which are found to be most acute, are also those which, from their position, are most used, it is highly probable that the difference between the sensitiveness of the hand and the other parts of the body, as organs of touch, may also be attributed to that cause. From early life our hands are almost incessantly employed to pick up, to hold, or to move objects, and, in short, to perform all the operations of physical agency, of which that important organ is capable. And as the attention of the mind is ordinarily directed to these manual operations, we have the greater reason to expect great improvement in the mental results accompanying them. It is probably to this want of attention that other portions of the body which are often brought into contact with various objects do not improve proportionably in sensibility; or, to speak more correctly, that the mind does not improve more in sensibility through them.

Whether the organ of touch should be separated from that of muscular effort, has been disputed. Perhaps they may, with more propriety, be regarded as one organ exerted in different degrees. The slightest possible contact, although it could not afford us the same amount of knowledge which we derive from stronger contact, and from the muscular tension caused by firm resistance, yet does seem to include in it the elementary idea of resistance in a small degree, and, therefore, also of muscular action.

By the organ of touch we obtain a knowledge of the different degrees of solidity or fluidity of bodies, their shape, extension, smoothness or roughness, heat or cold. The ideas embraced in this knowledge may probably be reduced to modifications of resistance and extension. We know that the ideas popularly expressed by these terms, as well as the feelings accompanying them, are derived through the organ of touch; and we know, too, that in obtaining them our organ meets with resistance perfect or imperfect, continuous or irregular. By the organ of touch combined with motion, we also acquire an idea of extension and shape; but individual touch does not afford us a general idea of the object causing it. The terms heat and cold properly designate our perception or cognitive idea of a greater or less degree of caloric in the atmosphere, or any other body with which we come into contact. Cold is a negative term, implying the absence of heat. In winter we perceive but little caloric in the atmosphere, and term the weather cold. In summer, when the reverse is the case, we term it warm. What caloric is we do not exactly know; but we employ the term to express the perception we have of it. Nor are we to suppose in this, more than in any other case, that either the perception of caloric, or the feeling attendant on it, has any resemblance to the caloric itself. This perception, however, does not teach us the nature of the radiating body, independently of the other organs of sense. It is a philosophic question, belonging to Pyronomics, rather than

Mental Philosophy, to determine the precise nature of caloric itself. But whether we suppose it to be an independent subtile fluid, or a mere modification of other bodies, all have the same perception of its influence on the human body, and of the feelings caused by it. The terms heat and cold, as expressing the sensation produced by this agent on our frame, are merely relative, the one being produced by our touching a body that has more caloric, and the other one that has less than our hand at the time possesses; and if, after having immersed one hand in hot water and the other in cold, we put them both into water of a medium temperature, to the one hand this water will feel warm and to the other cold at the same time.

In some cases of touch the contact may be so violent that the organ becomes injured, and that the feeling of pain is so great as to make us lose sight of the perception connected with it.

The feeling of exhaustion and fatigue, consequent on continued or violent exertion, seems not to belong to the sense of touch, but rather resembles the periodical appetites, and is a provision of the Creator to admonish us of the necessity of rest.

It has been denied by some recent metaphysicians that the idea of externity is a result of touch, and, consequently, affirmed that our idea of the real existence of the external world is not derived from this or any other organ of sense. This view we consider erroneous. Yet those who maintain it, admit that the idea of externity and of an external world occurs on *occasion* of the use of these organs, especially that of touch; but affirm that it then occurs by a separate law of the soul. We see no reason for the admission of such a separate law in this case, any more than in that of the ideas obtained by the other senses, and prefer regarding it as the appropriate information obtained by this organ. Neither of the other senses could afford us the idea of externity. By the ear alone we could obtain only ideas of sound; by the eye, only of colour, expansion, and direction; by the nostrils, only ideas of odours; but by neither, nor all of these combined, could we have learned the idea of externity in general, or of the existence of the external world. It is to touch and locomotion that we are primarily indebted for our knowledge of the objective reality of these objects.

The sense of touch has been improved to a most surprising degree by practice, and especially by the concentration of the powers of the mind upon it, in consequence of the loss of other senses. It appears to be well ascertained, that some blind persons have been able to judge of their distance from solid bodies by the action or pulsation of the air upon their face, to distinguish spurious coins from such as are genuine, and to distinguish and separate garments and other articles with which they were familiar, from a multitude of others of similar shape and texture. We are told that "Mr. Sanderson, the blind mathematician," could distinguish by his hand, in a series of Roman medals, the true from the counterfeit, with a more unerring discrimnation than the eye of a professed virtuoso; and, when he was present at the astronomical observations in the garden of his college, he was accustomed to perceive every cloud which passed over the sun. This remarkable power, which has sometimes been referred to an increased intensity of particular senses, in many cases evidently resolves itself into an increased habit of attention to the indications of all those senses which the individual retains. "Two instances have been related to me," proceeds Dr. Abercrombie, "of blind men who were much esteemed as judges of horses. One of these, in giving his opinion of a horse, declared him to be blind, though this had escaped the observation of several persons, who had the use of their eyes, and who were with some difficulty convinced of it. Being asked to give an account of the principle on which he had decided, he said it was by the sound of the horse's step in walking, which implied a peculiar and unusual caution in his manner of putting down his feet."

Thus, also, in the various institutions for the blind in this country and Europe, the sense of touch is employed as a substitute for sight, and by the use of uncial letters, elevated above the surface of the page, these unfortunate beings are enabled to distinguish the letters by following them with their fingers, and by practice to spell and read with tolerable facility. A communication has thus been opened for them to the world of intellect, and the literature of the past and present ages may eventually be brought within their view.

The organ of *taste* consists of a number of papillæ, distributed over the surface of the tongue, and particularly over its sides and extreme point, as well as the roof of the mouth or palate. This organ is thus wisely located by a benevolent Providence at the very entrance, through which all articles of food must pass, the healthy or unhealthy character or condition of which may by this means, in most cases, be tested. It serves as a guardian over the character of everything which finds access to the alimentary canal; and it is probable, that in its natural state, unvitiated by luxury and the artificial habits of civilized life, this organ, together with that of smell, would be an almost infallible safeguard against unhealthy food. It is, indeed, true, that these organs alone could merely teach us to distinguish the various odours and flavours of different objects, and to discriminate between the pleasant and the unpleasant feelings excited by them. But experience teaches us that articles of certain odours and flavours are healthy, while others are the reverse; and thus these flavours and odours become indices of the healthiness or noxiousness of edible objects. The pleasantness or unpleasantness of different flavours and odours is somewhat arbitrary and variable. What is pleasant to one man is often unpalatable to another; and a flavour, which at first was unpleasant, may become agreeable by use. Yet, Providence has wisely ordered that the staple articles of food, bread and meal, and also the natural beverage which springs from the mountain rock, and is everywhere met with by digging into the earth, are pleasant to all mankind.

It is, indeed, true, that if, with our eyes closed, we introduce a peach or apricot into the mouth we obtain not only the idea of the flavour which those species of fruit are calculated to excite, but also some knowledge of their solidity and shape. By flavour is meant that adjective entity (property) in the fruit itself, which is the subject of our knowledge, and the excitant of feeling pleasant or unpleasant. The word taste is used to designate our *knowledge* of the flavour, and the words pleasant and unpleasant express the *feeling* excited by it. Thus also the word *odour* means the adjective entity (property) in objects, of which the term smell expresses our knowledge, and the words pleasant and unpleasant the *feelings* excited by the odour.

But the knowledge of solidity and shape is, in the above-named instances also, obtained by touch, and the only thing of which the organ of taste is the medium is, 1. A knowledge of the flavour of the fruit; and, 2. A feeling, pleasant or unpleasant, connected with it. Oftentimes several of the bodily organs are acted upon simultaneously. Thus in eating a peach the several senses of smell, touch, and taste may be affected at the same moment, and each organ be the medium of the appropriate feeling and knowledge, which the entity peach is capable of producing. The flavours of different esculent entities are almost as various as the entities themselves; but it has not been found necessary in human language to distinguish many of them in any other way than by the name of the object itself. Thus, we speak of the taste of an orange, of a tomato, of an onion, of a peach, without having any other term to designate each.

Of *Smell.* The organ of this sense consists of numerous and minute ramifications of nerves, distributed over the interior surface of the nostrils, and the sinuses connected with them. The bony bridge of the nose, and the cartilaginous projection beyond it, serve as a protection to these delicate organs, and their location in the immediate vicinity of the mouth, through which all that is eaten must pass, affords peculiar facility for the exercise of their power in the choice of our food.

The odours of different objects are almost numberless in kind and degree. Indeed, almost every entity, that has any perceptible odour, has one in some respect different from all others. But, excepting a few general terms, such as fragrant, putrid, musty, &c., they are all designated by the name of the object by which they are emitted, and their precise nature learned by experience. Thus, we speak of the odour of a shrub, of a rose, &c.

Some odours are perceptible both to taste and smell. Those who have visited regions abounding in bilious miasma, well know that, on entering the infected region, the miasma may sometimes be tasted on the tongue, as well as smelled by the olfactories. The odour itself appears to consist of innumerable small particles, emitted in every direction from the object to which it belongs, and borne upon the surrounding atmosphere. When this atmosphere is inspired through the nostrils, the olfactories, wisely located by Providence, are touched by the odorous particles, and thus the smell is obtained. That such minute particles are emitted by the odorous body, is demonstrated by the fact, that if the most fragrant flower be placed under a glass receiver, no odour will be perceived by those around it, however near they may be to the glass, which is therefore impervious to these particles.

Although these particles cannot penetrate glass, and are therefore not so small as light, they are inconceivably minute ; for a grain of musk will fill the surrounding atmosphere for years with a pungent odour, without itself experiencing the least sensible diminution of weight.

This sense gives us no knowledge of the colour or shape of the entity to which the odour belongs, but only of the odour itself. In odours of a familiar kind, we instantly recognise the entity by which it is excited. But this we do by a recollection of the fact, that whenever we saw or felt a shrub or rose near us, we perceived the same odour ; and hence we discover the relation of analogy between the cases, and believe that the same entity is again the exciting cause of the odour. It is thus, that we can, by taste and smell, infer the entities by which they are excited, because almost every entity which can act on these two organs, excites a different idea or mental representative. That the organ of taste is the medium of knowledge, as well as feeling, is evident,

1. Because our ideas of the flavours of different objects, are almost as numerous as the objects themselves ; while the feelings excited by them are simply two, pleasant or unpleasant. There are some odours concerning which, though totally dis-

tinct from all others, and easily distinguished from them, as they have something very peculiar and striking in them, we may scarcely be able to determine, whether they are pleasant or unpleasant. But this does not arise from the fact of their having but little flavour ; on the contrary, their flavour may be very strong.

2. While all men agree in the knowledge, conveyed by the terms sweet or acid flavour, they very often differ entirely as to the question, whether a particular flavour, such as that of the tomato, is pleasant or unpleasant. Yea, the very same articles of food will at one time be pleasant, and at another unpleasant to the same person ; and yet, to that same person the flavours of these and other entities, will appear as distinct from each other as they ever did. In short, we perceive, that all these several organs are the vehicles both of knowledge and feeling to the mind.

The acuteness of our perceptions by any one organ, is not only augmented in a surprising degree by continued practice and the force of habit thus formed ; but is also greatly enhanced by the loss of one or several other senses. Indeed, when one organ is destroyed, the improvement of the residue often amounts to a virtual compensation for its loss. So acute does the sense of touch become in the blind, that some of them have been able to distinguish colours by it. And the sense of smell has been so wonderfully improved, that James Mitchell could distinguish by it the presence and location of a stranger in a room, and Dr. Moyse the black dress of his friends.

The different professional pursuits of men, as they give direction to the action of the individual during a large portion of his life, naturally lead to a correspondent improvement of particular organs. Thus, says Dr. Reid, " Not only men, but children, idiots, and brutes, acquire by habit many perceptions which they had not originally. Almost every employment in life hath perceptions of this kind, that are peculiar to it. The shepherd knows every sheep of his flock, as we do our acquaintance, and can pick them out of another flock one by one. The butcher knows by sight the weight and quality of his beeves and sheep before they are killed. The farmer perceives by his eye very nearly the quantity of hay in a rick, or of corn in a heap. The sailor sees the burden, the build, and the distance of a ship at sea, while she is a great way off. Every man accustomed to writing distinguishes acquaintance by their handwriting, as he does by their faces. And the painter distinguishes in the works of his art, the style of all the great masters. In a word, acquired perception is very different in different persons, according to the diversity of objects about which they are employed, and the application they bestow in observing them."*

In concluding this part of our subject we may yet remark, that although the body of man exerts so important a part in his perception of external objects, that any material derangement of the bodily organ often impedes, and sometimes entirely precludes the specific action of mind, to the perfection of which

* Vol. i., p. 286.

it is constitutionally necessary; these two parts of our being are nevertheless separate and distinct. That a degree of mind, even remotely approximating to that of man, is not necessary to the health or perfection of the mere animal economy, is demonstrated in the case of irrational beings. That mind can exist and prosper separate from body is also evident from the decided testimony of revelation concerning disimbodied spirits. Hence, it is by no means a necessary inference, that because body and mind co-operate in man, to qualify him for the purposes of his existence on earth, therefore they are amalgamated into one substance, or have undergone a reciprocal transfusion of properties; or are of such a nature, that the dissolution of the one, implies the death of the other. This fact is fully confirmed by the phenomenal appearances of every day's experience. The properties of the mind and those of the body, remain as perfectly and evidently distinct and different, in the most intricate and involved operation of which man is capable by their joint action, as they are in those of the simplest character. Often also we find the mind exhibiting its greatest vigour, after the body has been mutilated in every possible manner, yea, even after the greater part of the brain itself has been destroyed. On the other hand, the body is often found to vegetate best, after almost the last ray of intellect has been extinguished by misfortune or disease. Now a single case of this kind demonstrates, that mind and body cannot, as the materialist affirms, be one and the same substance; while all contrary cases only establish the fact of a strong sympathy between them in their present connexion.

As to the questions, how the soul, which is a spirit, can act upon the body, and also how the condition of our bodily organs can affect (as we know it does) the operations of the mind, it is not probable that a satisfactory solution of them will be furnished in this life. For, whatever progress we may make in ascertaining the minor ramifications of our bodily organism in the brain, there is just as great, as total a difference between the finest perceptible branch of nerve and the mind, as between the mind and the foot or hand. Nor has the finest nerve one single property in common with mind, any more than has the hand or foot. The most philosophic view of the subject, we think, is the following: As the fact of the reciprocal influence of mind and body on each other in this life is taught us by the testimony of our senses and of consciousness, we should admit it. As God is the author as well of our mind and body, as of their connexion with each other, we should refer their reciprocal influence on each other to his will. It is the Divine will that mind and body should, in this world at least, constitute one being, man. And He who formed them thus, established just such a connexion between them as was necessary to His purpose, as was necessary to make them act in unison, to make the material organ obey the mental impulse, and to subject that mental agent to sundry influences from the material organs. If, then, it be asked why, when I resolve to raise my hand, do the muscles of the arm obey the volition of my mind, the only philosophic, that is, reasonable and true, answer is, because God has so appointed, has so formed me.

The several theories of former days to account for the co-operation of soul and body, now find few advocates. Some writers of the seventeenth century contended that the soul and body have no immediate connexion, nor immediate control or influence over each other, but that God, when he beholds certain changes in the one, causes the correspondent changes to take place in the other by an immediate exertion of his power. But this hypothesis denies the reality of the reciprocal influence of soul and body on each other, instead of explaining it; and, moreover, by making God the immediate author of all human actions, necessarily represents him as the author of sin. It was termed "Occasionalism," because it represents God as causing human actions from time to time, as occasion required. Its author, as Dr. Krug informs us, was *Arnold Geulinx*, professor of Philosophy at Leyden, who died about 1664, or, according to another account, 1669; and Des Cartes embraced a modification of it.

Equally untenable, though for a season far more popular, was the theory of Leibnitz, termed the "pre-established harmony" (harmonia præstabilita). According to this system, soul and body were from eternity designed by the Creator for a series of perfectly harmonious changes, or actions, or phenomena. These changes or phenomena, both of the soul and body, are evolved separately in each, by virtue of an inherent necessity, without any connexion with the other; and these phenomena of the soul and the body do coincide or harmonize with each other in this life, so as to lead to the opinion of there being a reciprocal influence between them, not because they actually exert such a reciprocal influence on each other, but simply in consequence of the original purpose of God, that they should so coincide. To this hypothesis, Leibnitz was led by his well-known system of monads, according to which every monad, or ultimate atom, in the universe was thus separately predetermined; and he illustrated it by the supposition of two watches, both of which kept perfect time. They moved on together, they coincided in their indications of time, yet each moved by a separate intrinsic force, and there was no real connexion whatever between them. It must be obvious that this theory also denies instead of explaining the reciprocal influence of mind and body on each other, and by reducing everything to a state of predetermined fatality, destroys all moral agency and accountability in man.

We may, therefore, with the greater propriety recur to our first position, and while we, on the best of evidence, admit the fact of the reciprocal influence of the soul and body on each other, at the same time refer it wholly to the Divine constitution of our complex nature.

Of similar and equally unsatisfactory character are the later theories, which were designed to explain a part of the general connexion and influence between soul and body, namely, those intended to explain the manner in which thought results from cerebral action, from impressions made on the bodily organs, and conducted by the nerves to the brain.

Des Cartes, adopting the ancient notion of animal spirits circulating in the nervous fibres, conjectured these fibres to be so many tubes pervading the body, and thought he could show how the passage of these animal spirits through these tubes to and from the brain give rise to not only muscular motion, but also perception, memory, and imagination. Yet, as anatomical investigations demonstrate that the nerves are not hollow, and as the very existence of these animal spirits is yet unestablished, this theory has naturally and justly found few advocates.

Near the close of the seventeenth century, Sir Isaac Newton, who always carefully distinguished between the truths and facts which he considered as established by inductive evidence, and the mere conjectures which he uttered as subjects of future investigation for himself and others, proposed the inquiry, "Whether there may not be an elastic medium, or ether, immensely more rare than air, which pervades all bodies, and which is the cause of gravitation; of the refraction and reflection of the rays of light; of the transmission of heat through spaces void of air; and of many other phenomena." To these other phenomena he refers in "the 23d query subjoined to his optics, where he puts this question with regard to the impression made on the nerves and brain in perception, Whether vision is effected chiefly by the vibrations of this medium, excited in the bottom of the eye by the rays of light, and propagated along the solid, pellucid, and uniform capillaments of the optic nerve? And whether hearing is effected by the vibrations of this or some other medium, excited by the tremour of the air in the auditory nerves, and propagated along the solid, pellucid, and uniform capillaments of those nerves."*

On this conjecture, Dr. Hartley, regarding the nerves as solid and elastic substances, built his fanciful system, by which he accounts for the transmission to the brain of the impression made on the external organ, by the supposition that "such impression causes vibrations of the small, and, as one may say, infinitesimal medullary particles, first in the nerves, and then in the brain;"† and farther, that "the vibrations are excited, propagated, and kept up partly by the ether, that is, by a very subtile elastic fluid; partly by the uniformity, continuity, softness, and active powers of the medullary substance of the brain, spinal marrow, and nerves." But, if it were even true that the nervous fibre, which is now known to be unelastic and incapable of tension, were susceptible of vibrations, and that there is such a substance as this ether, of which there is no evidence, and that these vibrations were continued to the brain, does all this afford us the least assistance in understanding how the perception or sensation of the mind succeeds or is occasioned by the impression on the external organ? Certainly not.

* Dr. Reid's Works, vol. ii., p. 85, 86.

† Idem, vol. ii., p. 86.

That there is some communication of influence between the outward organ and the brain, through the medium of the nerves, seems to be certain, for the ligature to the nerve, or its total abscission, at once interrupts this communication, and destroys the sensibility of the nerve below the point of ligature or separation. But what the nature of this influence is, or how it is conveyed along the nerve, we know not. And if we did, this also would still leave us in the dark as to the mode of occurrence of the mental impression. For the brain itself, and the finest possible filament of it, is still matter, and approximates no nearer the attributes of mind than does the external organ, the hand or foot.

The last theory, which claims a passing notice, is that of *ideas*, as something intervening between the external object and the percipient mind. This view, with various modifications, has had numerous advocates both among the ancients and the moderns. The original term itself (*ἰδέα*, from *ἰδεῖν*, *to see*) signifies an image or form. In the Aristotelian philosophy, this term signified the original types or images of all created things in the Divine Mind, and also those higher conceptions of the human mind which correspond to these types. Subsequently among the ancients, and also by some moderns, the word idea was used to designate certain images, or shadowy films, sometimes also termed species, forms, phantasms, and, by Mr. Hume, impressions, which all objects were supposed to be constantly sending forth in every direction. These images, it was believed, came in contact with the brain through the organs of sense, and were the immediate object of perception to the mind. The particulars of this view are thus described by Malebranche:* "I suppose that every one will grant that we perceive not the objects that are without us, immediately or of themselves. We see the sun, the stars, and an infinity of objects without us; and it is not at all likely that the soul sallies out of the body, and, as it were, takes a walk through the heavens to contemplate all those objects. She sees them not, therefore, by themselves; and the immediate object of the mind, when it sees the sun, for example, is not the sun, but something which is intimately united to the soul; and it is that which I call an idea. So that by the word idea I understand nothing else here, but that which is the immediate object, or nearest to the mind, when we perceive any object. It ought to be carefully observed, that, in order to the mind's perceiving any object, it is absolutely necessary that the idea of that object be actually present to it. Of this it is not possible to doubt. The things which the soul perceives are of two kinds. They are either in the soul or without the soul. Those that are in the soul are its own thoughts; that is to say, all its different modifications. The soul has no need of ideas for perceiving them. But with regard to things without the mind, we cannot perceive them but by means of ideas." How far this theory has prevailed in past ages is a matter of some uncertainty, in consequence of the confused and often figurative

* Payne's Elements, p. 123.

manner in which writers on the subject often expressed themselves. Dr. Reid supposed it to have been common till the days of Mr. Locke, and to have been received even by that illustrious writer himself. The language of Mr. Locke on this subject is, doubtless, less perspicuous and discriminating than it might be. Speaking of his frequent use of the word idea, he says, "It serves best to stand for whatever is the object of the understanding when a man thinks. I have used it to express whatever is meant by phantasm, notion, species, or whatever it is, which the mind can be employed about in thinking. I presume that it will be granted me that there are such ideas in men's minds; every man is conscious of them in himself, and men's words and actions will satisfy him that they are in others." The former part of this quotation, it must be confessed, looks much like the ideal system, while the latter appears to sustain Dr. Brown, Dr. Beasley,* and others, who deny it, and to imply that by idea Locke may have generally meant, not any images or phantasms extraneous to the mind, and emanating from the objects perceived, but the perceptions of the mind itself, which inhere in the mind, and subsequently become the subjects of reflection. This ideal system was so fully exposed by Dr. Reid, that, at least since his time, it has found no advocates. Properly considered, it affords no real advantage in explaining the phenomena of sensation. As these images or phantasms

* See an excellent article by the Rev. Dr. Beasley, late Provost of the University in Philadelphia, in the Methodist Magazine for October, 1842.

emanated from external objects, they must have been material; and, however great their tenuity and refinement, they must have been matter still, and the transition from them to mind as difficult as that of any other matter. Nor is this theory at all applicable to some of our perceptions, such as those of sound and smell; for in what respect could these images resemble their original? But the fallacy ot this theory is most conclusively seen from the fact, that we have not the least shadow of evidence for the existence either of these phantasms, or of the impressions which they were supposed to make upon the brain. We must, therefore, revert to the view already given, that, in all our perceptions of external objects through any one of our bodily organs, it is the external object itself which is either directly or mediately the object of perception. And although we cannot explain the mode of communication between the external object and the mind, yet the mystery attendant on this subject is not greater than that belonging to ten thousand other objects and processes around us, the truth of which is certain, while the mode of their existence or occurrence is incomprehensible to us.

PART II.

SENTIENT IDEAS.

Having completed the discussion of the first species of mental operations, to wit, the *Cognitive class*, we now proceed to call the reader's attention to what we have ranked as the second general class, namely, *Sentient Ideas*, or feelings. We stated on a former occasion, that entities bear a threefold relation to the human mind; first, as subjects of our knowledge; secondly, as excitants of our feelings; and, thirdly, as motives or materials for our action. Assuming, for the present, that entities are the ultimate excitants of feeling in us, we describe feeling as follows: By *Feeling* is meant *those sentient states of the mind mediately or immediately excited by entities simple or composite.* This influence is immediately excited, when the objective entities themselves, are at the time acting on us through the appropriate organs; and it is excited mediately, when our feelings are either retrospective or prospective. In the case of present entities, which are, at the time, the subjects of our attention, the entity itself is the excitant of our feeling. But when the entity is retrospective or prospective, our cognitive idea of it seems either to be itself the excitant, or, in some way, the medium or conductor through which the external entity acts. Very often feelings accompanying our knowledge of some entities, are so feeble and indifferent, that we can scarcely pronounce them either pleasing or painful; yet, whenever they are sufficiently increased in degree, they will be found to assume this characteristic.

The criteria, by which feelings are distinguished, are such as these:

I. They have no object beyond themselves. If we have knowledge, it is a knowledge of something—of some entity. But, in feeling, we can distinguish nothing but the simple state of the mind itself, to which we attribute the name feeling. If we form a volition, that volition has for its subject some action, physical or intellectual, of which we judge ourselves capable. But in feeling, we can discover no such subjects.

II. Our feelings are not so absolutely dependant for their character on entities without us, as our knowledge is. Thus acids, when tasted, afford to some persons a pleasant feeling, and to others a contrary one; thus, also, the entity man, in the act of falling from his horse, excites a painful feeling in the breast of his friend, and, perhaps, a pleasant one in that of his inveterate and bitter enemy.

III. Feelings are always preceded by a cognition of the entity which mediately or immediately produces them.

In the farther discussion of our sentient ideas, we invite your attention to the following three topics:

I. To the classification of Feelings.

II. To entities as their ultimate excitants; and,

III. To the susceptibility of the mind for feeling: that is, to the laws of feeling.

CHAPTER I.

THE CLASSIFICATION OF OUR FEELINGS.

THE ideas expressed by the term feelings, being simple and primitive ideas, cannot be logically defined, but are learned by every individual through consciousness. All feelings are in their intrinsic nature much alike, and hence great difficulty has presented itself in all attempts to classify them. They are, however, distinguished by a variety of circumstances attending them and their occurrence, and these may furnish a basis for their division. On this principle, all the feelings of which the human mind is susceptible may be divided into two classes —*Individual* and *Relative* Feeling.

By *individual feelings* are meant those which have reference exclusively to ourselves; such as joy, contentment, cheerfulness, hope, sorrow, grief, despair, &c. By the phrase *relative feelings* we would designate those which have a relation to some other sentient being, or other object; such as love, hatred, friendship, compassion, gratitude, anger, envy, &c. We, therefore, present the following tabular analysis of human feelings.

ANALYSIS OF HUMAN FEELINGS.

Class I. INDIVIDUAL FEELINGS.

1. *Sensations*, that is, those feelings consequent on perceptions by the senses:

(*a.*) Sensations or feelings consequent on perceptions of sight, as those feelings attending the visual perception of any agreeable object.

(*b.*) of Hearing, as of a piece of music.

(*c.*) of Smell, as of a rose, a shrub.

(*d.*) of Taste, as of an orange or apple.

(*e.*) of Touch, as of any soft, smooth, or acuminated body.

2. Some of the *Emotions*, that is, of those transient excitements of feeling consequent on mental operations, direct or reflective, other than perceptions through the organs of taste, smell, or touch.

(*a.*) Intellectual emotions; viz., Emotions of the sublime, the beautiful, the ludicrous, of surprise, of wonder, of astonishment, amazement, &c., and other emotions resulting from the operations of intellect.

(*b.*) The moral emotions; or feelings included in the operations of conscience.

3. Some of the *Affections*, or of those habits or habitual states of feeling which are more durable than sensations or emotions.

(*a.*) Pleasant Affections, such as contentment, cheerfulness, patience, humility, joy, &c.

(*b.*) Painful Affections, some of which are also termed passions. Penitence, grief, sadness, discontent, despair, pride, vanity, fretfulness, &c.

4. The feelings connected with our *Bodily Appetites*, or those occasional feelings which are caused by periodical stimulus in our bodily organization, and are accompanied by desire. Such as Hunger—Thirst.

Class II. RELATIVE FEELINGS.

1. *Benevolent Feelings*, or affections; that is, those relative feelings which are favourable to the being on which they terminate.

Benevolence, hope, confidence, gratitude, respect, veneration, friendship, adoration, &c.

Filial love.

Parental love.

Love to God.

2. *Malevolent*, or defensive feelings; that is, those which involve hostility, or at least repugnance to the being on which they terminate.

Anger, hatred, ingratitude, dissatisfaction, suspicion, resentment, disdain, malignity, shame, cruelty, malice.

3. *Sympathetic* Feelings, or those expressive of similarity or congeniality to the feelings of the being on which they terminate.

Pity, condolence, compassion.

Sympathy of different kinds.

4. *Antipathetic* Feelings.

Envy, jealousy, fear, dread, horror, disgust, indignation, grudging, and what the Germans term Schadenfreude, a malicious pleasure in the misfortune or sufferings of others.

A division of relative feelings might also be made, into, 1. Those which refer to *animate*, and, 2. Those relating to *inanimate* objects. But this division would be based on the difference in the objects of the mental operations, rather than in the operations themselves.

Feelings may again be divided into the following three classes :

I. *Sensuous;* by which we mean those feelings obtained immediately through the bodily organs.

II. *Intellectual* or *Reflex*, or those resulting from the reflex operations of the mind ; including the pleasures of taste, the feelings connected with our views of the beautiful, the sublime, the ludicrous, &c.

III. *Moral* or *Religious ;* viz., those resulting from the consideration of the actions of moral agents in reference to the laws of man, and ultimately of God.

Feeling has frequently been divided, in relation to time, into *Present*, *Retrospective*, and *Prospective*. This division is clear in its nature, and distinct in its lines of separation ; although we do not consider it so useful as the one first given, nor at all inconsistent with it. It labours, however, under the difficulty of requiring us to assign feelings of essentially the same kind to different classes. Thus, those feelings of approbation or disapprobation which attend the judicial act of conscience, as to the agreement or disagreement of our actions with the law of God, that is, with our duty, will belong to one class when they relate to present actions, but to a different class if they refer to our past conduct. Upon the whole, we consider the first division as the most natural and the best, and therefore have adopted it.

Remarks on the different branches of the above classification.

CLASS I. OF INDIVIDUAL FEELINGS.

I. *Of Sensations.*

In a former part of this work, we remarked that the term sensation has been used by the major part of authors on this subject, with a degree of vagueness which cannot fail to cause obscurity in metaphysical discussions, if not avoided. Sometimes it has been employed as synonymous with perceptions, and, at other times, to designate feelings of various kinds, but especially those which are consequent on the perceptions through our bodily organs. It must be evident to all who reflect on the criteria which distinguish cognitive ideas from such as are sentient, that two kinds of mental phenomena entirely distinct and different are here confounded. And as the cognates of the term sensation, namely, sensitive, sensibility, &c., are universally employed in our language to express feelings and not cognitions, it will, we think, be best, in mental philosophy, to restrict this term also in a similar way. We therefore use the word sensations to express, not cognitions, but feelings of various kinds, and especially those produced through our bodily organs. When discussing the process by which we obtain ideas through the bodily senses, we proved that each of the five senses is a source of cognitions as well as of feelings. We easily perceive the difference between the idea obtained by beholding a beautiful landscape, and the feeling of pleasure which follows it. The former is cognitive, the latter is sentient, is feeling. But is not the idea derived from tasting an apple or orange equally distinct from the pleasant feeling attending the same process? And are not our ideas of the successive notes in a piece of music, different from the feelings, either pleasant or painful, cheerful or melancholy, which those notes also produce? There is, therefore, a necessity for both of these terms, for perceptions and sensations, in reference to the operations of each of our bodily organs; and if the one be used to express the cognitive result of their action, and the other more generally be confined to that which is sentient, much confusion will be avoided.

All these sensations are obviously *individual* feelings, because they terminate in ourselves, in the sentient subject.

II. *Of Emotions.*

The term emotion also is employed in several different significations by respectable writers. By some the words sensations, emotions, and passions are used to designate different degrees of intensity in one and the same species of mental operations. But there is certainly a fixed difference between these terms in the usage of our language. Thus, no good writer would employ the term emotion to express a higher degree of the sensation produced by the organ of touch, any more than he would use the term passion to designate a still higher degree of it. Some authors by emotion designate a state of feeling intermediate between sensations and desires.

Others define emotions to be those feelings which are consequent upon other mental operations than perceptions by the organs of sense. Yet this use of it is also not entirely correct; because we speak of the emotions of the sublime or beautiful, and yet these emotions are immediately consequent on our perceptions, through the senses, of those objects which we regard as beautiful or sublime. And other writers employ the term emotion with almost as much latitude as feeling itself. A more correct description of emotions and appropriate use of the term, we think, would be the following. Emotions are those transient excitements of feeling which are consequent on mental operations direct or reflective, other than perceptions through the organs of taste, smell, or touch. The very term emotion, in its primitive import, signifies a moving, a motion, an impulse; thus indicating its transient nature. Nothing more is necessary to the intelligent inquirer than to reflect on the testimony of his own consciousness, to enable him to perceive that those feelings of the mind which he denominates emotions are of brief continuance, that they come and pass away again in a short time, and are then known to us only by memory.

That they are different from cognitions and active operations, and that they are essentially sentient, are a species of feelings, is also a matter which cannot be rendered intelligible by words, but must be referred to the consciousness of each individual. When I behold a messenger, whom I had despatched on a journey of a hundred miles, in four or five hours again entering my room, I am filled with surprise at his unexpected return; and certainly I find no difficulty in distinguishing my perception of his personal appearance, and my knowledge of the unexpected circumstances under which he appears, from the feeling or emotion which attends it.

Emotions always succeed some cognition, or some active operation of the mind. Before I can experience the emotion of the beautiful or sublime, I must have had a perception of the object by which the emotion is caused; and if I feel emotions of regret or sorrow at my failure in any active process in which I was engaged, say in an attempt to finish a sermon or other piece of composition within a given time, the failure and the consciousness of it must certainly have preceded the emotion, the temporary regret. Emotions are sometimes motives to action, and then, of course, they precede the desires or volitions resulting from them. We do not recollect, however, that the word emotion is applied to the feelings, of any degree, which are consequent on our perceptions through the organs of taste, smell, and touch.

Emotions may be divided into *intellectual* and *moral.* Intellectual emotions are those which express and imply no reference to moral character or conduct. They are such as the emotions of sublimity, beauty, the ludicrous, emotions of surprise, wonder, astonishment, amazement, &c. The most important of these we will endeavour to explain in few words. It should, however, be distinctly remembered that, in popular language, the terms employed to designate these emotions, generally stand for a complex idea or state of mind, including a cognitive as well as a sentient element. Thus, when we speak of admiring the sublimity of a particular scene, we have reference as much, if not more, to our perceptions of its character and features, than to the emotions excited by it. And if we attempt to describe the ingredients of its sublimity, we describe our perceptions as well as our consequent feelings. The terms beauty, sublimity, &c., are used both objectively and subjectively, and in mental philosophy we must discriminate between these different significations. Objective beauty inheres in the object itself which is styled beautiful. Subjective beauty is the effect produced on the mind by the contemplation of a beautiful object. This effect is complex, and includes both our perceptions of the object and the feelings accompanying them.

Sublimity.

The emotion of sublimity is that delightful, solemn, and expansive individual feeling of the mind, which, to use the language of a distinguished writer of our country,* is excited by the "contemplation of whatever is vast in nature, splendid in intellect, or lofty in morals." Or, in the language of Dr. Brown,

* Dr. Wayland, in his Moral Dignity of the Missionary Enterprise

"Whatever is vast in the material world—whatever is supremely comprehensive in intellect—whatever in morals implies virtuous affections, or passions, far removed beyond the ordinary level of humanity, or even guilt itself, that is ennobled, in some measure, by the fearlessness of its darings, or the magnitude of the ends to which it has the boldness to aspire—these and various other objects, in matter and mind, produce the vivid feelings of sublimity." It has sometimes been disputed whether there is such a thing as *objective* sublimity; whether there is, in the objects which are regarded as sublime, any particular property calculated to excite the emotions in question; or whether they are not wholly the result of association of ideas. That is, when we hear the thunder rolling over our heads, and perceive the earth trembling under our feet, and the lightning flashing in the sky, is it these several appearances which call forth the emotions of sublimity that we feel, or is it *solely* the conception of resistless power associated with them? Mr. Payne, erroneously, we think, affirms the latter. That our reflections associated with the perception of these phenomena are also concerned in the production of these emotions seems evident; yet they are certainly not the sole cause of them. If the property of these phenomena, by which they cause the emotion of sublimity, be nothing more than their tendency to impress the mind with the conception of vast, resistless, and terrific power, still this would be a peculiar property of these objects, because others of a different kind do not possess it. Nor does the fact, that the rumbling of a cart may be mistaken for distant thunder, and excite emotions of sublimity, appear to disprove our position. It only shows, that the recollection of a scene of real sublimity may again excite emotions of the sublime ; and that any one feature of such a scene, or even anything nearly resembling it, may recall the essential circumstances of such scenes formerly witnessed by us. Thus the rumbling of the cart recalls our former impressions of thunder, and with it, all those circumstances which are calculated to excite ideas of vast and resistless power, and thus it excites the emotions of sublimity. If thunder had no property peculiarly calculated to excite those ideas which produce emotions of sublimity, then as the cart by association elicited our recollection of those same ideas, and thus produced these emotions, it would itself be regarded by us as a sublime object, even after it is known to be the cause of the sound. The sight of a fellow-mortal lying emaciated on a bed of sickness, scarce able to lift his hand, may, by the association of contrast, recall to our minds the resistless power of Jehovah, and thus the emotion of sublimity be excited. But does any man transfer this emotion from God to the feeble mortal? Certainly not. Therefore, whatever is the process by which certain objects or actions produce the emotion of sublimity, whether the effect be mediate or immediate, it is evident that entities or objects of this class do possess a peculiar tendency to produce these emotions, which objects of a different kind have not. If, then, it be inquired, is there any sublimity in external objects or actions themselves, we reply, there is that in them which calls forth emotions of the sublime; and as universal usage designates this something sublimity, we see no objection to the term. And this same train of remarks is equally applicable to objects exciting emotions of beauty.

The ordinary ingredients of sublimity in objects, or those attributes of them which are found by experience to excite in us the emotions of sublimity, are vastness in dimension, such as a boundless plain or the vast ocean; but especially height and depth, as a high mountain, a deep precipice, or the expanse of heaven, which is both high and boundless; resistless force, as the rushing of mighty waters, the devastating tornado, prostrating trees and houses in its course; extremes of colour, as the dazzling brightness of the sun, or the contrary extreme, in the dark and lowering clouds of a gathering storm; vast sounds, as the roaring of thunder, the sound of many waters; as well as vastness of power, physical, intellectual, and moral.

Beauty.

The emotion of beauty cannot be logically defined, but is known by consciousness to every individual. It may be described as that pleasant individual feeling of the mind which is excited by the perception of certain objects, termed beautiful, in the physical, intellectual, and moral world. The term beauty, like sublimity, is used both objectively and subjectively; to express a certain property in outward entities, and also to designate the perceptions and feelings caused by them. In reference to this emotion, also, the very existence of objective beauty has been denied, and the entire effect of objects of particular kinds in causing this emotion has been attributed to association. It is needless to say, that these emotions do not resemble the properties in the object which produces them, as no mental operation, either cognitive, sentient, or active, does or can in any one particular *resemble* any material object. But that there are certain characteristics, belonging to those numberless objects termed beautiful, which mediately or immediately cause our emotions of beauty, and lead us to regard those objects as beautiful, is as evident in the case of beauty as of sublimity; and the same arguments employed to prove it in that case are equally applicable to this. The emotions of beauty are augmented and multiplied by the influence of association; but, certainly, there must be some original basis for association to build upon, and even these associations must contain nothing inconsistent with the nature of beauty, or they impair instead of increasing the strength of the emotion. The influence of association is exhibited in the figurative language often employed to express these feelings, or, rather, the objects exciting them. We characterize landscapes as cheerful or gloomy; sounds as animated or mournful; forms as delicate or modest; colours as gay or grave, &c.

It is difficult to describe the precise characteristics of beauty; yet each individual possesses a natural susceptibility for objects of this kind, and can judge for himself. The influence of association and education causes the diversity of taste observable among different persons on these subjects; but there are some objects and characteristics pretty generally agreed on. Such are delicate rather than glaring *colours*, and also a particular variety of such colours. Some kinds of *motion* are beautiful, such as the gentle gliding of a bird through the air, the undulating motion of the surface of a lake when moved by a gentle breeze, or the waving of a field of wheat when a gentle current of air is passing over it. Some *figures* or *forms* are beautiful, either on account of their *regularity*, as in the case of a circle, a triangle, or a square; or on account of their graceful variety, as in plants, leaves, or trees. The waving line is termed the line of beauty, and the same character belongs to twisted pillars, or the vine or ivy gracefully entwined around the oak. Certain *sounds* are also found to excite the emotion of beauty, as well simply as in their combinations. All men who have a taste for music, characterize certain airs as beautiful. Some *works of art* also are beautiful, when they combine the natural elements of beauty in their form or colour. The creations of imagination, as seen in poems or other works of fiction, are beautiful when the writer has faithfully copied nature, that is, has employed the natural sources of beauty, and conformed to their principles. The *human countenance* is often among the most beautiful objects, not only on account of the beauties of form and colour, but also the expression of amiable, and cheerful, and benevolent feelings in its lineaments. This is, in part, a species of social, if not moral beauty. Intellectual and moral excellence is often exhibited in ways and under circumstances such as are felt to be beautiful by the corresponding emotions they excite. In some cases many of these sources of beauty are combined, and the general effect thus enhanced. "Perhaps," says Dr. Blair, "the most complete assemblage of beautiful objects that can anywhere be found, is presented by a rich, natural landscape, where there is a sufficient variety of objects: fields in verdure, scattered trees and flowers, running water, and animals grazing. If to these be joined some of the productions of art which suit with such a scene, as a bridge with arches over a river, smoke rising from cottages in the midst of trees, and the distant view of a fine building seen by the rising sun; we then enjoy in the highest perfection that gay, cheerful, and placid sensation which characterizes beauty." Some operations purely intellectual possess a high degree of beauty, and excite corresponding pleasing emotions; yet in some cases, especially when they border on the sublime, they derive most of their influence from association. Thus, while there is manifest beauty in many of the demonstrations of geometry, we doubt not that the ecstatic emotion felt by the great mathematician Bernoulli, as he followed Sir Isaac Newton in some of his great steps—a feeling which he, on his death-bed, informed Professor Robinson, of Edinburgh, gave him the liveliest conception he had ever enjoyed of the happiness of heaven—arose, not simply from the intellectual process of reasoning, but chiefly from the enlarged views thus obtained of the grandeur and overwhelming extent of the universe itself. But even with this allowance, it is to be feared his idea of heaven was essentially defective, as it appears not to have embraced that "holiness" of thought, feeling, and action which characterizes the inhabitants and occupations of heaven, and "without which no man can see God."

The Ludicrous.

The emotion of the ludicrous is that transient, pleasing individual feeling, excited in the mind by those entities or objects, physical or intellectual, which are calculated to cause laughter. The objective ludicrous, or that property in entities which is directly or indirectly the cause of the emotion, has been variously defined. Mr. Payne and others regard it as a strange mixture of congruity and incongruity, the unexpected perception of which occasions the mental emotion. This admixture of the congruous and incongruous is sometimes found in the language rather than the thing. Such is the case, for example, in puns and riddles; as when a barrister, on hearing it remarked what a large quantity of *ham* he had eaten, replied that he had only been taking *extracts* from *Bacon's Abridgment*. But in the couplet of Hudibras,

> "For rhyme the rudder is of verses,
> With which, like ships, they steer their courses,"

the incongruity is observed between the things compared, verses and a ship.

To the class of ludicrous emotions belong those feelings excited by what is termed *Wit*. Wit seems to be the sudden and unexpected association of ideas, natural, but novel, and often conveying an important fact or argument in few words, or by an allusion, the consequence of which flashes on the hearer's mind; or by an accommodation or play on some word or thing said before. Thus, Plutarch informs us, when Metellus Nepos told Cicero that he had ruined more persons as a witness than he had saved as an advocate, Cicero replied, "I grant it, for I have more truth than eloquence." And when a young man, who lay under the charge of having given his father a poisoned cake, was talking in an insolent manner, and threatening that Cicero should feel the weight of his reproaches, Cicero replied, "I would much rather have them than your cake."

Burlesque is a species of wit employed in rendering ludicrous that which is naturally grave or dignified, or which assumes to be so, by comparing it to things really mean and contemptible. Thus, Hudibras burlesques the adventures of his reputed hero:

"Ah me! what perils do environ
The man that meddles with cold iron;
What plaguy mischiefs and mishaps
Do dog him still with after-claps!
For though dame Fortune seem to smile,
And leer upon him for a while,
She'll after show him, in the nick
Of all his glories, a dog-trick."

The *mock-heroic* is another species of wit, which consists in making low or trifling persons or things appear ridiculous by speaking of them in lofty and grandiloquent language, or by representing them as speaking in such style. Thus, in the same poem, Ralpho is made to address the beaten and prostrate knight:

"You are, great sir,
A self-denying conqueror,
As high, victorious, and great,
As ever fought for the churches yet,
If you will give yourself but leave
To make out what y'already have ;
That's victory. The foe, for dread
Of your nine-worthiness, is fled ;
All save Crowdero, for whose sake
You did the espous'd cause undertake ;
And he lies pris'ner at your feet,
To be disposed as you think meet ;
Either for life, or death, or sale,
The gallows, or perpetual jail ;
For one wink of your powerful eye
Must sentence him to live or die."

Surprise, Wonder, Astonishment, Amazement.

These are all different modifications of the same individual feeling, under different circumstances and degrees. *Surprise* is that feeling excited by the perception of something novel and unexpected. This feeling is termed *wonder*, if the novel and unexpected object is also strange or unaccountable. *Astonishment* designates a higher degree of wonder. And *Amazement* implies something intricate or inexplicable in the object which caused the feeling.

These emotions may with propriety be termed *monitory* emotions, for they arrest for a season the action of the mind ; and, as Dr. Brown justly remarks, "It is in new circumstances that it is most necessary for us to be upon our guard, because, from their novelty, we cannot be aware of the effects that attend them, and require, therefore, more than usual caution where foresight is impossible. But if new circumstances had not produced feelings peculiarly vivid, little regard might have been paid to them, and the evil, therefore, might have been suffered before the alarm was felt. Against this danger nature has most providentially guarded us. We cannot feel surprise without a more than ordinary interest in the objects which may have excited this emotion, and a consequent tendency to pause till their properties have become in some degree known to us. Our astonishment may, therefore, be considered as a voice from that Almighty goodness which constantly protects us, that, in circumstances in which inattention might be perilous, whispers, or almost cries to us, Beware."

The Moral Emotions.

Moral emotions may be described as those individual feelings of the mind which are consequent on our cognition of moral truth, as well as moral character or conduct. The contemplation of the beauty of holiness in the Divine law itself, causes a delightful emotion in the Christian. The morality or immorality of an action, properly consists in its agreement or disagreement with the law of God. And our ideas of its morality will depend on our idea of that law, be it more or less accurate or defective. This relation of agreement or disagreement with our views of the law of God is, therefore, the entity which causes the peculiar feelings of pleasure or pain in view of moral actions, either our own or those of others. The terms moral approbation or disapprobation seem to include both the cognitive and sentient element, both our judgment that the act is right or wrong, as well as the concomitant feeling. Sense of moral obligation, more properly designates the *impulsive* part of conscience, and perhaps more or less feeling accompanying it. *The operations of conscience, fully considered, consist of three ingredients, the judicial, the sentient, and the impulsive.* The judicial ingredient is that judgment which we form of our actions, as being conformed or contrary to the law of God, and has found its place in the discussion of our cognitive ideas in the section on *Relative Knowledge*. The impulsive feature is active in its nature, and is discussed in the third division of our subject, when we treat of the first constitutional inclination. Our concern at present is wholly with the *sentient* part of these complex operations.

The moral emotions, like all other feelings, are original feelings of the mind, which imply a susceptibility in the mind for such feelings, and thus at once decide the point, that conscience, or our moral faculty, is an original part of the constitution of the soul. But it does not hence follow that its operations are not complex, embracing elements of different kinds. As they are original feelings, they must be learned from consciousness, and cannot be logically defined.

These feelings are neither numerous nor diversified. They are either *pleasant* or *painful*, the former consequent on a judgment of approval of a given action, and the latter resulting from a judgment of disapproval. From their intimate connexion with these judgments, some writers have confounded the two, and even designated the pleasant feeling a feeling of approbation, and the unpleasant one a feeling of disapproval, forgetful of the judgment included in the term. In popular language this may be allowed, but in philosophical discussions we should always distinguish the feeling accompanying the approval from the approval itself, which is always a judgment of the mind, that the act is right, is conformed to the will of God. Keeping in view this distinction, it may not be improper to retain the popular designation, and speak of judgments of approval or disapproval, and also feelings of approbation and disapprobation, meaning by the latter the emotions, either pleasant or painful, consequent on those judgments. Those feelings are also sometimes termed feelings of innocence or guilt, of self-approbation, or self-condemnation, or remorse.

As our moral emotions are consequent on the judgments of approval or disapproval to which they succeed, it follows, that if those judgments change, the feelings will change also. Thus, so long as Paul was conscious that his judgment approved of the persecution of Christians, he contemplated the act with pleasing emotions, and felt an inward impulse urging him to do it. But when his views on the subject of Jesus of Nazareth changed, and his judgment disapproved the act, he regarded with emotions of pain and regret the very conduct in which he had formerly delighted. Nor does this liability to change in our emotions imply that they are not to be depended on, any more than change of opinion in reference to any subject proves that our intellectual or cognitive powers cannot be relied on. It only proves that our moral nature, in ts cognitive, sentient, and active departments, is capable of improvement, and is a suitable subject of education.

The terms moral emotions may also be applied to transient impulses of some of our *relative* feelings, such as love and hatred, sympathy, &c., in as far as these feelings are matter of duty, and we have indirect control over them.

III. *The Affections.*

By the term affections we would designate those habits, or habitual states of feeling, which are more durable than sensations or emotions. Some of the affections refer only to ourselves, and some terminate on other objects. It is the former alone which belong to the individual feelings, now under discussion. They may be divided into pleasant and unpleasant.

The *pleasant* affections are such as joy, cheerfulness, contentment, humility, patience. *Joy* is a highly pleasurable affection, excited in the mind by the contemplation of something past, present, or prospective, which we regard as highly favourable to us or others. *Cheerfulness* is an habitual, moderate, pleasant affection of the mind, resulting from the view of our condition as on the whole favourable. It results from the habit of viewing the bright side of human affairs, and is of great importance in life, to ourselves and those around us. It often arises from constitutional temperament, but its purest source is true piety, which teaches us to dwell much on the numberless mercies surrounding us, and to believe that even the ills of life are designed for greater good. *Contentment* is a moderate, tranquil, pleasant affection, resulting from the conviction, that the circumstances of our situation are, on the whole, such as not to give us just cause of dissatisfaction. *Humility* is a moderate, pleasing affection, arising from a view of our unworthiness. *Patience* is a moderate, pleasing affection, resulting from our determination to endure the ills of life without murmuring.

The *painful* affections are by some writers termed passions, but this term is often applied to some relative affections both pleasant and unpleasant, to designate their existence in a high degree. Thus we speak of the passion of love and of anger. The painful individual affections are such as penitence, discontent, sadness, grief, despair, pride, vanity, fretfulness, &c. *Penitence* is that painful guilty feeling of self-condemnation, resulting from a violation of known duty. *Discontent* is a painful feeling arising from the conviction, that we have reason to complain of our condition or treatment. *Sadness* is a moderate, painful feeling of dejection, resulting from some loss or difficulty to ourselves or those we love. *Grief* is a more intense, painful affection than sadness, resulting from a higher degree of the same causes. *Despair* is an intense and settled painful affection, resulting from the belief that our condition is hopeless, or the object of our desire unattainable. *Pride* is that feeling of self-complacency which arises from an over-estimate of our own merits. *Vanity* is that affection of the mind which results from an over-estimate of our own merits, and a desire that they may be admired by others. *Fretfulness* is a painful feeling, resulting from losses or difficulties of minor importance.

IV. The feelings connected with our *Bodily Appetites.*

These appetites are such as hunger and thirst; the operations of which are connected with feelings, pleasant or unpleasant, of the individual class, the nature of which will be more fully discussed in a subsequent section.

We come now to the second general class of feelings.

CLASS II. RELATIVE FEELINGS,

OR THOSE WHICH TERMINATE ON SOME OTHER OBJECTS THAN OURSELVES

These we divide into *benevolent*, *malevolent*, *sympathetic*, and *antipathetic*.

I. *Benevolent Feelings or Affections.*

These are relative feelings, which are favourable to the being or thing, on which they terminate. These feelings constitute one of the noblest portions of our nature. When sanctified by Divine grace, they enter largely into the elements of true piety, and even in the natural man constitute one of the purest and principal sources of the happiness which he enjoys. The term affections is applied to this kind of feelings more generally than to any others, and in more specific accordance with the primitive import of the term.

Benevolence, or Love, is a relative affection of a very broad character, and embraces various modifications, according to the different circumstances under which it is exercised. In its widest acceptation, benevolence is a pleasing feeling of good-will and desire for the happiness of all sentient beings, irrespective of their character or conduct. With this affection a good man loves the whole human family, as well as irrational animals. This feeling appears to be much weaker in depraved human nature than the other modifications of love, and a career of sin very soon habitually overpowers it.

Love, in its other modifications, embraces in it a perception of something agreeable, praiseworthy, or desirable in the appearance, character, or conduct of the object beloved. It also implies delight in this object, a desire for its possession or enjoyment, and a disposition to promote its happiness. It is always, in its intrinsic nature, a pleasing affection. To a certain extent it is voluntary in well-balanced minds, and can be mediately controlled, by either shunning the presence and contemplation of the object which excites it, or by frequenting that presence and indulging in reflections on it when absent. All this, however, clearly proves that there is something in the beloved object itself which excites our affection, while, of course, it presupposes in the mind a constitutional susceptibility to be thus affected.

The principal modifications of this affection are the following: *Paternal* love, that affection which a father feels for his offspring, and which induces him contentedly to toil all day long for the support of his children, and to promote their welfare in every possible way. *Maternal* love is that affection felt by a mother for her children, which makes her watch especially over their defenceless years with ceaseless care, and willingly endure the loss of rest and convenience in protecting and rearing them. *Conjugal* love is the affection of husband and wife towards each other, which induces them to study to promote each other's happiness, to overlook each other's infirmities, and to lighten by mutual sympathy the ordinary troubles and afflictions of life. *Filial* affection is that love which children bear to their parents. These several species of affection form alike the basis of the domestic or family institution, and the cement by which its members are held together. A beautiful instance of conjugal affection is related by Xenophon in his semi-historical Cyropædia. Cyrus had taken captive Tigranes, the young Prince of Armenia, together with his wife, whom he had recently married, and of whom he was passionately fond. When both were brought before Cyrus, he asked the prince what he would pay to receive back his wife again, to which question Tigranes replied, "I will, if necessary, give my life to redeem her from servitude." Cyrus nobly gave liberty to all the prisoners, who, on departing, could not find words to express their admiration of their noble conqueror; some applauding his wisdom, others his bravery, others his clemency, and some his beauty and tallness. At length Tigranes thus addressed his wife: "And do you, Armenia, tell me, did Cyrus appear to you to be handsome?" "Indeed," said she, "I did not look at him." "At whom, then, were you looking?" said Tigranes. "At him, truly, who said that he was willing to lay down his life to purchase my freedom." Of maternal affection the history of every age is replete with examples. An interesting case is quoted from an anonymous writer by Professor Upham. "When the Ajax, man-of-war, took fire in the straits of the Bosphorus, in 1807, an awful scene of distraction ensued. The ship was of great size, full of people, and under the attack of an enemy at the time; the mouths of destruction seemed to wage contention for their prey. Many of those on board could entertain no hopes of deliverance; striving to shun one devouring element, they were the victims of another. While the conflagration was raging furiously, and shrieks of terror rent the air, an unfortunate mother, regardless of herself, seemed solicitous only for the safety of her infant child. She never attempted to escape; but she committed it to the charge of an officer, who, at her earnest request, endeavoured to secure it in his coat; and following the tender deposite with her eyes as he retired, she calmly awaited that catastrophe in which the rest were about to be involved. Amid the exertions of the officer in such an emergency, the infant dropped into the sea, which was no sooner discovered by the unhappy parent, than, frantic, she plunged from the vessel's side as if to preserve it; she sunk, and was seen no more."

Gratitude, friendship, respect, confidence, patriotism, and hope express pleasing relative feelings, the nature of which is so well understood as not to need farther elucidation.

Love to God is that pleasant relative feeling which the good man cherishes towards God as a being of infinite perfections, and as deserving of his supreme affection. This feeling, the Scriptures teach us, is supreme in the heart of the true Christian; and, as conversion does but restore the character of fallen man in some degree to its primitive condition, it seems reasonable to believe that it was the supreme affection of the soul in the state of primitive innocence. *Adoration* includes, besides its cognitive and active elements, a kindred feeling of more solemn kind, which accompanies our acts of worship, that is, our repetition of the truths of Scripture concerning the glorious character and relations of God, in an oral or mental address to him.

II. *Malevolent, Repulsive, or Defensive Feelings.*

Malevolent, or defensive affections, are those painful relative feelings which involve hostility, and a disposition to injure the beings on which they terminate. The malevolent affections appear to be a perversion of an original susceptibility, which is *per se* good, and purely defensive in its nature. Even in our fallen state the command of God to us is, in certain circumstances, "Be ye angry and sin not;" and, prior to the fall, the exercises of this power were all of that sinless kind. These feelings are consequent on the perception or contemplation of any person or object, which we deem hostile to ourselves, or to those with whom we sympathize, or to that which is right. In our unfallen state, our interests and feelings were in invariable harmony with the will of God: consequently, nothing could call forth these feelings but what was opposed to the will of God, or, in other words, was sin. Originally, therefore, our repulsive feelings were purely feelings of abhorrence or repugnance at sin. But, in the present state of man, it is undeniable that the love of self preponderates over the love of God, and we often cherish interests and desires opposed to his will. Hence, when our repugnant feelings are excited against others for opposing us, or our interests or desires, we are often wrong, and our opponents right, and these feelings are thus enlisted in opposition to right, in hostility to the will of God. Yet, in proportion as the image of God is restored in man, in proportion as he loves holiness and hates sin, his repugnant affections will always be opposed only to sinners and to sin; he will hate and feel anger only at that which God hates; and thus, in exemplification of the Scripture precept, he "will be angry and not sin."

The feelings belonging to this class are such as the following: anger, hatred, resentment, revenge, malignity, cruelty, and malice.

III. *Sympathetic Feelings.*

Sympathetic feelings are relative affections of the mind, which imply similarity or congeniality to the feelings of the being on which they terminate.

Sympathetic feelings do not differ in their general nature from the other phenomena of our sentient nature. They are all feelings excited in the mind by the contemplation of certain entities. They are both pleasant and unpleasant, according as they are excited by the happiness or misery of our fellow-creatures. It is alike accordant with the principles of our nature, that we should rejoice with them that rejoice, and weep with those who weep. Yet experience proves that we sympathize most acutely with those whose feelings are similar to the prevailing state of our own minds at the time. We do not, indeed, even in this case, literally participate in the feelings of others, because every man's feelings, like his other mental phenomena, are inalienable and untransferable. But in the similar state of our own minds, our susceptibility for feelings of that kind is peculiarly acute, and, therefore, deeper and stronger feelings are excited by the contemplation of the same entities than would at other times be the case. The impulses of sympathy are often sudden and unpremeditated, and lead to instantaneous action for the relief of those in danger or in pain, as when we rush to the relief of an individual who is sinking beneath the strokes of some ruffian. These sympathetic feelings have a most happy influence in harmonizing the differences which often exist among associates and in families, and thus making happy the intercourse of those who would otherwise be ever at variance.

Besides the general term sympathy, which is alike applicable to a fellow-feeling of a pleasing or painful nature, the terms compassion, pity, commiseration, are often used as synonymous terms, and at other times to express some shades of diversity in these feelings. Condolence signifies a fellow-feeling with others in suffering.

IV. *Antipathetic Feelings.*

To this class we refer all those relative feelings which, though they have reference to some other being, imply only opposition of feeling, but not intention of action. They are such as envy, jealousy, disgust, grudging, fear, dread, horror, and indignation.

Envy is that painful relative feeling which is excited in the selfish mind by the contemplation of some desirable property or possession of another. This feeling is excited more readily in some minds than in others, and the different susceptibility for it is proportioned to the relative preponderance of the second constitutional inclination over the first, that is, in proportion as the individual is in the habit of being influenced more by selfishness, the love of well-being, rather than by the moral fitness of things, his duty. It is the design and tendency of true religion to suppress and eradicate these feelings, and the truly pious man is rarely guilty of them.

Jealousy, in its primary application, has reference to amatory affection, and signifies that painful feeling of temporary or qualified displeasure against an individual whom we love or have loved, because we suppose some other person to be preferred to ourselves. The term jealousy is, however, more generally applied to that painful feeling which is excited by apprehension that some other person has or will obtain some object which we had hoped to acquire ourselves. It is in this sense of it that we speak of professional jealousy, and jealousy between competitors for any supposed good. This feeling has a particular tendency to warp the judgment, to make us place the most unfavourable construction on the actions of its object, and to magnify molehills into mountains; so that it may with truth be said,

" Trifles, light as air,
Are to the *jealous* confirmation strong
As proofs of Holy Writ."

Disgust is an unpleasant feeling of aversion to an individual on account of something low, mean, obscene, vulgar, or base in his person or conduct. *Indignation* is the same feeling, mingled with contempt and scorn for its object.

Fear is a painful feeling, resulting from the conviction of some impending or probable evil. *Dread* is a higher and more permanent degree of the same feeling. *Horror* is a still higher degree of fear, excited by the sudden and unexpected view of something very evil or dangerous in our condition or conduct.

CHAPTER II.

OF ENTITIES AS EXCITANTS OF FEELING.

SECTION I.

All feeling, like knowledge, may be traced mediately or immediately to entities without the mind. The eye could never afford us feeling if the rays of light were not reflected from external entities to it, or did not reach it from the surrounding atmosphere. The pleasing or painful feelings, excited by entities through the eye, are produced immediately by the rays of light which reach the eyes, and ultimately, in a certain sense, by the particular object from which the rays pass, and which give them their peculiar texture or combination of colours.

The ear could never be the medium through which either knowledge or feeling is excited, if the vibrations of the atmosphere were not permitted to reach the tympanum. The vibrating atmosphere is therefore the entity which immediately excites the feelings connected with sound, and the sounding body is the ultimate entity which gives the air its vibratory motion.

The nose could never be the vehicle of knowledge or feeling to the mind, if the effluvia emanating from surrounding odorous bodies were not permitted to touch the olfactory nerves.

Nor does *religious* feeling seem to be different in its nature. Thus, the Christian meditates on the glorious character of God, and the feelings of his heart are excited to the highest pitch. But what is this meditation else than an inspection of the entity God, and his relations to us? By these it is that our feelings are excited. The case is similar, when our feelings are occasioned by reading the Divine word; for the signs or letters read remind us of the sounds for which the letters stand, and the recollection of these recalls the ideas of real, objective entities. The daily habit of meditating on heavenly or Divine things, by the same law of mind, keeps alive our interest, or, rather, our feelings, on this subject, and increases the frequency of our reinspection of them; thus, a kind of rapport is formed between the soul of the Christian and that heaven which is his home, and that God who is his everlasting friend.

SECTION II.

Entities of every class possess some tendency, though very different in degree, to excite feeling in the mind. Our remark is not that this tendency is perceptible in every entity belonging to each class, but that it is perceptible in some of every class. With regard to solids and liquids, the truth of this remark is evident. It is self-evident, that all articles of food or drink possess it in some degree. Other objects of these classes, which at first view might seem incapable of exciting feeling, change their aspect when more closely examined. Thus, who would attribute to the earth and minerals the power of exciting feeling in the mind; and yet what else is the pleasure found by men in the pursuit of Geology and Mineralogy, than the result of this very feeling excited by a contemplation of the laws and principles of these sciences, as delineated in nature? The pleasures experienced in the study of optics, exemplify the feelings excited by the entity light, its laws, properties, and relations. Space and number, which would seem, from their nature, least capable of exciting feeling in the mind, are, in fact, found more operative than some others, and afford all the pleasures of geometrical and mathematical study.

Our retrospective and prospective knowledge of entities also produces feelings similar in kind, though generally inferior in degree, to the objective entity itself, when it is the subject of present attention; yet our retrospective ideas are also entities without the mind. I can reflect on a former interview with a long-absent and beloved friend, and derive the purest pleasure from the recollection. The various relations of entities often exert this influence. Thus, the pleasure experienced by the mind when contemplating the beauty of holiness, is excited by the composite entity, a perfect law, and the conduct of a moral agent; and the relation which excites this feeling, is that of agreement between them.

SECTION III.

The degrees in which different entities possess this exciting power are very different, and can be accurately learned only from experience. Nor can any organ originally afford us this information, except the one through which the feeling is produced. We should be unable, from the mere appearance of an orange or a peach, to know, à priori, that their redness or yellowness is indicative of superior aptitude to gratify the palate. Yet after we have by experience learned the fact of this tendency, and learned that the degrees of it are usually attended by these external appearances, they serve as indexes to the mind. But not only is the feeling, produced by entities of different classes, different in degree; the same diversity belongs to one and the same entity, when acting in different ways, and under different circumstances. So far as this arises from a different susceptibility in different minds, or in the same mind at different times, its discussion falls under a subsequent division of our subject; other circumstances only claim our present attention.

The influence of different entities in exciting our feelings.

(*a.*) Their strongest influence entities certainly exert when brought into contact with the particular organs of our body, through which, according to the divine constitution, they act upon the mind. Thus, a peach affords most pleasure, when brought into contact with the palate; a beautiful landscape, when actually viewed by the eye; an escape from the hands of a murderer, when really experienced by us; and the pains of disease, hunger, disappointed hope or ambition, when we are actually the subjects of them.

(*b.*) When we have a prospective knowledge, that we shall, at some future time, probably be the subjects of their influence, they exert their next greatest power; that is, when they are the subjects of hope or fear.

In many instances our prospective view is accompanied by stronger feeling than when we are the direct subjects of the influence of the entity. But this arises from erroneous ideas of the pleasures or pains which will be occasioned by actual experience. The law of nature seems to be that present feeling is stronger than retrospective or prospective.

(*c.*) When these entities excite retrospective feeling, they are again productive of a different degree of pleasure or pain.

(*d.*) Sympathetic feeling is, as a general rule, weaker than its corresponding direct class of feelings.

(*e.*) The least degree of feeling is excited by entities, when we view only their abstract tendency to produce pleasure or pain, without supposing ourselves or others to be actually the subjects of them. This might be termed their original degree of influence, and is, perhaps, the exact degree of strength which the Author of our being designed they should exert upon us as motives. It might also be termed their simple influence, because in all other cases additional principles, such as self-love, &c., are called into action.

SECTION IV.

Entities of the classes of solids and liquids excite more feeling, and exert more motive power, when near us than when far off. This circumstance may be demonstrated by a variety of cases, although it is not so easy to assign the philosophical reason of the fact. This appears to be the case particularly with those solids and liquids, which gratify our periodical susceptibilities of feeling, such as hunger and thirst.

SECTION V.

The manner in which entities act in exciting feeling, seems to be very similar to that observed in the production of knowledge. Each adjective or composite entity can originally excite feeling in the mind, only through that organ by which it becomes the subject of our knowledge. The flavour of fruit can excite pleasure in us originally only through the palate. Again; each individual property or relation of an entity acts independently and individually, in exciting feeling; so that the same substantive entity may produce different feelings in us, when we inspect different properties or relations of it. Hence, if I now love him whom I once hated, it is because I now contemplate different properties, or relations to me, or to others, from those which were formerly prominent in the same individual. This principle is extremely important to enable us to understand how it is, that the penitent and converted sinner finds very different feelings excited by the contemplation of the Divine Being, from those which he formerly experienced.

SECTION VI.

In feeling, as in knowledge, two things are necessary; first, *the action of the entity on its appropriate organ;* and, secondly, *the attention of the mind to that entity.* Thus, if a peach or pear be placed before my face, and my attention is firmly fixed on some other object of thought, the rays of light are indeed reflected from the peach to the retina of my eye, but the soul derives neither knowledge nor feeling from the peach, because my attention is otherwise directed. Hence attention, and the power of directing the mind to one or other object, are highly important active powers of the soul.

CHAPTER III.

THE SUSCEPTIBILITY OF THE MIND FOR FEELING, AND LAWS OF FEELING.

HAVING discussed the nature and classification of feelings themselves, and also the cause from which they spring, that is, entities as excitants of feeling, we now proceed to examine the susceptibilities of the mind for feeling, and the laws by which they seem to be regulated.

First law. *Sensation, no less than cognition, is an attribute of the mind*, and not of the body. That is, all sensation is in the mind. As sensations are obviously *ideas*, it must be admitted by all except materialists, that they are phenomena appertaining to the entity to which ideas belong, that is, to mind. As to the materialist, since he supposes cognitions also to be attributes of matter, or the result of bodily organization, he can without greater absurdity extend the same supposition to sensations. But, so long as all the known properties of matter are totally different from all the known properties of mind, we may well leave the absurd supposition of their being the same substance, to those who delight in philosophical nonsense and paradoxes. The popular impression, that sensations have some kind of local habitation in the organs, through the instrumentality of which they are produced, results from a confusion of the organ through which we perceive, and the thinking being itself. But obviously, there is little more propriety in regarding the eye as the being that sees, than the telescope through which we see; nor ear as the being that hears, than the acoustic tube by which the hearing of the partially deaf is improved. In like manner, the feeling produced by touch is wholly in the mind; although the antecedent perception, which is different for some different parts of the body, enables us, by practice, generally to tell what part of the body has experienced the contact.

Second law. *The original susceptibility of different minds for feeling is evidently very different in degree.* In this there is a striking similarity between the susceptibility for knowledge and feeling. Whether the ground of this diversity is seated partly in the mind itself, or wholly in the different texture or perfection of the bodily organs by which the operations of the soul are limited, it is difficult to decide. That there is a striking diversity in the texture or organization of different individuals, cannot admit of a moment's doubt; it is a subject of ocular and anatomical demonstration. The fact, moreover, is one of universal ocular observation, and its expression provided for in popular language. What else is meant by the phrases, a person of ardent feelings, and, a cold-hearted man, than persons characterized by a diversity in the degree of their habitual feelings; i. e., by a natural diversity in their original susceptibility for feeling. The diversity in the texture of the organs themselves is designated by the term temperament. It is a point doubted by no man of observation, that mankind are distinguished by those diversities, and that they may be reduced to several classes, such as the phlegmatic, sanguine, choleric, &c. The various commixtures of these temperaments are almost infinite; nor is the difference in the texture of the body which is designated by the word temperament, confined to any particular organ of sense; the characteristic pervades the whole organization of the body, the skin, the lymphatics, flesh, blood, bones, nerves, &c. Nothing, however, is more certain, than that the temperaments of men are hereditarily transmitted according to certain laws, which are fixed by the Author of our nature; but which are not, and probably never will be, fully understood by us.

Third law. *Excepting this diversity, which results from the different temperaments, the relative degrees of susceptibility for the influence of different entities is, in all minds, naturally the same.* Although A is twice as sensitive as B, yet, the difference of temperament excepted, an entity which produces twice as much feeling in A as another given entity would, also naturally produces in B twice as much as the other would. A will be operated upon twice as forcibly as B by all motives to good, and it might be supposed that he was favoured by Providence more highly than B, whose natural susceptibility is only half as strong. But it must be remembered that A is also operated upon twice as forcibly as B by all motives to evil, and therefore the relative degree of his susceptibility for feeling is, in effect, equal to that of B. The relative equality of the influence of different entities has an important bearing on the subject of the moral government of God; because feelings are motives to action, and, other things being equal, they naturally exert a power proportionate to this degree. That the above peculiarity of the natural susceptibility for feeling also occurs in feelings of a religious character, seems to be certain. This fact must be taken into consideration by every pastor, who wishes to form a correct view of the religious progress of his spiritual children, and also by every individual, who would judge with accuracy of the religious state of his own soul.

Fourth law. *Feeling is, in a great measure, involuntary at the time.* We cannot, when acted upon by an entity, and when our attention is directed to it, determine whether feeling shall or shall not, in the first instance, be excited in us.

Fifth law. *We can, however, at the time, add to the intensity and duration of the feeling, or subtract from both, by either confining our attention to the exciting entity, or directing it to another object.* Thus, the more wholly we fix our attention upon a piece of music performed within our hearing, the greater will be the feeling excited in us; and the more wholly and intensely we direct our attention to the truths pronounced from the sacred desk, the more fully will they exert their proper influence of feeling and motive power upon us.

Sixth law. When any particular feeling, or passion, or purpose becomes dominant in the soul, and absorbs in a great measure its other energies, all feelings at variance with this are impaired. Thus the sensualist, the miser, and the votary of ambition, are in most cases found comparatively insensible to objects unconnected with their favourite pursuits. In like manner, when men find it necessary to success in any of their habitual pursuits, to suppress those feelings which would endanger that success, they can, by a settled purpose and continued effort, succeed in steeling their hearts against those feelings, and can acquire an insensibility, which at first is artificial, but if persevered in, becomes habitual and natural. It is on this principle that the most benevolent physician from the best of motives, the desire of benefiting his patient, studies to acquire that control over his feelings amid scenes of the most distressing character, which is requisite to enable him to judge wisely of his patient's condition, and to select the most appropriate remedies for his case. And it is upon the same principle, though from far less honourable motives, that military chieftains and professional soldiers acquire the unenviable ability to wade in the blood of their nominal foes, and even to climb unmoved over the mangled bodies of their slaughtered comrades.

Seventh law. *The tendency of entities to excite pleasant or unpleasant feeling, when they are the subjects of prospective or retrospective knowledge, depends, in a great measure, on their accordance, or discordance, with what will hereafter be described as the* CONSTITUTIONAL INCLINATIONS *of the soul, especially the love of well-being or happiness.*

Eighth law. *The influence of an entity, in exciting feeling, is, to a mind of given susceptibility, stronger when it for the first time acts upon us, on account of its novelty.* We may here refer to an analogous case in medical science. A medicine, administered for the first time, produces a greater effect than the same dose does after having been repeatedly taken. How far this analogy is occasioned by similarity of cause, would be an interesting subject of inquiry, in which, however, we have not time to engage. This principle accounts for the fact, that the feelings of the newly-converted are so peculiarly vivid when the entities exciting them, that is, their new relations to God and his law, and to the Saviour, are first presented to their minds. Yet, as continued attention increases the constitutional susceptibility of feeling, the same mind may, by such attention, subsequently have feelings as vivid as those first experienced.

Ninth law. *Feelings produced by the same substantive entity, in the same person, at different times, are in some cases different.* This fact is explained by the principle adverted to on a former occasion, that every property or relation of an entity acts separately in the production of feeling. Every property, indeed, and every relation of an entity, produces a feeling peculiar to itself, and produces this feeling invariably; but, as entities have various properties and relations, the different properties and relations of the same entity, in many cases, produce contrary feelings. Hence it will always be found, that when an entity produces feelings diverse from those which it formerly excited, the reason is, either that the entity has changed its properties or relations, or that a different property or relation is now the subject of our attention, and the excitant of our feeling. At one time we habitually dwell on one property or relation of an entity, and our feelings are correspondent; but when our feelings change, it is because we dwell upon another relation of the same entity. Thus, reflecting on the death of my friend, viewing its relation to me as a social loss, I am grieved, that is, this relation produces painful feeling; but when I reflect on it as a means of his translation from a bed of long-protracted, painful, and hopeless sickness to a world of bliss, I rejoice; this relation of the same event excites pleasant feelings. When our feelings change towards any of our fellow-men, it is always because either their character has changed, or we have acquired additional knowledge concerning it, or, from a change in our own character, we now dwell on different relations of it. The character of men being so very mutable, changes in the relative feelings existing among them, are constantly occurring.

Tenth law. *The susceptibility of the mind for feelings of every kind is increased by* ATTENTIVE *practice.* Here the question arises, whether the cause of increased susceptibility from practice is occasioned by an improvement in the bodily organs or in the mental power. Probably it may be found jointly in both. This principle is exemplified in the pleasures of the glutton, the drunkard, the musician. In other words, the feelings of men are augmented by habit, just as all their cognitive and active operations are. The law of habit pervades the entire man physical and intellectual, and adds facility and strength to all his operations. Feelings of benevolence or of malevolence may be and are confirmed and increased by repetition; and it is owing to this principle that we are enabled, as moral agents, by repeated voluntary exercise of our affections on proper objects, to cherish and cultivate those habits of feeling and traits of character which we know to be good.

Eleventh law. *Intense and long-continued feeling produces a temporary exhaustion, and fatigues the system in a manner similar to intense cognitive mental action.* Yet it is difficult, as knowledge and feeling always go together, to distinguish what portion of the fatigue is to be attributed to each. The question might arise whether the sleepiness of the glutton after dinner be owing to the debility occasioned by this feeling during eating, or by the fact that nature has been compelled to concentrate her energies upon the stomach to digest the newly-received load.

Twelfth law. *The susceptibility for feeling naturally declines with age and with the decline of the constitution, even if that be premature.*

Thirteenth law. *A* NEGLIGENT *review of entities diminishes their tendency to produce feeling.* Upon this principle it is that religious formality tends to produce insensibility of mind.

Fourteenth law. *Time wears off retrospective feeling.* There are cases of exception to this law, such as in those persons who have become melancholy in consequence of severe afflictions, and of always pondering over their loss. But here there is a morbid state of the mind, which, therefore, does not disprove the general law. The ordinary fact is, that the retrospect of our sufferings is attended by feelings less acute than our original sufferings, and that each successive retrospect by the same individual is productive of emotions of diminished acuteness. This law must be regarded as a most benevolent arrangement of Providence. Life is a scene of not unfrequent trials and afflictions. Some of these, at the time of their occurrence, fill us with grief almost as great as we can bear. Now, if the suffering caused by these successive calamities were all accumulated, with undiminished vigour, as we advance in our earthly pilgrimage, life itself would in most cases become an intolerable burden, and man be disqualified for its ordinary duties. On the other hand, the death of friends or relatives could not affect us less at the time, without such a change in our mental structure as would make us place a far lower estimate on their value, and thus greatly diminish our social enjoyments. The result of such a change would necessarily be to weaken the strongest and most endearing ties by which society is held together. We are, therefore, wisely and benevolently so constructed that our suffering at the loss of friends and relatives is poignant, in order that we may take the better care of them when living; and time diminishes the eight of these sorrows, so that their accumulated pressure might not disqualify us for the duties of life.

Fifteenth law. *Feeling is, in general, not instantly excited*, as is knowledge, when an entity becomes the subject of our attention. Oftentimes feeling is elicited by continued application of the mind.

Sixteenth law. *The feelings connected with the gratification of our periodical appetites, such as hunger and thirst, have the following peculiarities.* (1.) They are stronger in proportion to the length of previous abstinence, unless that has been extreme, and has impaired the organs. (2.) They are increased by the frequent attention of the soul to the entities capable of gratifying these appetites. (3.) This feeling is diminished and eventually suspended by gratification. (4.) It is interrupted by the debility and increased by the vigour of the body.

From the preceding laws and considerations it is evident that the state of our feelings is, TO A CERTAIN EXTENT, under our own control. It is indeed true, that no man can instantly change his feelings by a mere volition to do so. But the end can be accomplished eventually, by his habitually directing his attention to those entities and truths calculated to produce the desired feelings. We are, therefore, justly held responsible by our moral Governor for the character of our feelings, *so far as they are under our control.* Nor is the case different with what is often termed the habitual *state of our feelings or affections.* As every feeling is *individual* and *transient*, as it continues only so long as our minds dwell on the entity or idea which excited it, and as it must, in every instance, be excited anew by the appropriate entity, or our knowledge of it, it follows that by the state of our feelings or affections must be meant our *susceptibility* for feelings from any particular entities. This susceptibility is *permanent*, being a part of our original mental constitution, and is either increased or diminished according as it is more or less frequently and designedly exercised towards any given object.

To this increased susceptibility must be added, the increased tendency to the spontaneous recurrence of the ideas of the objects, on which our susceptibility is most frequently employed. These two things, the *increased spontaneous recurrence of the ideas* of the entities which excite feelings of any given character, and *the increased susceptibility of the mind* to their influence when presented, constitute those different habitual *states* of feeling, or of the affections, by which different persons are characterized. In this, so far as known to us, consists the difference between the virtuous and the vicious, the pure and the impure, in regard to the state of their affections. The licentious, for example, by continued voluntary indulgence of criminal thoughts, if not actions, have formed the habit of frequent spontaneous recurrence of licentious thoughts. By the same course they have increased the susceptibility of their minds to be excited by thoughts of that kind; and thus they have corrupted the state of their affections, and made them far worse than they naturally were. For this corrupted state of their affections, they will justly be held liable by the Judge of all the earth.

Thus a person of malevolent disposition, is one who has formed the habit of indulging in such views of human character as are calculated to excite the malevolent feelings, and who has thus augmented the susceptibility of his mind for feelings of that description.

Persons of a benevolent disposition are those of a directly contrary habit. As our feelings are always preceded by a cognitive idea of the entity by which they are produced, we cannot determine whether there is any immediate connexion, any nexus rerum, between the several feelings themselves, by which their tendency to recurrence is increased, or whether that tendency is based only on the association between the cognitive ideas, while the recurrence of these superinduces the repetition of the feelings. If, however, the individual feelings themselves have this tendency, it is exerted only through the medium of our cognitive ideas.

The feelings connected with what are termed our periodical appetites, such as hunger and thirst, might at first view seem to form an exception to the remark, that all our feelings are transient and individual, and must be excited anew in every instance by their appropriate entity, or the recurrence of our idea of it; because they seem often to be permanent, at least for a season, and to continue even without the presence of the external entity or the thought of it, by which they are gratified. But, upon closer examination it will be evident, that during the whole time of their continuance, there is an objective entity acting on the organ and exciting the feeling. Thus, for example, in hunger, the exciting entity has been supposed to be the gastric fluid irritating the coats of the stomach, which in this case are the organ of sensation. This irritation is continued so long as there is not a sufficiency of food thrown into the stomach to absorb or occupy the gastric fluid, and divert it from the coats of the stomach. And just so long, and no longer, do we experience the feeling we term hunger, and the desire of food resulting from it, without its being excited by any external article of food or the thought of any. Still, even while this desire and feeling are excited by continued action of the gastric fluid within us, the idea of food of some kind or other is almost constantly present to the mind, and adds its excitement to the feeling and desire excited from within. The feeling of hunger thus seems simply to be that pain produced by the gastric fluid. The desire connected with it is the result of the motive influence of some article of food, or the idea of it, acting on the mind, and tending to a volition to procure it. The *feeling* of hunger can exist independently of any idea of food; the desire of any kind of food whatever cannot exist without either its presence, or the thought of it.

PART III.

ACTIVE OPERATIONS OF THE SOUL.

Having taken a brief survey of the various classes of entities around us, and having discussed the two kinds of mental representatives, which are obtained by the soul, when these entities are the subjects of our attention, viz., the cognitive and sentient, that is, those ideas which constitute our knowledge and feeling, we must next advance to the examination of those active operations of which the soul is capable, and which certainly constitute the most important feature of our character, as beings responsible to God. Our knowledge and feeling may be regarded mainly as our acquaintance with the universe which God created. They are what our Creator has made them, and, with the exceptions detailed in former portions of this work, we have in general little or no influence over them, so far as their mere original nature is concerned; but these entities, simple and composite, are the materials with which, and the motives in view of which, all the active operations of the soul are performed.

As these active operations are either directly or indirectly, mediately or immediately, under our individual control; as it is by these actions that we exert our influence on the other rational and sentient beings associated with us in this probationary world, an influence always operating for evil or for good; and as it is only through these active operations that the character of our cognitive and sentient states of mind, be they good or evil, can make their influence felt on others, it must be evident that these active operations constitute the principal and most important part of our mental phenomena, that part more immediately contemplated in the precepts and sanctions of the moral government of Jehovah. A man may harbour sentiments of the rankest infidelity, and so long as he keeps them secret, so long as he does not perform the active operation of communicating them to others, either orally or in writing, they will exert no direct tendency to contaminate those around him. Perhaps, if he could prevent his sentiments from influencing his own conduct in the neglect of duty and in giving direction to his agency through life, his opinions and feelings would injure no one but himself. But so soon as they are manifest in his active operations, which in most instances is very soon the case, their baneful tendency is seen and felt by his associates, and by all within the circle of his influence, either personal or literary. In accordance with this is the common sentiment of mankind, that propriety of conduct is more important than the extent of our knowledge or the acuteness of our sensibility; that to do right is more valuable and meritorious than to know accurately or to reason clearly.

Before we proceed in the attempt to enumerate the several species of active operations, we shall first call your attention to the *criteria by which mental operations of the third class are distinguished.* The more we compare the active operations of the soul with its knowledge and feeling, the more distinctly do we perceive that they are radically different in their nature.

The marks of distinction are such as the following:

(1.) One grand feature of this diversity is, that, while knowledge and feeling are effects, ultimately produced upon the mind by external entities, our active operations are mainly causes originating in the mind, or rather they are the mind itself, exerting its influence on the entities which are the subjects of its action. Knowledge and feeling are inward effects produced from without; the active operations are outward effects caused from within. In short, in the two former mental operations we are, to a certain extent, passive recipients of external influence; but in the third we are the active agents, ourselves originating the action.

(2.) The entities by which our cognitive and sentient ideas are excited, must have an existence before we can have either knowledge or feeling by them; but the action, which is the subject of our volition, is yet future, and cannot have an existence at the time when we resolve to perform it. I can have no knowledge of an orange or a peach which has no existence, nor can either affect my palate by feeling unless it exist; but when I will or resolve to perform any action, the act which I determine to perform has no existence at the time when I resolve upon doing it.

(3.) Our feeling is, in some measure, and our knowledge still more, dependant for its character on the entities which produce it. But when we resolve to perform an action, that action does not necessarily depend for its character on anything without us; it is what, within the limits of the laws of nature, we determine that it shall be.

Of Entities as the Materials on which our Active Operations are performed.

As the soul, in both cognitive and sentient operations, is the subject of the influence of entities without us; so the active operations of the soul have also their subjects on which the exerted action is performed. This subject is, in every instance, entities without the mind, which is the case even when some operation is performed upon ideas. Entities of every class and of every species are the materials which, in a greater or less degree, are within the range of our active influence; and on these all our active operations are performed. The soul, like a mechanist, goes to work on these materials, and is capable of producing various combinations, modifications, and alterations in them, limited indeed by the laws of its own nature, and the nature of these materials; but nevertheless important in themselves, and sufficient to enable us to accomplish the customary purposes of daily life, and the grand ultimate end of our existence upon earth.

In order that you may be prepared for understanding the active operations of the soul, it will be advantageous to fix in your minds a specific view of the various materials for *human* action. These are the following:

(*a.*) The external objective entities of the different classes.

(*b.*) Past mental operations of any class; that is, mental representatives of entities, and sentient ideas, and active operations either of our own or other minds.

(*c.*) The natural signs by which these representatives or ideas are expressed; such as, (1.) The sounds which constitute oral language, and (2.) The signs employed; such as the expression of the countenance, gesture, and pantomime in general. The artificial marks or letters by which these sounds are designated in written or printed language, might at first view appear to be an additional class of materials, but they are merely the results of physical action on paper or other materials, which are embraced in the class of external entities already designated.

CHAPTER I.

DIVISION AND DISCUSSION OF THE ACTIVE OPERATIONS OF THE SOUL.

ALL the active processes of the soul are essentially alike, so far as mere activity is concerned; but they differ in the end contemplated by each, in the operation performed, in the different results of the action, and in the different objects on which they terminate. The first place among these active processes seems, for various reasons, to be due to what may be termed the process of inspection, by which we mean the survey or investigation of entities.

SECTION I.

Of Inspection.

By Inspection we would designate *that active operation in which the attention of the soul is directed to some entity, simple or composite; prospective, present, or retrospective; with a view to acquire some knowledge concerning it.* Or, in other words, inspection is that active process of the mind by which we contemplate, either some external entity through the bodily organs, or some idea or operation of the mind, without employing the bodily organs, at least at the time. Some of the ideas thus inspected, are often ideas originally obtained through the bodily organs; although this is not always the case. Thus, we inspect the objects in nature around us, and the result of this act of inspection is a knowledge of the properties perceptible to us. Thus, also, we inspect a train of argument, which we lately heard, on the importance of phrenology; and the result is the belief, or knowledge, that the merits of that science are much overrated, and that it affords few instructions that can safely be relied on, beyond those general indications which have long since been established as a branch of physiognomy. Or, I inspect the abstract proposition, " That things equal to the same thing are equal to one another," and perceive, acquire a knowledge of its truth ; or the metaphysical proposition, " It is impossible for the same thing to be and not to be at the same time," and I judge, perceive, know its truth. The sphere in which this operation is conducted, embraces all the entities within our knowledge, including our own mind and its operations, as well as our ideas concerning all these entities. If the entities inspected were always present, external entities, and never retrospective or prospective, the definition might be altered thus : Inspection is that active operation in which, by a voluntary effort, the attention of the soul is directed to some one or more of the bodily organs, and that organ directed to a particular entity. Thus, when a man who is partially deaf, and does not hear the carriage that is rushing on at some little distance behind him, is called to by a person standing near him to look at the carriage approaching, the information conveyed to him through the ear induces him to look at, that is, inspect the entity by which his safety is endangered. By what action is this accomplished ? First, by volition or resolution to inspect; secondly, by a direction of the bodily organ towards the entity to be inspected ; and, thirdly, by directing the attention of the soul to the organ, or, rather, to the rays of light reflected from the carriage to the retina of the eye. But when we contemplate the mind itself or its operations, or when we take a retrospect of an external entity, that is, inspect our knowledge of a past entity, or when we view an entity, either past, present, or prospective, in its relation to some abstract truth, or proposition, or law. the bodily organ is not used at all; and to embrace such cases, the definition must be more general.

The specific objects of the soul in this inspection may be various. In present entities its object may be, and its results are, the following:

(1.) To obtain more correct mental representatives of the properties of entities. For instance, suppose the Capitol of the United States were the subject of our inspection. We direct our attention to it, and, in so doing, also our eyes, and the first glance gives us an idea of its general structure. We, however, wish to acquire a more minute acquaintance with its structure, and for this specific purpose continue to direct our eyes and our attention successively to every part of it. We may examine it with a specific design of ascertaining its general plan, or the execution of any particular part of the work, such as that performed by the mason, or the plasterer, or the carpenter; and thus, by repeated and continued inspection, we acquire more correct and minute mental representatives of the external entity.

(2.) The second object in inspecting present entities may be to give more vividness to our mental representatives of them. This vividness may perhaps consist in the additional feeling, excited by a reiterated and attentive inspection. After having examined all the features of a painting, we have a correct mental representative of it; but we may resolve to fix our attention successively on its different features, and exert the intensity of that attention on them; and thus, perhaps, it is in part, that our ideas of it become more vivid, because our feelings are more interested.

(3.) We may inspect entities with the express view of ascertaining their relations. Thus, we inspect different entities for the purpose of ascertaining their relation of sameness, or diversity, or contiguity, or causation. In all these examinations, the accuracy of our results will greatly depend on the deliberateness and degree of attention with which the process is conducted. Particular caution is requisite, when the design of our inspection is to ascertain the relation of causation between entities, or to decide, whether the relation be one of mere antecedence and sequence.

In inspecting the moral character of any action, that is, its relation of congruity or incongruity with some law of God, inferred by reason from the works of nature, or learned from Revelation, the relation may be so obvious as to be instantaneously perceived, and thus our judgment is intuitive. In other cases, the moral character of the action may not be so clear, and then continued attention and investigation are requisite, either to ascertain, by an induction of facts, the real tendency of the actions in question, or by continued exegetical investigations, conducted according to the laws of impartial hermeneutics, to ascertain the true sense of Scripture, to determine whether the disputed action is or is not interdicted in the Sacred Volume.

For the same general purposes, namely, to ascertain the relations of entities, the mechanist examines, inspects the materials which he designs to employ. Thus the carpenter inspects a piece of wood in order to discover its relation of fitness or unfitness for the specific purpose for which he intends it, or with a view to perform some voluntary action on it, such as sawing, planing, or cutting it.

In the case of retrospective entities, simple or composite. (1.) These we inspect, or rather our mental representatives of them, in order to revive those representatives, that is, as it is popularly expressed, to refresh our memory. Experience proves, that both knowledge and feeling have a tendency to vanish from the mind. Both become weakened by time, and, unless revived by retrospection, will be lost to us, at least in the present world. When we reflect on the instances of extraordinary memory on record, and combine with them the fact, that some persons of very ordinary powers of retention have, under the influence of disease, recollected facts which they had long forgotten, and rehearsed extended passages of authors in a language unknown to them, which they had heard repeated many years before, but which in health they were utterly unable to repeat, we may well be inclined to regard thought as indestructible, and think it probable that all the mental operations of our whole life will be recollected by us in eternity, and perhaps these reminiscences will be one of the principal bases of our future happiness or misery. But in the present life, there is a constant tendency in the mind to forget what is long past, if it be not revived by reinspection.

(2.) The second object of inspecting retrospective entities is to view their relations to each other; that is, to compare them with each other, or a present entity with a prospective one. Thus, we may inspect the relation of causation between the British Stamp Act and our Revolutionary War, both being retrospective entities; or we may examine the relation of causation between our Revolutionary War and our present enjoyment of free institutions; in which case we compare a retrospective and a present entity or idea. Finally, we may consider the relation of probable causation between our Revolutionary War and a future regeneration and remodelling of all the governments in Europe; here we compare a past with a future entity. In this last example we have an instance of the inspection of the prospective knowledge of entities. All the subjects of our prospective knowledge may be subjects of inspection. Indeed, this department of our knowledge, more than any other, seems to be the fruit of voluntary inspection. Every hypothetical case that can be imagined is, at least in part, an inspection of prospective entities.

The process of inspection embraces all the voluntary operations which, in former systems, have been attributed to the faculties of *perception*, *consciousness*, *conception*, *judgment* in moral as well as intellectual and physical cases, *voluntary recollection*, *analytic reasoning*, and *conscience*. That the operations of the mind termed *perceptions*, when voluntary, are embraced in the process of inspection, is evident from what was said on the subject of the inspection of present entities. That the operations usually ascribed to *conception* are nothing else than inspection, is evident from the remarks made on the inquiry, how many of our supposed faculties furnish us with knowledge, or how many of the operations of the supposed faculties are cognitive in their character. The only cases which might seem to militate against the classification of the operations of conception under the process of inspection are abstract ideas, such as virtue, vice, &c. But we have already exhibited to you the proof, that these terms designate our ideas of certain relations of real entities which are observed by inspection. The conception of the meaning of a proposition, is nothing more than the inspection of retrospective knowledge, aided by the signs called words, either written or oral.

In the inspection of present entities, the entity itself is the subject of inspection. In the inspection of retrospective entities, however, it is not the entity itself, but our knowledge of it, which is the subject of our inspection. This seems evident from the fact, that, if our original knowledge of an entity was incorrect, a review of it, however frequent, will not rectify it; unless we compare our knowledge with the original entity itself, or with a description of it by another, whose knowledge was more accurate, and in whose testimony we confide; whereas, every attentive review of a present entity tends to correct any error in our first idea of it. These facts also prove the fallacy of Dr. Brown's opinion, that all mental operations are merely the mind itself in certain states. When we review our knowledge, are not the passive, inert items of this knowledge manifestly different from the active being, or mind, which is at work on them? As well might we say that the wood, out of which the cabinet-maker is framing a desk or table, is nothing else than the workman himself, in a certain state.

The act of *memorizing* is an active operation embraced under the process of inspection. It may be defined thus: The act of memorizing is a voluntary, repeated, attentive review of some entities, or of our ideas of them, or of some signs of such ideas, in order that we may have a retrospective knowledge of either the ideas of the entities, or the ideas of the associated signs. Thus, if we commit to memory a piece of composition with a view to speak it verbatim, we make the recollection of our ideas of the sounds, which are associated with the ideas of the entities, the subjects of our chief attention. But if we wish to recollect only the ideas of the entities themselves, we pay little attention to the ideas of the sounds, and leave them to be recalled at the time of delivery by the ideas of the entities. Thus, it is evident, we are able to make different things the subjects of our aim in the act of committing to memory, and different persons have different habits on this subject. The man who, as it is usually expressed, recollects only ideas, is one who by habit, or possibly by a constitutional predisposition, recollects principally the ideas of the entities themselves about which he is speaking, and trusts to the association formed in his mind between the ideas of the entities and those of the sounds designating them, for the suggestion of words at the time of speaking. The man distinguished for verbal memory, on the contrary, is one who is in the habit of inspecting the ideas of the sounds as well as of the entities signified by them ; and to his mind, in the moment of delivery, the very words recur in which he had committed the speech. Perhaps, in the one case, the train of the ideas of the signs is the leading train, on which the retrospective energy of his mind is expended ; and this train of the ideas of sounds does, in the moment of delivery, recall the parallel train of the ideas of entities. In the other case, the train of the ideas of entities is the prominent one which recurs, and, by association, brings with it the train of the ideas of the connected sounds. Yet, as there is no relation at all between the ideas of sounds except that of contiguity, whereas the ideas of the entities are related by the additional connexion subsisting between them in a well-digested composition, it is not improbable that the ideas of the entities discussed are in most cases the prominent train in the recollection ; and the different degrees in which sounds are recollected form the difference between ideal and verbal memories.

That *analytic reasoning* is also chiefly a process of inspection, is evident from its nature, as it consists of the successive investigation of a series of particulars, from which eventually a general conclusion is inferred to be applicable to all other particulars of the same kind. Thus we learn from observation (inspection), that a number of material objects, such as trees, stones, portions of lead, water, earth, &c., gravitate towards the centre of the earth. Hence, as we find this property to belong to all material objects, without excepiton, which we have examined, we infer, with the greatest probability, that it belongs also to all other material substances. Our syllogism will then stand thus:

Trees, stones, lead, water, earth, &c., gravitate towards the centre of the earth:

Trees, stones, lead, water, earth, &c., are all the material bodies which are within the reach of our examination:

Therefore all the material bodies which are within the reach of our observation, gravitate towards the centre of the earth.

Should we invert this reasoning, and form our syllogism in the synthetic mode, it would run thus:

All material bodies, within the reach of our observation, gravitate towards the centre of the earth:

Stone is a material body within the reach of our observation:

Therefore stone gravitates towards the centre of the earth.

The analytic method is best adapted to the investigation of subjects, and the synthetic to the communication of knowledge already attained.

In all its reasonings, however, the mind is governed by certain principles of its own structure, or *Laws of Belief*, the most important of which it may not be unimportant to enumerate. These truths are, however, not abstract or general in their intrinsic nature or form, in which they operate on the mind. They are, indeed, often formed into general truths, and by some writers these general truths were supposed to possess greater strength of evidence than the individual cases from which they are derived. But this is incorrect. The general truth is merely an abstract statement, derived from the individual cases, and embracing them all, and, consequently, cannot possibly possess stronger probative influence than the individuals of which it is composed. With this explanation, we proceed to state the

Fundamental Laws of Human Belief.

All men make the following constitutional judgments, in each individual case as it occurs:

1. That the testimony of their *senses*, when clearly ascertained, is true. This truth has never been sincerely doubted by any man in his senses, not even by those skeptics who, in theory, professed to do so.

2. That the testimony of *consciousness* is entitled to our confidence in every case. This is, indeed, the fundamental source of our knowledge of all our mental operations, of our cognitions, of our feelings, and of our active processes of mind. If this channel, so to speak, through which all our knowledge passes, were unworthy of confidence, of course no other item of our knowledge, of any kind whatever, could claim a higher degree of certainty.

3. That the *testimony of memory*, when distinct, and so far as distinct, may be relied on as true. I am just as certain that I lately re-examined the prophecies of Daniel, and the Revelation of St. John, on the second coming of our Saviour, a subject now arresting so much attention in some parts

of our country, as that I see the pen with which I am now writing. Our confidence in our reminiscences is strong in proportion to the degree of distinctness which they appear to us to possess. Yet our recollection of a general fact may often be perfectly distinct, while we recollect but imperfectly some of its attendant circumstances. In this case our confidence in the former is unwavering, and our belief in the latter doubtful. I remember with great certainty my having read Dr. Channing's sermon at the ordination of Mr. Sparks upward of twenty years ago, and also Professor Stuart's letters in reply to it; yet of some of the arguments and explanations contained in these works, my recollection is indistinct. But I can, on this account, no more doubt that I perused these productions, than if it had occurred yesterday.

4. That all the *other operations of our mind*, such as reasonings and judgment, may be relied on with a degree of certainty proportioned to their nature, and to the circumstances under which they are performed.

5. That all men naturally *speak the truth*, when they have no motive to practise deception.

6. That every *act of consciousness presupposes or implies a conscious being*, *the soul.* On occasion of every such act we constitutionally judge the existence of a conscious subject, to whom these acts belong. The only case we have met with of an individual who disbelieved the existence of his soul, is that of Rev. Simon Browne, of England, a dissenting minister, of excellent character, who died about 1732. "He imagined, that in consequence

of an extraordinary interposition of Divine power, his rational soul was gradually annihilated, and that nothing was now left of him but a principle of animal life, which he held in common with the brutes." But no man can be at a loss for the proper solution of this melancholy phenomenon. All will just as readily regard it as the result of mental derangement, as if he had denied the axioms of mathematics, or disbelieved the existence of his body. The circumstance which so preyed upon his mind as to deprive him of reason, was the death of his wife and only son, in 1723.*

7. That *every act of memory, or succession of acts of consciousness, implies our personal identity*, and is the occasion which elicits the constitutional judgment of such identity. Nor is this judgment of our identity destroyed, even if consciousness and memory, yea, all conscious mental action, is for a season interrupted. A very singular case, illustrative of this fact, was reported to the Royal Academy of Sciences in France. " A nobleman of Lausanne, as he was giving orders to a servant, suddenly lost his speech and all his senses. Different remedies were tried without effect for six months, during all which time he appeared to be in a deep sleep, or deliquium, with various symptoms at different periods. At last, after some chirurgical operations, at the end of six months his speech and senses were suddenly restored. When he recovered, the servant to whom he had been giving orders when he was first seized with the distemper, happening to

* See the Narrative of his case in the Adventurer, No. 88.

be in the room, he asked whether he had executed his commission: not being sensible, it seems, that any interval of time, except, perhaps, a very short one, had elapsed during his illness. He lived ten years after, and died of another disease."* Dr. Beattie also cites his own experience in support of the same view. "That consciousness may be interrupted by a total deliquium, without any change in our notions of our own identity, I know by my own experience. I am, therefore, fully persuaded that the identity of this substance, which I call my soul, may continue even when I am unconscious of it; and if for a shorter space, why not for a longer?"†

8. In addition to the above constitutional truths, there are some other judgments, not intuitive, indeed, but early acquired and universally entertained, which also lie at the basis of much of our reasoning. Thus all *men judge that the laws of nature and the known properties of all entities or objects in the world will, with almost entire certainty, continue*, because they have found them to continue with absolute invariableness during the whole time of their observation and recollection.

9. *Different kinds of truth are found to be possessed of different kinds and degrees of evidence.* And we have reason to believe that the Author of our nature has invested every truth, which he has placed within our sphere of observation, with a degree of evidence sufficient, when fully and impartially weighed, to produce just as strong a conviction as he designs us to feel.

* Dr. Beattie, on Truth, p. 36. † Essay on Truth, p. 36

These principles are presupposed in all kinds of reasoning. The different species of reasoning are influenced by the nature of the subject or entity under investigation. Analytic reasoning may relate to physical, intellectual, or moral subjects or entities.

In the investigation of physical objects, the materials for reasoning must be acquired through our bodily senses, on the testimony of which we confidently rely.

In the investigation of intellectual objects, the phenomena of mind are the materials for reasoning, and these we acquire by the testimony of consciousness, which we judge to be true.

In the investigation of moral truth, in its most limited sense, the moral relations of rational beings to each other and to God, as well as the relation of their actions to the Divine law, are the materials for reasoning; and in the acquisition of our knowledge of these, we rely on the accuracy of consciousness and other powers of the soul, as well as on the testimony of our senses when the *actions* of men are concerned. But, as it is not our design to embrace Logic in this treatise, we shall not enter into the discussion of these different processes of ratiocination.

SECTION II.

Of Arrangement.

Arrangement is that active operation of the soul by which we select some from among the mass, either of external entities themselves, or of our mental representatives of them, and place them, as wholes or units, in a particular order, with a view to a specific purpose. In present entities, the entities themselves are the subjects of the arrangement. Thus, having a number of ivory balls of different colours before us, after having inspected them, the result of this inspection is a knowledge of their shape, colour, &c., and nothing more than knowledge. But when we select those of the same colour from the mass and place them together, we perform an additional and distinct operation, viz., that of arrangement. In addition to the present entities themselves, this operation is also performed on our mental representatives of retrospective and prospective entities. When, e. g., we resolve to arrange into classes all the various animals which we have ever seen, and of which we have a recollection, we can accomplish the work, though not one of those animals be present. But then it is not the animals themselves (present entities) which we arrange into different classes of quadrupeds, bipeds, carnivorous, graminivorous, oviparous, viviparous, &c., but only our mental representatives or cognitive ideas of them. The purposes of this arrangement, and the principles on which it is made, may be various.

(1.) We may arrange them according to any one of the various relations of entities to each other; such as sameness, diversity, contiguity, causation, majority, minority, progression, proportion, &c. Thus the mental act of comparison in language is nothing else than the arrangement of two entities according to the relation of similarity, together with an expression of their relation in words.

E. g., "Virtue is the pillar of a republic." This sentence means, that virtue in a republic resembles the pillar of an edifice, which supports the fabric. Comparison may be performed on present entities, or on our ideas of them.

The arithmetical processes of addition, subtraction, division, multiplication, are so many species of this second active operation, arrangement, performed by man on different numbers. Addibility, subtractibility, &c., i. e., the capacity of being thus operated on, are properties of the absolute entity number; but the operation of addition, &c., is an active process of the mind of man on these properties. Addition is the arrangement of several numbers into one class or sum; division is the arrangement of a certain number into a given number of parts; subtraction is the arrangement of some of the integral parts of a given number into a separate class or number; and multiplication is the addition of a sum a given number of times.

(2.) The second principle according to which the process of arrangement may be conducted, is that of genus, species, class, &c. The difference between this and the first mode of arrangement is, that in the former only one classification is embraced, whereas, in the latter, there are several grades of similarity. The arrangement of entities differs from the mere reinspection of them, in the fact, that the latter always embraces merely the view of entities, without including any change effected in their relations to other entities or ideas. Inspection can only view the universe of entities as it exists at the time of inspection, but arrangement changes their order, or connexion, or relation, by bringing those into contiguity which were separate before, and by separating such as were before contiguous. By this process, we form all the varieties of mental associations which are based on any natural principle or affinity; while unnatural and arbitrary associations are the product of what we term the third active process, modification.

The musician, who *composes* a piece of music, performs this process of arrangement. He takes the several individual notes or sounds, and places them into such relation as, by the constitutional influence which they exert on our minds, will produce the effects at which he aims. The act of recording such composition by writing is a process of physical agency.

(3.) This arrangement may be made according to the probative relation of entities to a given proposition or to the human mind. The order in which evidence, that is, related entities are arranged, gives them more or less force or influence upon the mind. This is well understood by the advocate, the logician, and the intelligent and faithful preacher. The successful arrangement of our knowledge or arguments according to their probative relations to the human mind, constitutes the all-important operation of synthetic reasoning, so far as its object is to produce in others, conviction of truths already known to the speaker or writer. The capacity of reasoning clearly, in a public speaker or writer, is nothing else than the ability to arrange his ideas or arguments in their best probative order, and in that order in which they produce their greatest convincing effect, to enunciate them in words, or record them in written signs, which will recall those words to all who read (i. e., inspect) them. Thus we see that *analytic reasoning*, or, more properly, *investigation*, is an operation of *inspection*, while *synthetic* reasoning, that is, the logical arrangement of the result and evidences of our investigation, is chiefly an instance of the second active operation, viz., *Arrangement*. The *formation of generic propositions*, in which the results of our investigations are synthetically proposed, is a *process of abstraction* or generalization, and thus belongs to the active process, *modification*. The presentation of the whole to others in oral or written language belongs to the last active operation, namely, the communication of our ideas to others, or *intellectual intercourse* with other minds.

Evidence, objectively considered, is the tendency or fitness of any one entity in the physical, intellectual, or moral universe, or of its relations, to make the reality of another supposed entity credible, that is, apparent to the mind. Evidence, subjectively considered, is the tendency of our knowledge of some entity, or its relations, to make our knowledge of other entities, or their relations, appear true. Here is presented to our view one of the grandest features of intellectual science—truth based upon the rock of the universe, which God founded, while our knowledge is but the shadow or reflection of it, merely its mental representative.

The probative order or relation of entities to a certain proposition, seems to consist in their being detached from all irrelevant appendages, and placed in such connexion of contiguity or succession, in relation to the proposition, as is best calculated for the inspection of the hearer, so as to present the greatest facility for the operation of inspection by the auditors or readers. The more completely arguments are separated from everything irrelevant, the more easily can they be inspected by the mind.

Every species of syllogism is nothing else than a particular arrangement of certain entities, or rather of propositions expressing our ideas of them, such as is best calculated to facilitate their inspection; and the art of reasoning well is nothing else than the habit of arranging the related ideas in this way for easy inspection. Before we exemplify these observations by the examination of the process of reasoning itself, we would remind the student of the classification of composite entities, that is, of relations as the bases of verbs in human language; for, as all syllogisms embrace verbs, an accurate idea of the nature of verbs is essential to the comprehension of the subject. We have, on a former occasion, remarked that the words in human language originally and most naturally expressing substantive entities are in grammar substantives, and those standing for adjective entities are originally adjectives. But it is the verbs which alone most naturally express the *relations* subsisting between different entities. In pursuing our examination of syllogisms, we begin with the several parts, and first inquire, What are they? They consist of human language, of propositions. These describe some of our mental representatives or ideas; and the question is, Of what entities are they representatives, of substantive, or adjective, or composite entities, or of all combined? An example will best illustrate these observations in their application to the structure of the syllogism.

Major proposition: If there is a God, he ought to be worshipped.

Minor proposition: But there is a God.

Conclusion: Therefore he ought to be worshipped.

Here the term God, or letters G, o, d, express the sound, which, in our language, is the sign of a certain idea, which idea is our mental representative of a real entity, viz., the great Author of the universe. This is a substantive entity. The phrase "ought to be worshipped" is a verb, and expresses our idea of a certain composite entity, viz., the relation of moral fitness or obligation between the two parts of a composite entity, viz., God (a Being of a certain character), and his rational creatures worshipping him. The major proposition, therefore, expressed in the language of our system, would run thus: "If there be an entity corresponding to the idea designated by the sound which is spelled by the letters G-o-d, he ought to be worshipped;" i. e., we see the relation of suitableness between him and those actions of his rational creatures called the worship of him. The major proposition, when closely examined, seems evidently to be nothing else than a sentence expressing in words our ideas of a composite entity, i. e., of the relation of two simple entities to each other. The simple entities are, (1.) A Being corresponding to the idea designated by the sound and word *God;* and, (2.) Those actions of his rational creatures, which they perform with a view of worshipping him; and the relation between them is that of suitableness. The process by which this relation is known is none other than that of inspection. The result of inspection is, in all cases, knowledge; and in this case likewise we can trace no other operation than the act of inspecting the two parts of a composite entity, God and the worship of him by rational creatures, and the result of this inspection is, conviction of the relation. This knowledge or conviction is not optional, but necessary. The minor proposition, philosophically stated, runs thus: "But there is an entity corresponding to the mental representative designated by the sound, which we describe by the letters G-o-d;" "hence he ought to be worshipped" is the conclusion or relation perceived by the mind. It is evident that the only point to be proved in this syllogism is the minor, viz., that there exists an entity which we designate by the term God, and this must be done, and can be done, only by the successive inspection of the entities which constitute the proof.

SECTION III.

Of Modification.

The third active operation or process is termed modification, and embraces a class of operations distinct in their nature from those which have preceded. *Modification is that active operation of the soul, by which we take some from among our mental representatives of real entities* (rarely the objective entities themselves), *and bring them into such forms or combinations as do not correspond to realities;* that is, *make arbitrary substantive and composite entities out of them.* The materials on which these operations are performed are seldom objective entities themselves, but generally are our mental representatives of them. This operation is distinguished from the two preceding by the following distinct peculiarities: (1.) The operations of *inspection* and *arrangement* act as generally on objective entities themselves, as on our mental representatives of them; whereas, that of *modification* is conversant chiefly about our ideas. (2.) The former two operations take our mental representatives of substantive entities as wholes or units, and leave them such throughout all the process of their influence; take our ideas of the combination of properties found coexisting, and leave these combinations unaltered; but modification changes them from their natural state, and brings their constituent parts or elements into forms and combinations which do not exactly correspond to real entities. This operation embraces, among others, the following processes:

1. The process of *abstraction* and *generalization*; that is, the process of framing ideas and combinations of ideas, which do not fully represent any one entity, but are used to express a whole class of individual entities which have, in common, the properties expressed by the generic idea and term. Thus the idea quadruped is formed by the process of abstraction. We take the combinations of our mental representatives of the properties found coexisting in each of the several animals, horse, cow, sheep, dog, &c. We compare with each other our ideas of these several combinations of properties, each one of which combinations is found coexisting in one or other of these animals. Thus comparing these several combinations of ideas, we omit from each every individual idea which is peculiar to itself, until at last we have nothing remaining but the idea of four legs, as the property or peculiarity which they have in common, and by which they are distinguished from animals of a different class. In considering this process, let it be recollected that our mental representative of each one of the different coexisting objective properties is separate and independent. We can therefore, with the greatest ease, abstract from our ideas of the combination, any one or more of its elements at option, and use the residue as a substantive entity in our ratiocinations. It is in this way that all generic *terms* are formed.

If we examine the ideas conveyed to the mind by the term *quadruped* and the phrase *four legs*, we instantly perceive a great distinction between them: the latter designates our idea of a part of an animal, while the former signifies not only a whole animal, but a whole class of animals each of which has four legs. But it is evident that the idea expressed by the term quadruped does not correspond with any individual entity intended by it, any farther than the circumstance of its having four legs. The term quadruped, therefore, expresses one of those general ideas which we refer to the process of abstraction. Thus also the idea expressed by the term *all*, when definitely used, does not correspond fully to any real entity, but is a generic idea embracing a great number of entities.

Of the same character, generically, are negations, and the ideas expressed by particles of speech which have no objective entity in nature corresponding to them. They are, though of different kinds, the product of this power of modification. Thus the word "nothing" expresses a negative generic idea, and is equivalent to not a solid, not a liquid, not a gas, not light, not caloric, &c., &c. The idea is acquired by the perception of the absence of one entity after another, and ultimately the supposed absence of all entities. Generally, however, when we use the term nothing, we employ it in a qualified sense. About absolute nothing we seldom speak, and can say but little intelligently.

Generic *propositions* are formed by striking out from a specific proposition, the name of the individual objective entity of which the predicate of the proposition may be affirmed, and substituting in its stead some generic name, which comprehends all the individual objective entities to which the predicate is believed to be applicable. One of the most important rules of correct reasoning is, that the utmost caution be always observed not to introduce into our general proposition a term more generic than our actual examinations warrant, not so general as to include any entity, *of which we are not certain that the predicate really belongs to it*, or in regard to which our experience is not sufficiently extensive, and also uniform so far as it goes. This process of generalization or abstraction is one of the most important among all our mental operations.

Among its results are embraced, (1.) Geometrical axioms; (2.) Metaphysical axioms; (3.) Mathematical truths; (4.) Moral general truths or principles; such as, virtue is productive of happiness and vice of misery.

Hence the opinion of Kant and many other German philosophers, that knowledge of this kind is *à priori*, that is, inherent in the mind, is erroneous. There are, indeed, many truths which may be characterized as universal and unchangeable, which are the properties assigned by him to the truths of pure reason (Reine Vernunft). And there can be no objection to calling them transcendental. But they do not differ in their nature from other ideas. Viewed *subjectively*, these general ideas are phenomena of our minds, are mental representatives of actual relations in nature, abstracted from the entities in which they are found. Viewed *objectively*, general truths are relations actually existing in nature, not in an abstract, but in a concrete state, between different individual entities. Thus the axiom, "Things which are equal to the same thing are equal to one another," is nothing else than a proposition expressing the relation of agreement between different entities, and especially the truth taught by experience, that any two of them which are equal to a third, will also be found equal to each other. But if it be inquired whether these truths are *à priori* knowledge, we reply in the negative. The *individual* relation of equality between the different objects existed before we perceived it; but the general, abstract, subjective idea of this relation, having been formed from the ideas of the individual relations perceived, must necessarily be subsequent to our (empyric) perceptions of the individual relations. The general truth has nothing in nature corresponding to it; because all actual relations and entities are individual. It therefore exists only as an idea in the mind of man. There are, indeed, some laws of the mind itself, which regulate and limit its operations, our knowledge of which is not derived from the observation of external nature. These laws, it is admitted, exist prior to our knowledge of them. But so do the laws of the material universe. And just as we derive our knowledge of the laws of the physical universe by observation of external nature, so we acquire our knowledge of the laws of mind by observing the phenomena of mind. Yet, there is as much difference between the laws of mind and our knowledge of those laws, as there is between the laws of matter and our knowledge of them. Nor can we perceive any reason why the one should be regarded as *à priori* knowledge, rather than the other; for in reality neither possesses any claim to that character.

2. Fictitious combinations of ideas: (*a.*) Fictitious simple entities, either substantive or adjective, i. e., fictitious persons, things, and properties. (*b.*) Fictitious composite entities, or relations, or actions performed by one on the other, or existing between several. This process brings different entire substantive entities into imaginary combinations, and attributes to them imaginary actions. To this species of modification belong all the operations of *imagination* and *fancy*, the active element of many specimens of wit and burlesque; all specimens of painting, and all works of fiction, either in poetry or prose; and also, what is of the same character, though of different design, every species of misrepresentation, falsehood, or lying.

The operations of what is termed *imagination* are clearly specimens of *modification*. The definitions of imagination, adopted by the best writers, sufficiently prove this. "It is the province of imagination," says Mr. Stewart, "to make a selection of qualities and of circumstances from a variety of different objects, and by combining and disposing these, to form a new creation of its own." What is this else than modification, which, according to our definition, "is that active operation of the soul, by which we take some from among our mental representatives of real entities (rarely the objective entities themselves), and bring them into such forms or combinations as do not correspond to realities." Still more accordant with our definition of modification is that given of imagination by Dr. Abercrombie, who says, "In the process of imagination, we take the component elements of real scenes, events, or characters, and combine them anew by a process of the mind itself, so as to form compounds which have no existence in nature." But the process of abstraction, or generalization, also consists in an operation of the same general kind, but for different purposes. Some of the processes termed wit, burlesque, and the ludicrous, partake of the same nature. Hence, as these several processes differ only in minor circumstances, while they are generically the same, it is more philosophic not to regard them as entirely different operations, but to adopt one general process of modification, and regard these as its different species. Thus, when the painter designs to paint an imaginary landscape of perfect beauty, how does he proceed? He recalls to his reminiscences all the most beautiful scenes which he has witnessed in nature, and selecting from them his ideas of those traits which strike him as most beautiful, he forms these into one imaginary landscape in his own mind. After this, he tries successively to imitate these several features with his pencil, that is, he records this new creation of his imagination on the canvass. The poet passes through the same process, more or less formally, only he makes his record in words instead of colours, with the pen instead of the painter's pencil. "Milton," says Mr. Stuart, "has, in his garden of Eden, created a landscape more perfect, probably, in all its parts, than has ever been realized in nature, and certainly very different from anything that this country (England) exhibited at the time when he wrote. It is a curious remark of Mr. Walpole, that Milton's Eden is free from the defects of the old English garden, and is imagined on the same principles, which it was reserved for the present age to carry into execution." But it was no peculiarity of Milton, that he depicted his garden as more beautiful than any which nature presents to us. This is characteristic of poets and novelists generally. They exhibit their heroes and heroines either as elevated above the bounds of human perfection, or sunk below the dregs of our race. For this very reason, a fondness for works of this description is no promising trait of character, especially in the young; and the habitual indulgence of it almost invariably disqualifies, in a greater or less degree, for the sober realities and the active scenes of real life. But another and still more serious objection to the great mass of popular novels, romances, tragedies, and comedies, is, that they familiarize the mind with scenes of pollution, and thus destroy the moral sensibilities of the soul; and they often present vice arrayed in so many circumstances of interest, as to make the reader insensibly forget its deformity. Nor does the unfortunate end which is sometimes made to close the career of wickedness, and which is the reputed moral of the tale, at all compensate for the corrupting influence exerted on the reader's mind by long familiarity with scenes of impurity throughout the book. Even when scenes of affliction or misfortune are presented, and the sympathy of the reader becomes deeply interested, as the whole is confessedly fictitious, and no opportunity is afforded to him to exercise his sympathy in efforts to relieve the unfortunate, the practical benevolent tendencies of his nature are impaired, and even his sensibility to real misfortune blunted.

The sudden and arbitrary combinations of thought, which constitute the intellectual part of wit and burlesque, are in many cases different species of the process of modification, while the sentient part of these complex efforts of mind constitute the feeling or emotion of the ludicrous.

The architect and the sculptor, likewise, first make a creation of fancy, and then endeavour to realize it by erecting some splendid and tasteful edifice, or an animated, almost living statue.

SECTION IV.

The fourth active process is that mental agency which immediately regards and regulates the action of our bodily organs. It may be termed *the mental direction of our physical action.* It embraces all voluntary control over the entire muscular system, by which alone motion is produced in any part of the body. The intrinsic connexion between mind and matter, and the manner in which the latter is made to obey the former, is a mystery to us. The fact of the obedience of the body to the mind is of daily and hourly, yea, of incessant occurrence; but is as incomprehensible to the greatest philosopher, as any other mystery in nature or religion. I will to hold the pen in my right hand, and so to move it as to form letters and words; but why my right hand takes the pen rather than the left, why my fingers move the pen so as to form alphabetic letters rather than mathematical figures, I know not. I can assign no other reason than my antecedent volition, that they should do so. And a man who has suffered a paralysis is surprised when, for the first time, he finds that the muscles of his arm or leg refuse to obey the volitions of his mind.

This connexion between the mind and body, this obedience of the muscles to the will, in healthy persons, being assumed as one of the best-established facts in nature, our next inquiry is, how far is so-called physical action really physical, and how far is it mental? It seems evident that everything about it, except the simple tension and relaxation of the muscles, and consequent locomotion of the body, or some of its parts, is mental. Mechanical skill is an improvement of the mind in directing bodily motion. Intelligence, memory, wisdom in the selection of appropriate materials, and appropriate bodily motions, to effect an end, are involved, as are also other mental processes.

This agency might be divided into different kinds, according to the different organs to which it more immediately relates; or it might be divided into the different processes effected by the hands, by the feet, the eyes, the whole body, &c. Under the operations effected by the hands would be embraced, (1.) The different species of mechanical and agricultural labour; (2.) The manipulations requisite to performances on musical instruments, in which there is, combined with much physical activity, remarkable intellectual skill. Of the operations of the feet, walking is the most remarkable. It properly results from the combined muscular effort of the whole body, and consists in balancing the body by leaning forward so far that the centre of gravity is brought beyond the base, and sustaining the body from falling by the continued position of one foot after another in advance of the whole. In all cases of voluntary physical action, we can distinguish the following mental processes: (1.) Selection of the end to be accomplished; (2.) Knowledge of the ways and means for its attainment; (3.) The volition to exert the bodily organ; (4.) The attention of the soul to the organ; (5.) The inspection of the material on which the agency is to be performed; and, (6.) The active process of the mind conducting and regulating the physical action.

SECTION V.

The fifth process is that of holding intellectual intercourse with other minds; or, as it is commonly, though incorrectly termed, *the process of communicating our ideas to others.*

Philosophically speaking, this process consists in exciting in others the ideas which they themselves have already obtained from those entities on which we wish them to think, and exciting them in such order, and in such combinations, and with such adjective properties annexed, as we wish them to entertain. When we utter articulate sounds, these sounds, by their exact similitude to those which the person whom we address has heard in connexion with certain ideas, first recall his idea of the similar sound formerly heard by himself, and this recalls the idea of an entity then connected in his mind with that idea of the sound. Thus, by speaking to others, that is, by successively pronouncing the sounds corresponding to the train of thought in our own minds, we not only excite in others the similar ideas which they have received from entities, but we bring them into new connexions, and add epithets to suit our purpose.

This process of intellectual intercourse is carried on in different ways:

I. *By speaking, or expressing our ideas by articulate sounds.* We are born with organs of articulation, by the voluntary action of which we can so modify the expiring breath as to produce specific articulate sounds. The air on which the action of these organs is exerted is only the expiring breath, the breath as it is in the act of passing out from the lungs. The constant inhalation and expiration of breath is, within certain limits, involuntary, and goes on during sleep; but whether we will or will not modify this breath by the organs of speech, and emit it with such force as to produce sound, is voluntary. The scope of voluntary control which we have over respiration, seems to be just as much as is necessary for speaking, and yet not sufficient to destroy life by a total interruption of breathing. If it were possible to withhold respiration entirely, a man might at any moment easily put an end to his existence. If, on the other hand, we had no control over our respiration, but were compelled to inspire and expire at regular intervals, our sentences would all have to be of a certain length, or our enunciation could have no reference to their punctuation, and the operation of speaking would be subject to such monotonous interruptions, as would be unpleasantly mechanical. Hence, it is evident, this voluntary control was given, and this voluntary respiration withheld, for these very purposes.

Children find the same pleasure in exercising their organs of articulation on the expiring breath, that they do in using their arms and legs. God has so constituted animals, that the use of their organs is, in itself and for its own sake, pleasant. The fishes skipping about in their watery element, the birds in the atmosphere filling it with warbling notes, exhibit such signs of enjoyment as to leave no doubt, that if the vocabulary of their language were intelligible to man, the feelings would be joyous which they express. For the same reason, children, when they find themselves able to talk, are prone to talk incessantly. Even before they can articulate correctly, they find, by crying, that they can in some measure control their organs of speech, and thus they learn the rudiments of oral action. By continued practice they increase this ability, and in due time they learn to articulate, that is, to speak, with tolerable accuracy.

The following appears to be the manner in which

words become connected with things, or, rather, in which the ideas of oral words, that is, sounds, be come connected in our minds with the ideas of external entities. Children see an entity, and hear a certain sound pronounced in connexion with it. The idea of an entity, for example, an apple, obtained by sight, and the idea of the sound obtained by the ear, are received almost simultaneously, and thus, having the relation of contiguity of time, the one, by virtue of this relation, recalls the other. Thus a father approaches his child with an apple; he stretches out the fruit that the child may take it, and, in so doing, pronounces the word *apple.* The child's mind thus receives, almost simultaneously, two ideas, viz., that of the colour of the apple, obtained by the eye, and that of the sound indicated by the written word *apple,* acquired by the ear. Originally the child perceives no connexion between these ideas, the one of sound and the other of colour; but finding the two generally connected by other persons, that is, hearing the same sound pronounced by all who seem to be speaking of the same entity, the child soon learns that the one, viz., the sound *apple,* is used as a sign or name to designate the other, the thing apple. Thus both these ideas, or items of knowledge, having been obtained together, have the relation of (temporal) contiguity, and become so closely related, that if the attention of the mind is by any means directed to the one, it spontaneously pursues this relation, and is conducted to the other. The idea of the colour of the apple may also at any time be recalled by the presence of another apple, which will afford a similar idea, and thus, by the relation of similarity, recall the first. The visual idea may likewise be mediately recalled by seeing the letters which spell the sound which stands for that idea.

These remarks show us that, parallel to our train of thoughts, the subjects of which are objective entities, runs another coequal train of thoughts, the subjects of which are sounds, viz., those sounds which, by experience, have become associated with those entities. But speaking is an active operation of the articulating organs consequent on a volition to communicate our wishes, commands, or other ideas, to those whom we address; experience having taught us that others associate with certain sounds the same ideas that we do, and, therefore, that the utterance of sounds by us, similar to those which we have heard uttered by others, will excite in others the same ideas which we attach to these sounds.

Properly speaking, however, we neither do nor can excite in others the same identical ideas which we connect with our words. The ideas which all men connect with words are the mental representatives of entities which they originally derive from entities themselves, and which they can derive from no other source. When they hear others pronounce the same, or, rather, exactly similar sounds, they, by the relation of similarity, recall the recollection of the sounds which they formerly heard; and the recollection of these former sounds recalls the ideas formerly associated with them. Thus, when a speaker addresses an audience, there is a truly remarkable train of collateral and parallel operations running on with the train of the speaker's ideas. Every idea of the speaker is succeeded by the following operations before it accomplishes its design.

(1.) The idea of the speaker himself. (2.) The speaker's recollection of the idea of the sound formerly associated with that idea by himself. (3.) His volition to articulate a similar sound. (4.) The articulating action of his organs on the expiring breath to produce a similar sound. (5.) The hearer's idea of the sound produced by the speaker's voice. (6.) The hearer's recollection of the similar sound which he himself had often made. (7.) The recurrence of the idea which he formerly connected with the similar sound made by himself. All these parallel trains of operations attend every thought conveyed by the speaker. The security that men by this process will substantially understand each other, rests on the fact, that all men derive from an inspection of the same entity substantially the same representative; otherwise there could not be any common language or communication of thought among men.

Our ability to make just such sounds as correspond to our recollection of sounds made by others, results from our being able to make at option coarser or finer, dental or labial, lingual or guttural sounds, and from our ability to discern whether the sounds which we make, and of which we have an idea so soon as we hear them, exactly resemble those which we heard from others.

The structure of the human articulating organs is such, that all men naturally make certain elementary sounds. These sounds are expressed by the letters of the alphabet, and are substantially the same in all languages. Even the difference observed in the number of letters in different languages is often the result of the imperfect state of the art of designating these elementary or alphabetic sounds, and two languages whose alphabets differ most, may, when spoken, bear much greater similarity to each other in their elementary sounds. So far then, at least, as the elementary sounds are concerned, we must answer the long-disputed question in the affirmative, and maintain that language is of Divine origin ; because the nature of these elementary sounds results from the structure of the organs which God gave us.

We learn, by early habit, to articulate nearly all the elementary sounds with great promptness and certainty ; and it is thus that we learn new languages ; because we can form relations of contiguity between our ideas and the words of a new tongue. Nay, although it is a rare attainment, we may, by frequent repetition and long-continued habit, form so close a connexion between old ideas which we were wont to express in our vernacular tongue, and the words of a new language, that we spontaneously think in it ; that is, as we reinspect the old ideas, the corresponding words of the newly-acquired language will spontaneously recur to our memory as we advance, instead of those of our vernacular tongue. In the exercise of articulation the breath is voluntarily modulated into those sounds: one lungs' full after another, leaving only short intervals for inspiration, just as long as we wish to convey our ideas to others; and when this volition is accomplished, the articulating organs become motionless, and the breath is inhaled and exhaled without any sound, except what is termed audible breathing.

II. The second means of communicating our ideas to others is by gestures and muscular action of the countenance correspondent to the thought. How far this kind of communication may be carried, is forcibly exhibited in pantomimic exhibitions, in which a regular succession of scenes is intelligibly represented by gestures and muscular expression of the countenance, without the utterance of a single word. This process it is not necessary for our purpose to examine in greater detail.

III. The third mode of communicating our thoughts is by WRITTEN SIGNS. These signs are of different kinds. (1.) *The regular alphabetical letters.* These designate the elementary sounds which belong to languages in general, and are virtually the same in them all. These signs, or letters, constitute the most perfect form of the alphabet, and in point of time were probably later than the hieroglyphic and syllabic signs. In the Chinese language the written signs do not designate elementary sounds; but at least many of them stand for whole words, and designate those elementary objects which men find it necessary to express in the infancy of knowledge; additional words being formed by a combination of these. You will easily perceive, that the accumulation of signs in this language must be unusually great, and very inconvenient. So much is this the case, that it is said very few of the most learned men in China itself are fully acquainted with all the marks of their own language, and the exact import of their numerous combinations.

Of the syllabic alphabet, intermediate between the Chinese and European languages, we have a modern instance in the invention of See-qua-yah (George Guess), a North American Indian of the Cherokee tribe, which deserves notice. It consists of an alphabet of eighty-six letters, each of them designating neither an elementary sound, as in European languages, nor an entire word, as in the Chinese, but a syllable or part of a word.

(2.) *Arithmetical figures and signs*, which stand for sounds designating our ideas of the entity number. (3.) *Musical notes*, which designate our ideas of such sounds as are used in musical composition.

IV. The fourth mode of expressing our thoughts is by SINGING. This is a voluntary effort to make certain sounds in accordance with different principles, with a view to excite in ourselves or others certain feelings, and sometimes to give interest to certain truths. This mode might, indeed, be regarded as a subdivision of the first or oral sounds.

The exercise of Composition is a complex operation, consisting of an act of voluntary inspection and arrangement of ideas of entities, simple or composite, together with the act of expressing the ideas thus arranged, by signs on paper; that is, writing the ideas as arranged by us. Thus, e. g., we resolve to compose an essay on the evils of intemperance. We reflect on the entity a drunkard, or our idea of him, that is, inspect it in all its various melancholy and disgusting relations, and arrange our ideas with reference to the object in view, and then write them as arranged. We do not write every idea which the mind lights on in its voluntary inspection, but only those which are particularly suited to our purpose. Here the question arises, What are the new ideas, not retrospective, which we never had before, but which thus oftentimes occur to the mind? Are they not merely cognitive representatives of relations; of new combinations of simple entities, which were known before, but never precisely thus combined by the mind? Now from these new combinations result new relations, which, when viewed by the mind, are called original or new ideas. This feature of suggestion presented some difficulty to Dr. Brown; but, according to this view of it, its nature would be sufficiently plain. It is incorrect to say that the new idea recurred to the mind. The true statement is this: the simple entities thus viewed together by the mind are inactive, as are also our ideas of them; but the mind itself is the active agent, which, in voluntarily contemplating, that is, inspecting the entity and its relations, perceives this, to it, new relation, which, however, existed before it was viewed, and was perhaps perceived by many others before, and which would exist in nature if it had never been viewed by any one.

The preceding five operations, viz., Inspection, Arrangement, Modification, Physical action or agency, and Intellectual intercourse with other minds, appear to constitute all the specific active operations of the soul. To one or other of these every operation of the mind may be referred which is in its nature active, excepting only what remains to be discussed under the mode of their occurrence.

SECTION VI.

Of Attention.

We shall first make a few remarks on the subject of attention before we inquire whether it is entitled to the rank of a distinct active process. Whatever be the active operation in which we are engaged, the clearness, success, and mnemonic tenacity attending it, will generally be in proportion to the degree of attention exerted in the operation. Every one must have observed, that an inattentive perusal of a book leaves an indistinct impression, figuratively speaking, of its contents on the mind; while an attentive perusal produces a directly con trary effect. In conducting an inquiry, if the pro cess be negligently conducted, the result may be a total failure to obtain a clear conviction; but an attentive review, that is, reinspection, of the very same evidence, will often produce clear conviction, and dispel every doubt.

The influence of attention on the degree of feeling excited in the mind is equally striking. Indeed, in most cases, there can be very little feeling, that is, little pleasure or pain, without attention. The same remark is equally true of knowledge. Thus, the rays of light may be reflected from an object to the retina of the eye, and form the image there, but it will fail to convey knowledge to the mind, if the attention be not directed to it. So also the same entity can produce no feeling unless the attention be directed to it; or, in other words, unless it be observed. There are, indeed, cases of disease in which painful feeling is irresistibly produced, and we are not able entirely to divert our attention from it; but in so far and so long as we can divert it, the pain is greatly diminished.

Attention also greatly improves every active operation to which it is directed. The success and accuracy of *inspection* are obviously improved by it in the highest degree. *Arrangement* can also be performed with an accuracy and facility proportioned to the attention bestowed on the operation. The abstractions and generalizations of the active process of *modification* are in like manner greatly improved by attention. Who can doubt, that the excellence of mechanical operations, or of the execution of instrumental music, requires the attention of the performer? Or who would be guilty of the absurdity of denying, that the communication of thought on any subject, whether performed orally or in writing, can be executed with greater accuracy, and system, and effect, when the energy, the attention of the soul, is expended on the effort?

In complex operations, also, the influence of continued attention, that is, of attention combined with *habit*, is strongly displayed. Some talented individuals have thus acquired the ability to conduct a simultaneous train of several operations, each of which ordinarily engrosses the attention of men separately. Thus, of Julius Cæsar it is said, that he could at the same time dictate seven letters to as many secretaries, and that even when engaged in writing himself, he could dictate to four others.

Attention, too intensely exerted, and too long continued upon any one subject, sometimes induces monomania. But it is a benevolent law of our nature, that the lassitude arising from continued attention unlooses, as it were, the grasp of attention, and enables the mind to resume the natural and salutary self-control and equipoise of its powers.

That attention, however, is not a distinct and separate operation, will appear evident from the following facts: (1.) We cannot conceive of it as acting by itself, but only in connexion with some other operation of the mind. (2.) It does not give us any results of its action, distinct from those of the active operation with which it is combined. (3.) It is common to all the active operations. (4.) It seems only to be a property of the active operations conducted at the time. We therefore define *attention to be the energy of the soul exerted in some active operation.*

The causes which excite attention appear, in general, to be these. (1.) A volition to bestow attention on the performance of some active operation. (2.) The present interest or pleasure felt in the operation itself. Thus, we commence the perusal of a book incidentally met with, not knowing what its contents may be, but soon become so interested, that the most intense attention is excited in our breast. (3.) Some impression from without made through the bodily organs. Thus, we may be engaged listening to some interesting narrative; but, a band of musicians passing by, their music makes an impression on the organs of hearing, and it attracts and diverts the attention. This we suppose to be a correct view of the character of attention, which we, therefore, cannot regard as a separate or distinct active operation.

CHAPTER II.

THE MODE OF OCCURRENCE OF THE FIVE ACTIVE OPERATIONS.

If it be asked, *why does the soul engage in active operations at all rather than not*, we reply, the reason is, because the nature of the soul is active. By this we mean, that the Divine Author of our nature has so constituted the mind of man, that, during his waking hours, it is unavoidably and incessantly engaged in some one of these five active processes. Of this we can be convinced by an examination of our own mental operations. On such an investigation we find, that it is not optional with us whether our minds shall be engaged in thinking or not; we are constitutionally thus engaged, and can at best, by the most determined voluntary effort, interrupt the succession of thought for a few seconds only.

As to the manner in which this continued action is mediately sustained, several theories might be suggested; but the fact, which is beyond dispute, is all that is requisite to the accuracy of our system; and as we have endeavoured to avoid mere theory heretofore, we shall not at present call your attention to either of these.

If it be inquired, in the second place, *why does the soul, at any given time, engage in one of these active operations rather than another*, the experience of every individual will unhesitatingly reply, that these operations are engaged in in one of two ways: either from deliberate choice or from habit. The testimony of every man's own consciousness, if we mistake not, is decided and conclusive on this subject, and teaches that in one of these two ways, and in no other, do active operations at any time take place.

The mode of occurrence in the active operations of the mind is twofold:

I. Voluntary. II. Spontaneous.

SECTION I.

Of the Voluntary Occurrence of the Active Operations.

The active processes of the soul are voluntary, when we engage in them in consequence of a volition so to do, or, to express the same in popular language, when they are undertaken from deliberate *choice*. That we do perform such acts of choice every hour of the day, must be evident to every impartial inquirer, from the testimony of his own consciousness.

(1.) The certainty of our performing such acts of uncontrolled choice is just as evident and indubitable to every individual, as is the certainty of his performing any other mental act. All men agree as to the existence of our other mental operations, such as knowledge and feeling; nor do any doubt in practice the existence of our acts of choice, because it rests on the same basis.

(2.) As to the nature of this act of choice, our ideas must be derived from the same source by which we become acquainted with the nature of knowledge and feeling. It is probable, too, that all men agree in fact and practice, though not in theory, in their views of these acts of choice, as much as in their ideas of knowledge and feeling. The differences of opinion which exist do not relate to the existence of the power of willing, nor to the idea which consciousness furnishes of our volitions as mental acts, but to the supposed relations between volitions and precedent operations, and to other powers and principles of the mind. (*a.*) All men agree that these acts of choice differ from acts of necessity, and are in their nature opposite to them. When the fiendlike assassin has deliberately sent the fatal ball through the heart of his victim, we do not censure the bullet that penetrated his heart, nor the rifle which contained the powder, nor the spark which ignited it, nor the cock which elicited the spark, nor the trigger which moved the cock, nor even the finger which moved the trigger: but instantly perceiving that all these are not voluntary agents, we attribute the blame to the malicious mind, which originated the whole train of second causes. Nor does the common sense of mankind discriminate merely between the voluntary actions of man and the actions of mechanical and irrational agents; the distinction between the voluntary and involuntary actions of man himself is equally clear, and universally acknowledged. What different feelings from those produced by the voluntary act of the cold-blooded assassin, are excited in every bosom when, as two intimate companions are running through a thicket in pursuit of game, their guns cocked and hands applied to the trigger, the foot of the hindermost is caught in a brush; he stumbles, and in his effort to regain himself presses unconsciously the fatal trigger, and prostrates his friend, a corpse, before him. (*b.*) It is only for such actions as are voluntary that we accuse or excuse ourselves, and for these alone can we feel true penitence, if they are contrary to known duty. When we have yielded to the force of temptation, we are conscious of our guilt, because we know that the force of these temptations was not irresistible; we know that we could and ought to have resisted it. (*c.*) All men agree, that for their own acts of choice alone, and the consequences of them, can they really and justly be held responsible either by God or man. (*d.*) Every reflecting man who has attained mature development of mind, is conscious of the fact that he can and ought to regulate the voluntary actions of his life according to certain fixed rules and principles.

The question now arises, Is the soul, in choosing and refusing from among the acts possible to it, entirely free from any and every bias, and left to make its choice uninfluenced by anything whatever, or do we perceive in the voluntary actions of the soul any evidence to the contrary? If we find, that the great majority of the acts of deliberate choice in all men of every character, under all circumstances, and of every age, are of a particular kind, are calculated to promote a particular general end, and made with a view to accomplish the same general purpose, we are irresistibly led to the belief, that there is in the soul itself a *constitutional* impulse, or *bias*, or *inclination* to that end. This inclination must be prior to the actions themselves, and is among the causes which produce them. It must belong to the structure of the soul itself, and may therefore with propriety be termed a constitutional inclination. If we are not grossly mistaken, the conduct of all men does present evidence of such inclinations in every situation of life, from the cradle to the tomb. Though these inclinations at first view appear numerous and complicated, on closer examination they resolve themselves into the following two constitutional inclinations:

I. THE INCLINATION TO ACTION IN ACCORDANCE WITH THE FITNESS OF THINGS, *moral, intellectual, and physical.*

II. The inclination to well-being, or the enjoyment of pleasure, present and ultimate; and the avoiding of pain.

These inclinations are not *faculties*, because they are not sources of distinct species of mental operations. Nor are they themselves mental *operations*, in the ordinary sense of the term, because they exist constantly, and prior to action. Nor are they *habits* of the soul, for habits are merely a facility for the performance of actions of particular kinds, and a tendency to their spontaneous performance, which facility is acquired by practice, and may be changed; while the constitutional inclinations are permanent and immutable. They are therefore natural characteristics of the soul, and belong to its constitutional structure. This bias seems to have been impressed upon our minds by the great Creator, to determine, in some degree, the general tenour of our voluntary actions; and experience teaches us that the great mass of all human actions is in accordance with one or the other, or both of these inclinations.

I. *The first constitutional inclination*, viz., *the inclination to action in accordance with the physical, intellectual, and moral fitness of things*, is an attribute of the soul, the existence of which is clearly established by a multitude of facts. All mankind do habitually evince the existence of this disposition, in a greater or less degree, in their unpremeditated actions. It is this inclination which leads all men, even from their earliest years, naturally to speak the truth rather than falsehood, unless they have acquired the habit of misrepresentation from deliberate and self-interested calculations. The truth of this fact is not only admitted by men on ordinary occasions, but is incorporated into their criminal codes and judicial proceedings. It is an admitted rule of testimony in all our courts. Accordingly, if the testimony of a stranger be offered in a trial, we inquire whether he has any interest in the issue, which his testimony may tend to produce. And if it be fully ascertained that no interest of his, even of the most remote kind, can possibly be affected by the decision, we naturally expect, in the absence of contrary evidence, that he will not designedly swerve from the truth.

All mankind have a constitutional sense of obligation, a constitutional inclination to obey the moral fitness of things. Whatever men naturally judge to be right, they also feel some impulse to do. This impulse is, alas! too often, and in many persons habitually resisted; yet its existence is clearly taught in the occasional unpremeditated actions, and in the deathbed confessions of the most abandoned. And all who pay the least attention to the moral dictates of their nature, will not only freely admit its existence, but also acknowledge that its empire is justly unlimited; that wherever, throughout the whole range of creation, they perceive a trace of moral fitness, there they also find this impulse accompanying it, and feel a constitutional monition to obey its dictates. This obligation, too, though so often resisted, is seen by all men to be paramount in importance, and in the strength of its claims, to everything else. It is this inclination which leads men, when travelling in a strange land, to keep the road rather than pass through an adjoining grain-field, where they would destroy the provision which God has made for his creatures. This inclination also urges us to obey the intellectual fitness of things in general; such as, to yield submission to those who have a right to direct, and to receive instruction from those who are older and wiser than we; to arise in the morning when we awake; to take care of things belonging to unknown persons, rather than to destroy them. In short, when we examine the whole sphere of human agency, we find that the crimes of men alone are exceptions to the observance of this constitutional inclination, while the precepts of the law on all subjects exhibit its appropriate dictates. The tendency to observe the physical fitness of things is witnessed throughout the whole sphere of physical action, in every department of life. Thus, apart from every self-interested motive, who can doubt that there is a natural disposition in persons engaged in mechanical or commercial pursuits, to make things right rather than wrong? to make them according to the principles of physical fitness rather than the reverse?

From the above considerations, it is evident that the first constitutional inclination is one of the *most important features of our moral nature*, and embraces all that is monitory or impulsive, in what is termed the *moral sense*, in the widest import of the term, and also in *conscience*, in its stricter acceptation. As the operations of conscience are complex in their nature, their several constituent parts belong to different branches of our subject. There is in conscience something that is *judicial*, something that is *sentient*, and something that is *impulsive*. The first was discussed in the observations made on relative knowledge; the second, when treating of moral emotions; and the third, or impulsive part, belongs to this place.

The monitions or impulses of conscience are original and constitutional. If we attend to the testimony of our own consciousness on this subject, we think all will admit that these impulses arise spontaneously in the soul, whenever we contemplate our relations to the beings around us in the universe, in their bearings on our own conduct. Whatever we thus perceive to be dictated by these relations, to be our duty, to be right, to be conformed to the moral fitness of things, we also feel an imperative monition to perform. It follows, therefore, that conscience, in its principal, its impulsive feature, is an original faculty or power of the soul, although the operations generally designated by the term are complex, and several of their elements referable to cognition (judgment) and sensibility. The very structure of all different languages, proves alike the existence and the universality of this principle. Whenever we use the term "ought," or any others equivalent to it, we express an impulse of this constitutional inclination of conscience; and where is the language on earth that is destitute of terms equivalent to these; or where is the individual, in any nation under the sun, which never employs them?

All men also judge the impulses of this monitor, whom God has implanted into our breasts, to be *supreme* in the authority of its dictates. If at any time we yield to the solicitations of passion, and violate the prescriptions of conscience, we feel guilty and degraded; we feel that we have done that which is unworthy of our nature, and have violated the relations we sustain to the great Author of our being.

This principle of our nature is one of the fundamental bases of our moral responsibility. Without it, man could not be a moral agent; for, however lucid might be his views of the relations of the different beings in the universe to God and to each other, and of the influence of his conduct on their happiness or misery, he certainly could not be responsible for the conduct he pursued, if he felt no sense of obligation, no impulse to select the one and shun the other.

The impulses of this principle of our moral nature, though strong enough in all to make us justly responsible for our conduct, are not, in any case, irresistible. They never destroy our liberty, although they are strong enough to justify conscience in "excusing, or else accusing, us" for our conduct.

Like every other power of the soul, the constitutional inclination can be strengthened by faithful exercise, and it may be weakened by the neglect or violation of its dictates. The first entrance into the paths of known sin is generally made with a tremulous step. The first oath, or the first act of theft or violence, is perpetrated with uncomfortable feelings, and followed with a sense of guilt and self-condemnation. Happy would it be, if erring, guilty man would then listen to this kind, monitory voice, and return to virtue's paths, for they are paths of pleasantness and peace! But the repetition of crime soon impairs the strength of these monitory impulses, and every subsequent transgression makes farther violations easier. On the other hand, sincere and faithful obedience to the dictates of conscience, both in ascertaining what our duty is, and in labouring to perform it, will increase the strength of its impulses, and make subsequent obedience the more easy.

II. *The second constitutional inclination*, viz., the *love of well-being*, acquires different names in popular language, according as it is habitually indulged in reference to any particular class of entities. This inclination embraces the following, among other modifications: (1.) *Love of life.* This is one of the fundamental principles of the soul, and is implied in all the subsequent modifications of this constitutional inclination. Independently of its superadded pleasures, life itself is regarded by man as a great good. "Skin for skin, and all that a man hath, will he give for his life," is a sentiment which, notwithstanding the source whence it proceeded, is undeniably true. The afflictions of life have sometimes made men willing to leave this world; but it was always in the expectation, true or false, that a hereafter would restore them to life and pleasure.

So much is man attached to his existence, and so deeply ingrafted on our nature is the love of life, that we can scarcely find, even among the most miserable of the sons and daughters of affliction, one who would be willing to purchase release from his sufferings at the expense of his being, one who would be willing to be blotted out from existence. In the beautiful language of Grey, we may confidently inquire,

> "For who, to dumb forgetfulness a prey,
> This pleasing, anxious being e'er resigned;
> Left the warm precincts of the cheerful day,
> Nor cast one longing, ling'ring look behind?"

This love of life leads us to a proper care of our health, and to all necessary acts of self-defence in time of danger. As this principle is an inherent part of our mental nature, it seems to be right that man, when assailed by violence, should defend himself to the utmost extremity, unless by the laws of God he has forfeited his right to live. And if in this defence his own life cannot be preserved except at the risk of that of his assailant, this constitutional principle seems to dictate a preference of his own existence to that of others. The propriety of this position is not doubted if the assailant be a serpent or some ravenous beast, nor can we perceive why it should not be equally proper in reference to robbers and murderers. We have no right to submit to be murdered, and by doing so we would often cause two deaths instead of one, as the murderer will generally also, and justly, be executed. But "if he has done anything worthy of death," then, like Paul, he ought "not to refuse to die." (2.) *Love of esteem or power*, which is the inclination to gratify our love of well-being by the pursuit of such entities and the performance of such active operations as acquire for us the applause and admiration of men. A desire for the approbation and esteem of others is in itself, when regulated by a proper regard to the first constitutional inclination, an important and useful principle of our nature. It tends to make us observe the decencies of life, and to pursue such a course of conduct as will commend us to others. It is only when it becomes inordinate, and is indulged in violation of the fitness of things that it becomes sinful and pernicious in its consequences.

So, also, the desire of possessing influence or power is in itself commendable, if that influence be desired not to promote any selfish ends, but chiefly as a means to advance the welfare of the community and the glory of God. When this principle becomes inordinate, it is termed *ambition*, in the unfavourable sense of that term. (3.) *Love of property or possession*, which is the inclination to gratify our love of well-being in the pursuit and possession of wealth. So long as the love of property is controlled by the first constitutional inclination, the fitness of things; so long as it is not pursued contrary to right, contrary to the relations we sustain to others, it is a useful principle, and leads men to industry and exertion to provide comfortably for themselves, and those of their own household; but when it degenerates into *avarice*, it becomes not only morally wrong, but also detrimental to the interests of society. (4.) *Love of novelty, or curiosity*, which is the inclination to gratify our love of well-being by the pursuit of frequent change in the objects of our attention, having learned from our experience that any entity excites the greater feeling for being novel to the mind. (5.) *Sensuality*, which is the inclination to gratify the second constitutional inclination by the pursuit of objects adapted to the indulgence of the sensual propensities. (6.) *Love of science*, which is the inclination to gratify our second constitutional inclination by the pursuit of the different objects of human knowledge. (7.) *Social inclination*, which is the inclination to gratify our love of well-being by seeking the society of others. These, and various other modifications of the second constitutional inclination, are exhibited in the actions of mankind generally.

This second constitutional inclination, the love of self, or of well-being, was, in its original condition, morally good, and of salutary tendency. The Scriptures often address our love of happiness, and the Saviour expressly commends it: "Thou shalt love thy neighbour *as thyself*."

These two constitutional inclinations of the soul exert more or less influence on the character of our acts of choice, but never destroy the ability to choose; that is, they never act irresistibly. When an individual act of choice is in harmony with both these inclinations of the soul, both as to motive and outward form, it is right in the sight of God. But it is evident that the great mass of human actions is an indulgence of the second inclination at the expense of the first, that is, consists in actions which are an indulgence of our love of pleasure or well-being in violation of the dictates of the physical, intellectual, or moral fitness of things. All such actions are sinful. Among this class must be reckoned, also, some actions which, in themselves considered, that is, so far as the outward acts are concerned, are right, but which originate from a motive of pure selfishness. Thus, that modification of the second constitutional inclination termed ambition, induces many men of the world to observe outward morality of deportment, and even to perform acts of beneficence, and to support the institutions of religion, in order that they may secure the public approbation, and be successful in their aspirations after fame or power. Such morality is, indeed, less unfavourable in its influence on the community at large than open vice; yea, it may even tend to support the order and promote the well-being of society; but it evidently cannot secure the Divine approbation, because a regard to the moral fitness of things, a regard to what is morally right, and duty, did not enter into the motive with which it was performed.

It is greatly to be feared that a large portion of the morality of the world is of this kind, is the result of selfishness in some one or other of its modifications. This may even be the case without the person himself being fully aware of it, because he has not carefully and faithfully examined his heart, and tested the motives of his conduct by the light of truth, either natural or revealed. Thus multitudes deceive themselves as to their real character. The first *constitutional inclination* is manifestly the more noble; but it is evident to all impartial observers, that in the natural state of man the second greatly preponderates: and in this, so far as the mind is concerned, may at least in part consist the natural or constitutional depravity or disorder of man. Self preponderates over God, pleasure over what is right. This constitutional bias of the soul itself, let it be remembered, determines only the general end; but not the specific means by which, in any case, we accomplish that end. Thus, the second constitutional inclination, in the form of self-interest, inclines our fellow-citizens to seek the melioration of their temporal condition by the construction of internal improvements; but it does not decide whether they shall do it by making railroads or canals. This latter point the soul itself decides, after an inspection of the relative properties and advantages of both these means of gratifying our constitutional inclination. The several volitions of the mind, resulting from these different sources, are different in regard to comprehensiveness. Some of them are of the most generic kind, as they relate indefinitely to the general end; others, which contemplate some particular method of accomplishing the generic one, are specific in their character. Resolutions in regard to our general conduct are generic volitions, and exert an important influence on the specific volitions, and other operations of the mind, concerned in executing them.

Besides these constitutional inclinations within the soul itself, by which the Author of our nature has given a general direction to the agency of man, there is also in entities themselves without the mind, a certain degree of motive influence, that is, a certain degree of adaptation to influence the mind to action, in view of which the soul exercises its powers of choice.

All entities without the mind may be divided, in reference to this subject, into two classes:

1. *Our own bodies.*
2. *All other entities in the universe.*

In our own bodies we find certain phenomena, termed *bodily appetites*, which possess a strong motive power. By bodily appetites we here strictly mean the corporeal part, the material part of those appetites. Thus by the bodily appetite, hunger, we mean the periodical action of the gastric fluid on the coats of the stomach (or, as this theory has of late been impugned, whatever other physical change that may be the true cause of the feeling), which results from the structure of our bodily organisms, and was designed by the Creator as a periodical motive to urge us to take the necessary food. The same remarks are applicable to thirst, which is nothing else than that peculiar condition of the throat and fauces, occasioned by the want of a liquid, and causing a desire to obtain it, or some other substance, in order to relieve the pain felt; and also sometimes in order to enjoy the pleasure occasioned by the reception of the liquid. The fluid thus taken into the stomach is consumed by the progress of the bodily functions, and its want occasions a painful feeling termed thirst. Both these appetites are the work of God. They are the necessary results of the bodily organization of man, and may justly be considered by him as clear indications of the Divine will, that they should lead to the course of action by which they are relieved, though under the limitations of reason.

The second general class of motives embraces all other entities except the above. The pleasure we expect to derive from eating any fruit, or from perusing the work of a well-known author, acts as a motive to procure the object of our desire. Entities of every class seem to possess some motive influence on the will, e. g., all kinds of food, a landscape, a beautiful passage in any author, literary or scientific. To the mathematician, the pleasures found in the discussion of the relations of space and number are a strong inducement to the repetition of the exercise.

The question here arises, Have these entities any certain motive power which they exert on all minds, and how is their relative strength determined? It is certain that every entity does possess a definite, invariable, intrinsic desirableness, or the contrary; and one entity is more or less desirable than another. Again, when we view these relatively, they all have certain fixed relations to each other, and to human actions and interests, as means to an end. After having weighed the merits of a case or a plan, we can practically decide which is most suitable, and which presents the strongest inducements to its adoption; and we are seldom in doubt as to what we ought to do, that is, on which side the strongest inducements lie.

But these inducements or entities do certainly not act with irresistible force or mechanical power on the will; otherwise men would always act in obedience to the strongest consideration, that is, to truth, and thus they would act virtuously. It is evidently the duty of all men thus to do; God has made the inducements to virtue stronger than those to vice, the evidences of truth stronger than those of falsehood; hence it is the duty of all men voluntarily to obey the truth by pursuing virtue. But have they no power to act otherwise? The fact that they do, must forever set this point at rest. And it is certain even with regard to our bodily appetites, that we can resist their cravings. A sensible man can refuse to satisfy the most ravenous appetite, when he knows that abstinence is necessary to the recovery of health. In this case, regarding health as a greater motive than present gratification, he wills to obey the stronger motive, and declines eating; while another, under the same circumstances, wills to prefer present gratification to ultimate health.

It seems evident, therefore, that, though men generally do, in matters relating to temporal interests, will in accordance with the strongest motive, yet they certainly can will contrary to conviction and to a sense of duty. Hence it is evident that, though the determinations of the will are made in view of motives, that is, of a knowledge of entities, they are nevertheless made freely.

The spontaneous recurrence of retrospective knowledge of certain entities exerts an important motive influence upon the soul. When this recurrence is habitual, it will constitute a particular trait in the character of its subject. A certain sphere of this knowledge and feeling, retrospective, present, and prospective, is constantly at our command, and some item or other of it is constantly recurring to us spontaneously, when the attention of the mind is not occupied in some active, voluntary operation. When we are not engaged in any voluntary active process, the tenour of this spontaneous recurrence is regulated by the impressions made on the organs of sense, or by other principles to be enumerated in the discussion of spontaneous inspection. Some such impression is made almost every moment, and each object, seen, or heard, or felt, educes a train of related spontaneous knowledge. Thus each item of present knowledge or feeling gives rise to a train of related ideas, which runs on according to certain laws, until interrupted by some other impression on the organs of sense, or by some process of voluntary action. Peculiar pursuits in life, also, form habits of peculiarly frequent spontaneous recurrence of our knowledge of the particular entities connected with them, which also exert an important influence on the will, by bringing the entities referred to more frequently to bear on it by their retrospective influence. Hence the incalculable advantage of a good, a religious education. And as knowledge can influence our active operations only so long as it is recollected, the advantage of early good instruction is manifest; because what is learned in early life is longest recollected. And, finally, as a daily, or, at least, frequent attentive review of such truths, tends to rivet them on the mind, and make them the subjects of frequent spontaneous retrospection, we cannot fail to perceive the salutary tendency of the habit of daily perusing a portion of the Sacred Volume, or reading it in our family circle.

Desire is that state of the soul in which an entity, that is the subject of inspection, is exerting its motive power, but the will has not yet made a decision. Hence desire may be regarded as incipient, but suspended volition. Nor is the decision of the will always, or at any time necessarily, in accordance with the desire. Oftentimes we decide against the solicitations of the present desire, in consequence of our recollection of other and more influential considerations to the contrary. And if we direct our attention to these preponderant considerations or objects, and dwell upon them, they will gradually excite desire in us. *Desire is therefore a state of soul, tending to a volition to choose the object by which it is excited, but not necessarily producing it.* Various objects possess different degrees of desirableness in our view; and each one, when it is made the subject of our deliberate attention, will excite its appropriate degree of desire in us.

Desires differ from feelings in this particular, by which they may easily be distinguished. The *immediate* object of desire is always some *action;*

while the immediate object of relative feelings, with which alone it may be confounded, is always some person or thing. If I desire, I always desire to do, to be, or to possess some person or thing; but if I have love, it is towards some person or thing; and if I hate, I hate something or some person. Or, in the language of our system, relative feeling immediately contemplates substantive or adjective entities, while the *immediate* object of desire is a composite entity.

The strength of our desires for particular objects is not the same in all men, nor in the same person at all times of life. It is very much influenced by the preponderance of the one or the other constitutional inclination in reference to the objects in question, and the strength of the constitutional inclination is influenced by the habitual voluntary conduct. To the miser a purse of gold will appear more desirable than to another man; because the second constitutional inclination has become stronger in consequence of his long-continued voluntary pursuit of money, and seeking his enjoyment in its possession.

Desires always presuppose a cognition of the object desired, and generally, also, a pleasant emotion or feeling in reference to it. Yet this pleasant feeling does not appear to be always present; for we may desire a dose of medicine that is nauseous to us and makes us shudder; but here the end which we hope to accomplish by it appears desirable to us.

Desire is a state of mind, which is sometimes of long continuance.

With regard to our power of choice, usually termed power of volition, we may yet remark, that it is confined, in the intended objects on which it determines to act, to some future time. However various the actions which we resolve to do or not to do, they must be done or avoided hereafter. Yet this future time admits of various modifications in relation to the will; we can resolve to do an act immediately, or at some future time more or less distant; we can resolve absolutely or conditionally. The object of every act of volition or choice is the performance or non-performance of some one or more of the five active operations; and one trait of difference between them is, that, while some one or other of the five active operations is always going forward in the mind, the act of choice occurs more rarely and at intervals, either to give a new direction or continued energy to the current active process.

Our entire view of the will therefore resolves itself into the following features.

I. The soul of man does possess the power of free, uncontrolled choice.

II. In the exercise of this power, the soul is influenced (but not certainly or irresistibly determined) by the following things:

1. By its two constitutional inclinations, which relate only to the general end to be aimed at.

2. By the motive power of entities without the mind. These relate to the specific means for the

attainment of the ends pointed out by our constitutional inclinations. These entities are the following: (*a.*) Our bodily appetites. (*b.*) All other external entities.

3. By our knowledge of these entities, either retrospective or prospective. This knowledge embraces truth of every kind, which, by generating conviction and exciting feeling, exerts a definite motive influence.

4. By the habitual state of our feelings on similar or related subjects, or, to speak more accurately, by the state of our *susceptibility* of feeling from the object in question; that is, from the degree in which our feelings are susceptible of being excited by said object. Every feeling is individual, and more or less transient in its nature. Every individual feeling must be excited anew in each individual case, either by its appropriate objective entity, or by our knowledge of it, retrospective or prospective. But our *susceptibility* for feeling is permanent, and is increased or diminished, in each individual, by his mental habits. Thus the ambitious man habitually seeks the gratification of his second constitutional inclination, the love of well-being, by the pursuit of human applause. By this habit, the susceptibility of his mind to pleasure from demonstrations of popular approbation, and pain from the reverse, is augmented.

Thus also the sensualist habitually seeks the gratification of his second constitutional inclination, the love of well-being or pleasure, in the pursuit of objects of licentious indulgence.

His mental associations cluster around such

scenes, and his spontaneous mental operations recur to them. By this habit the susceptibility of his mind to be influenced by such objects is greatly increased. Thus, every circumstance, however remotely connected with such scenes, becomes a temptation to him, and every exposure to direct temptation acquires a double influence on his mind. And thus it is that his volitions, in view of such circumstances of temptation, will obviously be influenced by the state of his susceptibility for feeling in reference to them.

The native activity of the soul prompts us to action.

The constitutional inclinations of the soul determine the general character of the ends, or results, at which we aim.

Our knowledge presents to us the various entities, with their different and relative properties, by active operations upon which the proposed end may be attained in various ways and in different degrees.

The different entities exert a motive power proportional to their relative adaptation to accomplish the end proposed, and influenced by the habitual state of our feelings on related subjects; and, finally, in view of all these circumstances, the soul freely determines in its choice of the different possible means of attaining the desired end. We therefore define the will as follows:

The WILL *is that power of the soul by which it freely determines, in view of motives, either now or hereafter, absolutely or conditionally, to perform or not to perform some one or more of the five active operations.*

SECTION II.

Of the Spontaneous Occurrence of the Active Operations.

When the attention of the soul is withdrawn, the greater part, if not all the five active operations, are carried on spontaneously, viz., inspectiou, arrangement, modification, the intellectual agency concerned in physical action, and intellectual intercourse with other minds.

The difference between the voluntary and spontaneous active operations seems to consist chiefly in the following circumstances:

1. The former are the results of volition in their commencement, that is, are always begun in consequence of volition; while the latter are not commenced in consequence of volition, but result from an inherent constitutional disposition of the mind to be always, during waking hours, engaged in some active operation. The reason why one active operation is spontaneously engaged in rather than another, or why one entity is the subject of its action rather than another, seems to be a previous habit formed by frequent or late voluntary action of the same kind, on the same entities, or on our mental representatives of them. Habit is an increased facility in the performance of any active operation, resulting from repeated acts of the same kind. Habit not only renders the performance of any operation more easy, but also enables us to perform it with greater perfection and success. It is truly surprising with what facility and perfection we are

able to perform many active operations when long-continued practice has rendered them habitual; which at first we could perform at all only with the greatest difficulty. After years of continued practice, a student will commit to memory a given piece of composition, in one fifth of the time at first requisite for the task. An expert performer on the pianoforte will with ease execute some of the most intricate and difficult pieces of music, which he could not perform at all, in proper time, before long practice had established the habit from which his ability results. The same is true of all intellectual operations: habit makes them easy, and, in most cases, pleasant. This principle of habit seems to be nothing more than the progressive development of the powers of the soul by continued practice, and is applicable more or less to every part of our mental and bodily organism, not excepting even the constitutional inclinations of the soul. It is witnessed in the rapid reasonings, the almost intuitive conclusions of the experienced logician, in the declamation of the orator, and in the skill and expertness of every species of mechanical operation. It must, however, not be supposed, that these processes, which have become habitual to us, and in which continued practice has enabled us to make great improvements, are always performed spontaneously. The contrary is obviously the case. Even the celebrated Paganini, when performing a difficult piece of music, which he has never before seen, must certainly exert a volition to strike every individual note; although the execution may be so rapid that he will have no recollection in reference to any single note, and will merely remember his generic volition to play the piece, that is, to follow the series of notes, as he sees them before him. The same is also the case when a familiar piece of music is designedly performed by the most skilful artist. He has, indeed, no recollection of a volition in reference to a score of things, a knowledge of which is implied by every note that he strikes, and each of which he had at first to perform by deliberate volition. But then he has learned to produce musical sounds on an instrument with as much facility as he utters oral sounds when reading the printed page. And who, in reading, can recollect the separate volitions to articulate each individual letter, and to combine these sounds into syllables, and these syllables into words, as he is rapidly reading? These operations are spontaneous only when attention is withdrawn, and they are performed negligently, without deliberate purpose to do so. And even when thus negligently commenced, there is probably some effort of will occasionally exerted in the progress of such spontaneous exercises.

The improveableness of the different bodily and mental powers by practice is a subject of great extent and peculiar interest; but we shall not pursue it farther in this place.

The formation of these habits is voluntary, but their subsequent action is spontaneous. When we say, the formation of these habits is voluntary, we do not mean that there are not, in the constitutional structure of our minds and bodies, more opportunities, yea, constant temptations, to the formation of some particular habits rather than others. The contrary is evidently the fact. There seems to be, even in the mind itself, a greater aptitude for the formation of sinful habits than of such as are holy. Fewer voluntary acts will create or form a sinful habit, and the habit resulting from any given number of voluntary sinful acts is stronger than would result from the same number of acts of a different character. The perverted state of our bodily propensities, since the fall, also leads men into frequent temptations to sin. The bodily propensity is involuntary, but the indulgence of the inspection of objects to which it prompts is voluntary and sinful, and is one cause of the formation of sinful habits.

2. Voluntary active operations are carried on with much more attention and energy than those which are spontaneous.

The spontaneous operations of the mind in many persons constitute far the greater part of all their mental action; and in all persons, even in those most constantly engaged in duties or labours, mental or bodily, they occupy much of their time. Indeed, it is the spontaneous action of an individual that exhibits his real character. Hence, as the spontaneous action results from that which is voluntary, and is correspondent with it, either holy or unholy, it is evident that we are responsible to God, not only for our voluntary action, but also for that which is spontaneous, i. e., for the mental habits by which we are characterized. It might, at first glance, appear as if our view of the spontaneous operations tended to remove them from the sphere of responsibility; but, on a more careful examination, we think this difficulty will vanish. The grounds of our responsibility for spontaneous action, and the reasons which will make it evident, are the following:

(*a*.) The fact, that any particular active operation is spontaneously engaged in rather than another, is owing to the circumstances of our having, by previous *voluntary* action, formed a habit, or facility, and inclination for such action. As it is thus ultimately caused by our voluntary acts, responsibility justly attaches to it.

(*b*.) We can, moreover, prevent much of our spontaneous mental action, by keeping the mind constantly employed in voluntary engagements.

(*c*.) Although spontaneous operations are commenced without deliberate volition to do so, there is often some slight degree of volition exercised in their progress.

(*d*.) Spontaneous operations are at all times under the control of the will as to their continuance. We can at any moment put a stop to any spontaneous operations of the mind, by a volition to do so, and to engage in some other mental process. Spontaneous operations are, therefore, continued by consent of the will. Since, therefore, the commencement, continuance, and termination of these processes are at all times under our voluntary control, it seems evident that we are justly held responsible for their character by our great moral Governor.

Spontaneous action has for its materials, like our voluntary action, entities, simple or composite, past, present, or future.

An important fact of a physiological nature touching this subject is, that spontaneous active operations are much less debilitating to the mind than voluntary. The more entirely we can withhold the mind from voluntary action, and even from intense attention to a process of spontaneous thought, the more complete is this state of rest. Hence, riding on horseback or walking in company with others, by presenting a series of changing objects to the mind, and preventing us from entering on a very attentive inspection of any of them, is excellent relaxation. A solitary walk of a student, in which he becomes absorbed in the customary subjects of his pursuit, is but an ambulatory study, and affords very slight relaxation to the mind. On this principle, the different debilitating tendency of various species of mental exercise can be regularly graduated. Each mental process will debilitate in proportion to its difficulty to the student, and to the degree of attention requisite to its performance.

When the mind is fatigued, or, for any reason whatever, does not engage by volition in any of the five active processes, some of them will invariably occur in a spontaneous, indifferent, and careless manner; so that we have little, and sometimes no, recollection of the operation so long as it proceeds in this spontaneous way. The operations which occur spontaneously with the greatest frequency belong chiefly to the process of inspection, and they are generally such as are most frequently, or have been most recently, engaged in in a voluntary manner.

I. *Spontaneous Inspection.*—In the spontaneous

inspection of entities, or their mental representatives, the mind is found generally to proceed in several uniform ways, or *laws of association.*

(1.) It seems to follow the *relations* of the entities, which are the subjects of its inspection. The relations which are most frequently followed are sameness, contrariety, contiguity—temporal, local, or numerical—and causation. But all the other relations are also occasionally pursued in our spontaneous inspections. Perhaps the relative frequency with which each of the relations is pursued in spontaneous inspection, is not materially different from the order in which those relations have been enumerated. But the course of the mental train of action is often changed by one or more of the principles yet to be enumerated.

(2.) There is a tendency in spontaneous inspection to pursue, in preference, the train of those entities which have *most frequently* been the subjects of its voluntary attention. Thus, the mind of the mathematician pursues its spontaneous rambles in the regions of mathematical science; the mind of the sensualist recurs to the objects of his sinful gratification; and the mind of the faithful Christian delights to dwell upon the topics connected with his high and holy calling. And if several persons, of different pursuits, were requested to give us some account of their reminiscences of a recent tour which they had made, the memory of the farmer would spontaneously recur to the agricultural productions of the country through which he had passed; the painter would think first of the landscapes, the statesman of some political intelligence which he had obtained, and the Christian, of an interesting conversation which he had heard on the subject of the Redeemer's kingdom.

(3.) The mind more readily recurs to those objects which have lately been the subjects of its attention.

(4.) It pursues more frequently those entities which excite the most pleasant feelings and gratify the second constitutional inclination. This inclination, or love of well-being, is not, in itself, sinful; on the contrary, the joys and pleasures of religion itself are sought in accordance with its dictates. But it becomes sinful when it is so inordinate as to outweigh the sense of obligation to obey the fitness of things, to obey the strongest evidence, that is, to obey truth. This preponderating influence is found in all unconverted persons by nature, and thus all by nature are sinners.

(5.) The mind is diverted from the pursuit of the above-mentioned relations in its spontaneous operations, by the immediate action of some entities, at the time, through the bodily organs.

(6.) It is interrupted by volition. While engaged in spontaneous action we may, for some reason or other, resolve to do something, i. e., to engage in some active process, and thus the spontaneous character of our mental action is instantly interrupted and succeeded by a process of a voluntary nature.

These spontaneous retrospections have, by some recent metaphysicians, been termed suggestions.

This word, though it conveys something of the character of these operations, seems not to be well selected as their generic and characteristic appellation. It seems to represent one item in a train of consecutive reminiscences or associations, as the agent that causes the occurrence of the other, while the mind is regarded rather as the passive recipient of these influences. In reality, however, the mind is the active subject; its spontaneous rambles result from the constitutional activity of its nature, while in these rambles it, by a law of its nature, pursues in preference the channel of those natural relations between the different entities or objects which really subsist between them, or those artificial relations constituted in the course of events, or those habits of mind which proceed from individual voluntary action. The principles regulating these associations are therefore intelligible, and it is also evident that, to a certain extent, they are the result of our most frequent voluntary actions. Their character is therefore, though not immediately, yet ultimately, in a great measure under our control And just so far as this is the case, we are evidently responsible for the moral character of our spontaneous reminiscences and other spontaneous mental operations.

II. The operations of *Arrangement* are also sometimes carried on spontaneously. If, in passing along the road, we see any animal, and especially one of rare occurrence, how often do we not spontaneously arrange it with the class of quadrupeds, or bipeds, &c., as the case may be; how often do we not compare it to other similar animals, and thus spontaneously arrange the two by the relation of sameness. Every figure of comparison used by extemporaneous speakers, consists of spontaneous arrangements according to the relation of similarity, expressed in words. And when a person of well-disciplined mind hears a fact which has an important probative bearing, he instantly and previous to volition, even in the act of rapidly reading a book, arranges it with other facts bearing on the same subject.

III. The process of *modification* very seldom occurs spontaneously, especially in persons of veracity and conscientious character; yet, doubtless, the mind of the novelist, who has habituated himself by voluntary effort to the very frequent fabrication of fiction, will, when left unoccupied, sometimes form such combinations spontaneously.

IV. The *mental process regulating our physical action* is very often exercised spontaneously. How many motions of the hands, or feet, or entire body do we not daily perform from mere habit, without volition. How often does the musician find himself engaged in the spontaneous act of singing, and the ambitious orator, in practising emphatic and peculiar pronunciation. How often do some men spontaneously fumble their watch-key, or play with their penknife, without being aware of the fact. In short, all those actions of the body, which are said to be performed from mere habit, are spontaneous operations. Men sometimes, and with truth, assign it as an excuse for particular actions, that they did them without thinking, did them unintentionally; doubtless some of these acts are spontaneous. Sometimes, however, physical action is performed in a manner which does not properly fall within the division either of spontaneous or voluntary action, but is properly attributed to instinct.

V. The process of *intellectual intercourse* is sometimes carried on spontaneously, in a revery; as is evident from our making articulate sounds in the same spontaneous manner to express our ideas. How often do those who are in the habit of talking much, such as children and some talkative superannuated persons, talk not only without a volition, but even contrary to a resolution not to do so.

A PRAGMATIC VIEW

OF THE

OPERATIONS OF THE WAKING MIND;

FOR THE PURPOSE OF EXEMPLIFYING THE PRECEDING PRINCIPLES.

I. WHEN a superabundance of animal and mental vigour has been accumulated during sleep, we make a transition from the sleeping to the active, conscious, waking state. This transition is, in general, independent of our wishes, and seems to be the result of the stimulating or exciting influence of the principle of animal vigour, accumulated during sleep. In some cases the act of awaking is produced by the uneasiness resulting from the accumulation of some of the products of the animal economy, such as a painful stricture on the bladder in persons advanced in years, and some other cases which might be cited; but these we should regard as mere exceptions to the general rule. Persons labouring under such difficulties, awake before the time in which the system would spontaneously return to the condition of cerebral preponderance or waking action. And if the accumulated vigour is not yet sufficient to produce this effect by itself, the auxiliary stimulus of the light of returning day will aid in exciting us to a waking state. This is demonstrated by the fact, that all persons can sleep longer and more soundly in a dark, than in a light room. Thus the adorable Author of our being admonishes us, that night is the proper time for sleep, and that the artificial perversions of day and night, which are met with in some of the more fashionable ranks of society, are not only contrary to the constitution of our nature, but also detrimental to our health.

II. The moment we make the transition from the sleeping to the waking state, the mind begins to act, and the body, particularly the muscles and organs of sense, become subservient to the mind. The first action of the waking mind seems generally to be spontaneous; in most cases it consists in the spontaneous inspection of the objects surrounding our bed. Sometimes this spontaneous inspection gives rise to voluntary action, such as the reflection, i. e., the voluntary retrospection, of some entities related to those spontaneously seen by us and recalled by them. Thus, from the light perceived in the room, the mind of pious habits will revert to the great Father of lights from whom it comes, and to the value of that spiritual light, which constitutes the Christian's greatest and most constant source of happiness on earth and expected bliss in heaven. The worldly-minded, from the inspection of the same light, will be led to reflect on some profitable business or pursuit which this light enables them to prosecute. In this manner more or less time is spent until the next prominent active operation is engaged in, viz.,

III. The *voluntary actions of physical agency*, such as rising, dressing, washing, &c. If we inquire in what manner these voluntary actions take place, we trace them to the constitutional inclination to obey the fitness of things actively prompting us to perform what is right, fit, suitable, profitable, or agreeable to the Divine will. We have a knowledge that it is right or fit to rise in the morning, and, invited by the joint influence of these several considerations, we voluntarily determine to perform the active operation. Here, then, we distinguish the following several things:

1. Our constitutional vigour compels us to act either spontaneously or voluntarily, i. e., it keeps the mind always engaged in some active process during waking hours.

2. The constitutional inclinations of the soul incline us to the end, viz., obedience to the fitness, or propriety, or constitution of things, or pursuit of pleasure.

3. Our knowledge of the manner in which that end will be accomplished, determines the means or individual acts to be performed. Inasmuch as duty, fitness, profit, love of pleasure, often all dictate the performance of the same action, persons of different character will frequently do the same act from different motives. This is a very important fact, and shows that the moral worth of actions must be judged by the view or motive from which they were performed. Those who are in the habit of being influenced by the love of gain, i. e., of self, and personal advantage, will rise early, because

they know early rising to be a means of enabling them to transact more business, and accumulate wealth.

4. The same view seems to be exemplified in the daily duties of men. The Christian is prompted, by an habitual regard to the first constitutional inclination, to obey the moral fitness or obligation, i. e., to obey the Divine will. He knows that the act of offering up his morning and evening sacrifice to the Author and Preserver of his life, is a means or instance of obedience to his will, and thus performs it with benefit and delight. With the same motive he pursues his daily business, because he regards it as a means of supporting his family and of glorifying his God. The man of the world engages in the same various occupations of the day from different motives, some more and others less honourable in their nature.

Thus, throughout the day, various active operations are voluntarily engaged in and pursued. The intervals between these voluntary operations are filled up with spontaneous active processes, the nature of which, as has been already explained, will be influenced by the prevailing habits of voluntary engagement of each individual. Thus, between the voluntary and spontaneous processes, between labours and intermissions of labour, the day is passed. To the several customary meals the individual is invited, partly by the recurrence of stated times, partly by the solicitations of his periodical appetites, and partly by other circumstances.

The close of the engagements of the day and

evening, ordinarily finds every individual somewhat languid, and finally a feeling of exhaustion or drowsiness ensues, and sooner or later the cerebral gives way to the preponderance of the ganglionic action, and he relapses into the state of sleep in which the vigour of his system, if he be in health, is again recruited, and he prepared to pass through the same routine of another day.

OF DREAMS.

Before closing the discussions of this volume, it may not be improper to add a few words on the subject of another species of spontaneous mental operations, which, though properly belonging to the *diseased* action of the soul, is of such frequent occurrence, and oftentimes attended by so slight a derangement of the bodily functions, that it is popularly, though erroneously, regarded as a healthy state of mental action.

The existence of mankind in this life, is divided by a clear and definite line into two very different states; that of dormancy, and the waking state. Between these two conditions, the life of man and of every other animate being is spent. It is our waking action that properly belongs to us as moral beings, and constitutes the appropriate agency of man in life. Indeed, it seems to be the design of the Author of our nature, that sleep should be, as in healthy subjects it actually is, an entire cessation from all conscious mental action. Habitual, deep sleep is a characteristic of sound general health; and those who enjoy the highest degree of it are not conscious of dreaming at all. It, however, not unfrequently happens, that disease affects our bodily functions, and disturbs the exact relation which ordinarily subsists between them and the soul, thus rendering less distinct the line of separation between our sleeping and our waking hours.

Sleep being properly a physical phenomenon, belonging in common to man, to irrational animals, and, in a subordinate sense also, to the vegetable kingdom, its particular discussion does not fall within the design of our work. In animals it is a most important and salutary restorative process of nature. It is a fact of daily observation, that the performance of the various mental and bodily operations, during our waking hours, exhausts the animal vigour of the system, and that this exhaustion in a healthy subject naturally predisposes to sleep, and results in it. Equally well established is the position, that the healthy subject awakes with the returning light of the morning, refreshed by sleep, and conscious of the feelings of renovated life and vigour, but without any recollection of having been disturbed by dreams. Yet it may, perhaps, be possible to excite dreams in a healthy subject, by designedly acting on his bodily senses during his sleep, and the same effect may with equal probability be produced, when such impression is made accidentally. But we suppose that no healthy person will have any recollection of dreams, unless thus acted on from without.

As we recollect some dreams ourselves, and as others have discovered from our talking, and walking, and other actions in sleep, that we did dream when we had no recollection of it ourselves, the probability is, that the soul is essentially active, that active operations are always going on spontaneously when we are asleep. This is rendered the more probable, because many of the dreams recollected by us, occurred, while others who observed us saw that our bodies were perfectly motionless, and supposed us to be enveloped in profound sleep. The most perfect repose of the body, therefore, affords no argument against the supposition of constant, spontaneous, mental processes.

Dreams may be regarded as those spontaneous trains of mental operation, which occur, when sleep has, in a great measure, suspended that self-control, through reason and volition, which we possess, and ordinarily exercise when awake. The term dream has often been confined to those trains of thought, of which we retain some recollection in our waking state. But it is also applied to the cases observed by others, though not recollected by ourselves, and is in its nature equally applicable to all other instances of mental action in sleep.

The correctness of this view of dreams is strongly corroborated by the fact, that we often have no recollection of them until some time after, when they are recalled to our memory by some related thought or occurrence, which would, on the principles of association, have recalled the same train, if it had first occurred when we were awake.

In dreams the exercise of reason and volition is not entirely suspended; although it is probably more in a defect of the exercise of these powers than in anything else, that dreams differ from our waking reveries or unrestricted spontaneous mental trains. We can and do sustain conversations either mentally or orally; we enact scenes, and perform various achievements; in short, all the different powers of the mind appear sometimes to be exerted in dreams, though with various degrees of imperfection. The farmer has sometimes engaged in threshing his grain, the lawyer has prepared his argument, and the preacher has imagined himself in the great assembly, and proclaimed to listless walls the truths of his holy religion. Such cases of somniloquism and somnambulism are within the knowledge of all. Other instances of still more singular and extraordinary morbid action of the mind are on record; but, as they do not properly fall within the limits of our science, we pass them in silence. From the map of the mind in its healthy state, which we have endeavoured to present, we perceive evidence enough that we are "wonderfully and fearfully," and, at the same time, benevolently "made;" and that we "should praise the Lord for his goodness and his wonderful works to the children of men."

It is an interesting peculiarity of dreams, that they often disregard the exact relations of time and space. Though the scenes are passed through with the utmost rapidity of waking thought, we sometimes suppose them all to have been real, and imagine that months, and sometimes years, have transpired in their occurrence. This singular circumstance may be owing, among other things, to two causes; to the fact, that in sleep we hold no communion with the visible world through the senses, by which, especially through the succession of night and day, and the aid of memory, we have learned to measure time, even in its minor fractions, and also the fact, that the exercise of judgment is chiefly suspended, by which, in our waking state, we can distinguish between fact and fiction.

From this view of the nature of dreams, it follows, that however fantastic and unnatural they may sometimes be, yet there will, on the whole, be some analogy between the dreams of any individual, and the habitual traits and peculiarities of his mind when awake. The poet, the mathematician, the lawyer, the politician, the agriculturist, the mechanic, and the minister of religion, will all find in their habitual dreams some special relation to their waking pursuits. Even the peculiarities of genius may often be traced in dreams. The moral character, which is frequently concealed during waking hours, will sometimes be betrayed in dreams; and the Rev. Mr. Young, in his "Record of Providence," relates an instance of a murderer in England, whose dreams led to his arrest and conviction, seven years after he had committed the crime, for which he was eventually executed.

It is also evident from the nature of dreams, that there can be nothing *ominous* or *prophetic* in them. We do not affirm that no dream was ever of this character. The Almighty doubtless can, and, as the Volume of Inspiration teaches, has communicated his will to some individuals in the form of dreams. But this was as certainly miraculous, as if the same communication had been made in open day by a voice from Heaven. What we maintain is, that dreams have nothing ominous or prophetic in their own nature. As they are spontaneous processes of the mind, they depend for their character, in some measure, on the voluntary waking habits, from which they result. As the peculiarities of these spontaneous processes arise from the suspension of the exercise of judgment and reason in sleep, they must evidently be entitled to less confidence than our waking thoughts. And the adventitious influences on the senses, which tend still farther to modify them, cannot fail to divest them of all claim to confidence. Such are our natural dreams. The fact, that one dream in a million has some resemblance to an event that succeeds, only proves that in these cases men may form somewhat correct anticipations of coming events when awake, and that the same conjecture may recur to them in their sleep, and constitute the burden of their prophetic dreams!

CHAPTER III.

RECAPITULATION, FOR THE PURPOSE OF REVIEWS.

Introduction. Methodology of Mental Philosophy. Difference between Mathematical and Mental Science, p. 13–20.

Mental Philosophy is that science which discusses the properties and operations of the human soul, p. 21. Various names have been attached to this science, such as *Metaphysics*, *Anthropology*, *Psychology*, p. 21, 22.

The proper materials of this science doubtless are, not the supposed faculties, of which we know nothing directly, but the known phenomena of the mind, and all those other entities, or existences, which exert an influence upon these phenomena, or are concerned in their production, p. 22, 23.

In the classification of mental operations, various systems have been adopted. The first, and most generally received in the English philosophical world, is that into *Nine Faculties of the Mind:* viz., Perception, Consciousness, Conception, Judgment, Memory, Reasoning, Conscience, Feeling, and Volition, p. 23, 24.

Dr. Reid, adopting in the main this classification, separates these faculties or powers into two general classes, viz., *Intellectual Powers* and *Active Powers*.

Mr. Stewart adds to these a third general class, viz., *Social Powers.*

Dr. Brown's celebrated division is into two classes: *External* and *Internal Affections or States of the Mind*, p. 25, 26.

The German division into three faculties, *Sensibilities, Understanding*, and *Will.* Professor Upham's view, p. 26.

Unable, after mature deliberation, to adopt either of these divisions, we propose another, founded, not upon the unknown and supposed faculties or essence of the mind, but upon those mental phenomena which are known to us. It is a threefold division, into *Cognitive Ideas, Sentient Ideas*, and *Active Operations*, p. 27.

Difference between this and the German system. (*a.*) In its principle. (*b.*) In its lines of division. (*c.*) In the contents of the different parts, p. 29.

On the extent of the several parts of this division, p. 30.

I. The *Cognitive class* embraces Perceptions, Acts of Consciousness, Conceptions, Judgments, Recollections, Results of Reasoning, and the Dictates or Decisions of Conscience, p. 31.

II. The *Sentient class* embraces Sensations, Emotions, Affections, and Passions, p. 34.

III. The *Active class* embraces Volitions, Processes of Reasoning, the Act of Memorizing, the Intellectual Act of communicating our thoughts to others, and some other processes, p. 36.

PART I.

COGNITIVE IDEAS.

Cognitive Ideas are acquired by the mind through the medium of certain parts of the body called organs of sense, when these organs are brought into a particular relation to external objects, and from the operations and powers of the mind of which we are conscious. In this acquisition we distinguish three things, p. 38, 39.

First. The external entity, or object of knowledge;

Secondly. The knowledge itself; and,

Thirdly. The process by which the knowledge is obtained.

CHAPTER I.

OF OBJECTIVE ENTITIES AS SUBJECTS OF OUR KNOWLEDGE, p. 39.

SECTION I.

Of the different classes of Entities, p. 40.

We constitutionally judge external entities to be possessed of real objectivity, i. e., to have an actual existence out of our minds. An *entity* is anything whatever, of which we can have an idea, p. 39.

The reality of the material universe, in general, is proved by the testimony of our senses, which we constitutionally judge to be true.

No reasoning is necessary on this point; nor could it make the testimony of our senses more certain.

The universe, as known to us, consists of nothing else than various combinations of properties.

Each of these combinations, as found in nature, is individual, and in some respects different from all others.

There are, nevertheless, gradations of similarity in these properties, which form a just basis for classification.

On such classification human language is framed, having words not for each individual substantive object, but (*a*) for the different properties, (*b*) for the relations subsisting between them, and (*c*) for the different *classes* of substantive objects, more or less generic, as stone, tree, quadrupeds, &c.

All objects known to us in the universe are either substantive objects, that is, objects to which several coexisting properties appertain, or they are individual properties, or relations between them.

All substantive objects may be referred to the following classes:

Solids, Liquids, Gases, the Ethereal or Incoercible Fluids, such as Light, Caloric, Electric Fluid, and the Magnetic Principle; Mind, Spirit, Glorified Bodies, Deity; together with Time, Space, and Number.

The relation of the properties of mind to mind itself is not different from that of the properties of other objects to their substratum, the objects themselves. Supposed plastic power rejected. Our knowledge of the Divine Being, how acquired, its nature.

The peculiarities of Time, Space, and Number:

as three universal, fundamental entities created by God, of entirely peculiar properties, in which, or in the forms of which, all other created entities exist, p. 55.

No one denies that we have ideas relating to all these classes of entities.

Not all are agreed as to the question whether they are ideas of reality, many supposing them to be mere ideas of the mind, without anything in nature corresponding to them, or causing them.

SECTION II.

Division of these Classes, p. 56.

All these classes of entities may be referred to two generic kinds, viz., *Absolute* and *Concrete* Entities.

Absolute are those of which we can conceive without reference to the concrete class. They are Space, Time, and Number.

Concrete are those of which we cannot conceive except as existing in the absolute class, or being related to it. They are all the others except Space, Time, and Number.

SECTION III.

Subdivision of Individual Entities, p. 57.

Entities may be subdivided into *Substantive*, *Adjective*, and *Composite*.

A *Substantive Entity* is that to which any number of coexisting properties appertains.

An *Adjective Entity* is any one property of a substantive entity.

A *Composite Entity* consists of two or more adjective entities, viewed in regard to some relation existing between them.

SECTION IV.

Relations of Entities.

1. Of Absolute Entities, p. 61.

(*a.*) Equality, diversity, antecedence, subsequence, &c., of *Time.*

(*b.*) Equality, difference, progression or ratio, plurality, minority, &c., of *Number.*

(*c.*) Equality, diversity, contiguity, remoteness, superiority, and inferiority of *Space.*

2. Of Concrete Entities to each other.

(*a.*) Similarity and diversity.

(*b.*) Contiguity or remoteness, as to space, time, and number.

(*c.*) Fitness, physical, intellectual, and moral.

(*d.*) Analogy.

(*e.*) Causation or agency. (*a.*) Mechanical, either uniform or contingent; (*b.*) Instinctive; and (*c.*) Moral.

3. Between Absolute and Concrete Entities.

These, (*a.*) in regard to number, are Addition, Multiplication, Subtraction, and Division; which are active relations of agency performed by the concrete entity man on our ideas of the absolute entity number. (*b.*) Space. (*c.*) Time.

These Relations are, (*a.*) Transitive or Intransitive.

(*b.*) Absolute or Hypothetical.

(*c.*) Retrospective, Present, or Prospective.

CHAPTER II.

OF OUR COGNITIVE IDEAS, OR MENTAL REPRESENTATIVES OF ENTITIES.

SECTION I., p. 69.

Of the exact Nature of those of our Ideas which are Knowledge.

They belong to the class of entities termed *Mind*, but are distinct from the mind, and are, with certain qualifications, representatives of things actually existing.

SECTION II.

Of the Criteria by which the Cognitive Class of Ideas is distinguished, p. 70.

I. The Cognitive Ideas have for their objects entities existing out of the mind, or some mental operation of our own or other minds.

II. The Cognitive Ideas are dependant for their character on the entities themselves.

III. The Cognitive Ideas presuppose the previous existence of the entities, from which they are derived.

SECTION III.

On the Nature and Sources of Error in our Cognitive Ideas, p. 74.

In order to obtain a correct view of this extremely important subject, it is necessary first to make some remarks upon the nature and divisions of truth.

All truths may be divided into three classes; viz.,

I. *Real* or *Objective Truths;* that is, objective entities existing in nature.

II. *Idealistic* or *Subjective Truths;* i. e., correct mental representatives of objective Entities.

View of the ancient Realists and Nominalists, and of modern German Realism and Idealism; Transcendental Idealism of Kant.

III. Nominal Truths; i. e., correct mental representatives expressed by proper words.

1. Sources of Involuntary Error, p. 80.

I. *Incorrect original mental representatives of entities.* These may arise,

(*a.*) From a hasty, superficial inspection of entities.

(*b.*) From forgetfulness of the exact mental representative originally obtained, and a consequent misstatement of it.

(*c.*) From listening to one part of a statement, and neglecting to listen to the whole.

II. *Incorrect selection of sounds and written words, to express to others the true mental representative which we really have.*

III. *The real imperfection of language,* which does not furnish words to express our ideas exactly on all subjects.

IV. *Mistakes in judging of the motives of others.*

V. *Unintentional illogical reasoning.*

VI. *Misapprehension of a correct sentence,* through ignorance of language.

2. Sources of Voluntary Error, p. 82.

I. *Intentional misstatement of entities, simple or composite.*

II. *Indulgence in the habit of mere high colouring, without directly stating a falsehood.*

III. *Errors resulting from voluntary ignorance.*

IV. *The indulgence of prejudice in regard to persons or things.*

V. *The indulgence of passion.*

SECTION IV.

Division of our Cognitive Ideas, p. 84.

They may be divided in two ways:

First, into Individual and Relative; and,

Secondly, into Retrospective, Present, and Prospective.

I. *Individual Knowledge.* To this class belongs our knowledge of every individual substance in nature, and also of every individual property belonging to any entity.

II. *Relative Knowledge.* To this class belongs our knowledge of composite entities; the greater part of our conceptions; geometrical axioms; the relations of numbers; metaphysical axioms; moral abstract propositions; and belief, immediate and acquired.

I. *Retrospective Knowledge*, p. 89. This is our knowledge of all our former cognitive, sentient, and active ideas, and is usually termed memory.

It may be divided into *spontaneous* and *voluntary.*

The extent of our spontaneous retrospective knowledge depends on,

(*a.*) The natural aptitude of the mind for this exercise; i. e., the natural retentiveness of memory.

(*b.*) The different degrees of logical accuracy with which our knowledge is arranged on paper, or in the mind, according to the different relations themselves which subsist between the entities.

(*c.*) The frequency with which the knowledge to be retained was reviewed by the mind, and the interest which was felt in it.

Our *retrospective knowledge* will be increased by the following methods :

(*a.*) By thinking frequently of the ideas intended to be recollected.

(*b.*) By reviewing those ideas together which we wish to recollect together, and in the very same order in which we wish to remember them.

(*c.*) By connecting them, in the act of memorizing, with some idea which we will be sure to recollect at the intended time.

(*d.*) By the habit of studying subjects rather than books.

(*e.*) By interesting our feelings in the subject.

Cases of extraordinary memory in persons in health, Kepler, Des Mesmes, Pascal, Cyrus, Themistocles.

There is reason to believe that the soul of every man naturally possesses a degree of mnemonic power, equal or greater than was exhibited by these distinguished men ; but this power is restrained by our bodily organs. Yet in eternity it will be released from the shackles of these organs, and will develop its expanded powers.

Remarkable cases in proof. A man in St. Thomas hospital.

Case cited by Dr. Pritchard ; another remarkable case cited by Coleridge :

Probable inference, that thought is indestructible,

and will be a prominent ingredient in the future retribution of the righteous and wicked.

Mnemonics; different systems.

The inventor of the earliest system, Simonides. Cicero's account of him. Account of the system.

The greater part of modern systems are based on the same principle.

Numerical mnemonics, Feinagle's system and table.

Dr. Niemeyer's directions to teachers and pupils for the improvement of memory.

Case of Rev. Mr. Uhlhorn, as an example of a well-trained memory.

II. *Present Knowledge*, p. 99.

III. *Prospective Knowledge*, p. 100. This is all our knowledge of the probable future existence of entities and their relations.

(*a.*) The *Subject* of our prospective knowledge is *always a composite entity;* viz., the relation between a present entity and a supposed future entity.

(*b.*) The *Bases* of prospective knowledge are *Analogy*, *Causation*, and *Revelation.*

CHAPTER III.

OF THE ORGANIC PROCESS BY WHICH WE OBTAIN OUR IDEAS, p. 105.

The influence of entities upon the mind is exerted either through the medium of every part of the body, such as shape, &c. ; or through particular parts of the body, called organs of sense. *In all cases*, actual contact of some kind is necessary.

Nervous connexion between the different organs and the brain. Phrenology, its results, when once fully settled, will not conflict with a correct system of mental philosophy.

The *Eye:* description of its constituent parts, the sclerotica, choroid, cornea, optic nerve, pupil, &c.

The eye affords us knowledge of colour, local direction, and expansion. Light is the medium, or, rather, the object of vision. The different colours. Distance not an original object of vision, but acquired.

Proof that extension is an original object of vision.

Solid shape is not originally perceived by sight, though peripheral shape is.

Apparent and relative, but not actual size, is taught by the eye. The distinctness of objects affords some indirect criterion of their distance. The image formed on the retina of the eye, inverted.

The objects of our perceptions are also excitants of feeling.

Variety and different degrees of feelings excited by the works of nature.

Attention necessary to the recollection of our perceptions.

The connexion between the image on the retina and the perception of the mind unknown.

The *Ear:* description of its parts, the external ear, the auditory passage, the tympanum, the auditory nerve, &c.

The atmosphere is the principal medium of sound; other elastic bodies. Sound is an idea of the mind, caused by the vibrations or pulsations of the agitated air upon the tympanum of the ear.

The various feelings attending our perceptions of sounds.

Sound the exclusive original result of our auditory organs; yet by practice we learn also to judge of local direction and distance. Of echoes. Improvement of the sense of hearing in the blind.

Organ of touch is the whole body, especially the hands. By this organ we acquire a knowledge of the solidity or fluidity of bodies, their shape, extension, smoothness or roughness, heat or cold; together with the feelings accompanying these perceptions.

Feeling of exhaustion from violent effort does not belong to the sense of touch. The idea of externity is the result of touch. Improvement of this sense, especially in the blind. Examples, Sanderson, &c. Method of printing for the blind.

The organ of *Taste:* description of its parts. Benevolent location of this organ. Different flavours; cognitive and sentient results of this sense.

Organ of *Smell:* description of it. Different odours—emitted by all objects that can be smelled. Knowledge of odour alone is the original cognitive result of smell; but by experience we learn to recognise different objects by their odour. Improvement of this sense. Quotation from Dr. Reid.

The different theories on the mode of the reciprocal influence of the body and the soul upon each other in general.

The theory of Occasionalism. Theory of pre-established harmony by Leibnitz.

Theories to account for a part of this influence, viz., in sensation through the bodily organs. Des Cartes's theory; Newton's view; Dr. Hartley's theory of nervous vibrations. The last-named theory is that of ideas, as something material, as films, or images, or phantasms, emanating from outward objects and passing through the medium of the organ of sense to the brain, and there perceived by the mind. Malebranche's account of this theory. This view charged on Mr. Locke by some writers, and denied by others. Result: no theory can explain this subject. The facts we know, and must admit—the mode we must refer to the great Author of our being.

PART II.

SENTIENT IDEAS, p. 146.

Feelings are those sentient states of the mind mediately or immediately excited by entities, simple or composite.

Feelings are known by the following criteria:

I. They have no object beyond themselves.

II. Our feelings are not so absolutely dependant for their character on entities without us, as our knowledge is.

III. Feelings are always preceded by a cognition of the entity which mediately or immediately produces them, p. 147.

CHAPTER I.

CLASSIFICATION OF OUR FEELINGS, p. 148.

All Feelings are either,

I. *Individual;* viz., those which have reference exclusively to ourselves; or,

II. *Relative;* viz., those which have a relation to some other sentient being, or other object.

Individual Feelings.
1. *Sensations;* feelings accompanying the perceptions of sight, touch, smell, &c.
2. Some *Emotions:* (*a.*) Intellectual emotions, of the sublime, beautiful. (*b.*) Moral emotions, connected with conscience.
3. Some of the *Affections:* (*a.*) Pleasant. (*b.*) Unpleasant.
4. Feeling attending the bodily Appetites.

Relative Feelings.
- *Benevolent* feelings: love, friendship, gratitude, veneration, &c.
- *Malevolent* feelings: hatred, malice, anger.
- *Sympathetic* feelings: condolence, pity, &c.
- *Antipathetic* feelings: envy, grudging, and what the Germans term Schadenfreude.

Remarks on the Analysis of Feelings.

CLASS I.

INDIVIDUAL FEELINGS.

1. Of *Sensations.* Twofold use of the term, both cognitive and sentient. The latter use preferred, and perception for the cognitive result.

2. *Emotions* are those transient excitements of feeling which are consequent on mental operations,

direct or reflective, other than perceptions through the organs of taste, smell, or touch. Emotions succeed cognitions or active operations; and sometimes are succeeded by desires or volition.

(*a.*) Intellectual emotions—of the sublime, its nature, objective and subjective; beautiful; ludicrous; wit; burlesque; mock-heroic—surprise, wonder, astonishment, amazement.

(*b.*) Moral emotions are those individual feelings of the mind which are consequent on the cognition of moral truth, conduct, or character. Moral emotions are the sentient part of acts of conscience. It is consequent on the cognitive or judicial ingredient of conscience, and precedes the impulsive.

They are either pleasant or painful, and, in popular language, termed feelings of approval or disapproval, though, strictly speaking, the approval or disapproval is judicial and cognitive.

Our moral emotions, in reference to particular acts, change if our judgment concerning them does.

3. The *Affections.* By affections we mean those habits, or habitual states of feeling, which are more durable than sensations or emotions.

They are either pleasant, as joy, cheerfulness, contentment; or painful, as penitence, discontent, sadness, despair.

4. Feelings connected with our bodily appetites, such as hunger and thirst.

CLASS II.

RELATIVE FEELINGS.

1. *Benevolent* feelings: those feelings which are favourable to the object on which they terminate.

Importance of these feelings to piety and social happiness. Benevolence; love, parental, filial, conjugal; gratitude, friendship, respect, confidence, &c. Love to God, adoration.

2. *Malevolent*, or defensive feelings, are those painful relative feelings which involve hostility, and a disposition to injure the beings on which they terminate. These affections were, before the fall, purely defensive and good: in our fallen state, often offensive and sinful.

3. *Sympathetic* feelings are those relative affections of the mind, which imply similarity or congeniality to the feelings of the being on which they terminate. They are either pleasant or painful. We sympathize most freely with those whose feelings are similar to the prevailing state of our own minds at the time. They are such as compassion, pity, commiseration.

4. *Antipathetic* feelings are those relative feelings which, though they have reference to some other being, imply only opposition of feeling, but not intention of action, such as envy, jealousy, disgust, grudging, fear, dread, horror, &c.

Feelings may also be divided into Sensuous, Intellectual, and Moral; and into Present, Retrospective, and Prospective.

CHAPTER II.

OF ENTITIES AS EXCITANTS OF FEELING, p. 178.

SECTION I.

All feeling, like knowledge, may be traced, mediately or immediately, to entities without the mind, p. 178.

SECTION II.

Entities of every class possess some tendency, though very different in degree, to excite feeling in the mind, p. 180.

SECTION III.

The degrees in which different entities possess this exciting power are very different, and can be accurately learned only from experience; nor can any organ originally afford us this information, except the one through which the feeling is produced, p. 181.

I. The strongest influence is exerted by entities when they are brought into contact with their appropriate organ.

II. The next strongest, when we have a prospective knowledge that we shall, at some future time, probably be the subjects of their influence.

III. The next strongest, when they excite retrospective feeling.

IV. Sympathetic feeling is weaker than its corresponding direct feeling.

V. The least influence is exerted by them, when we view merely their abstract tendency to produce feeling.

SECTION IV.

Entities of the classes of solids and liquids excite more feeling, and exert more motive power when near, than when far off, p. 183.

SECTION V.

The manner in which entities act in exciting feeling, seems to be very similar to that observed in the production of knowledge, p. 183.

SECTION VI.

In feeling, as in knowledge, two things are necessary; viz.,

I. The action of the entity on its appropriate organ; and,

II. The attention of the mind to that organ, p. 184.

CHAPTER III.

SUSCEPTIBILITY OF THE MIND FOR FEELING, AND LAWS OF FEELING.

First law. Sensation, no less than cognition, is an attribute of the mind and not of the body, p. 185.

Second law. The original susceptibility of different minds for feeling is very different in degree. Influence of temperament: phlegmatic, choleric &c., temperament, p. 186.

Third law. Excepting this diversity, which results from the different temperaments, the relative degree of susceptibility for the influence of different entities is in all minds naturally the same, p. 187.

Fourth law. Feeling is, in a great measure, involuntary at the time, p. 188.

Fifth law. But we can add to or subtract from the duration or intensity of the feeling, by confining our attention to the exciting object, or directing it to another, p. 188.

Sixth law. When any one feeling or purpose becomes dominant and habitual in the soul, all others inconsistent with it are impaired, p. 188.

Seventh law. The two constitutional inclinations of the soul exert an influence upon the tendency of entities to excite feeling in the mind, p. 189.

Eighth law. Entities always exert a greater influence when first presented, on account of their novelty, p. 190.

Ninth law. Feelings produced in the same person, by the same entity, at different times, may be different, p. 190.

Tenth law. The susceptibility for feeling is increased by attentive practice, p. 191.

Eleventh law. Intense and long-continued feeling exhausts and fatigues the system, p. 192.

Twelfth law. Susceptibility for feeling declines with age and with the decline of the constitution, though that be premature, p. 192.

Thirteenth law. A negligent review of entities diminishes their tendency to produce feeling, p. 192.

Fourteenth law. Time wears off retrospective feeling, p. 192.

Fifteenth law. Feeling is, in general, not instantly excited, as knowledge is, p. 194.

Sixteenth law. The feelings connected with the gratification of our periodical appetites are peculiar, p. 194.

I. They are stronger in proportion to the length of previous abstinence, unless that be extreme.

II. They are increased by the frequent attention of the soul to the entities capable of gratifying those appetites.

III. This feeling is diminished, and eventually suspended, by gratification.

IV. It is interrupted by the debility and increased by the vigour of the body.

(*a.*) From the preceding considerations, it follows that we are responsible in a great degree for our individual feelings, as also for the habitual state of our feelings or affections, p. 194.

(*b.*) That feelings are individual, and transient, and continue no longer than the attention of the mind is directed to the entity or to the cognitive idea with which they are connected, p. 195.

(*c.*) By the *state* of our affections or feelings, is meant the increased or diminished degree of habitual susceptibility for feelings of any particular kind, produced by continued voluntary practice, and also the increased or diminished tendency to the spontaneous recurrence of the ideas of the entities, which produce the feelings in question, p. 195.

PART III.

ACTIVE OPERATIONS.

Active Operations constitute the most important feature of our character as beings responsible to God, p. 198.

The *criteria* by which they are known:

I. Knowledge and feeling are inward effects produced from without. Active operations are outward effects, or operations tending *ad extra*, produced from within.

II. Knowledge and feeling require the entities exciting them to have a previous existence; but the active operations contemplated by our volitions, are future.

III. The character of our active operations depends but little upon the entities upon which they are exerted.

The *materials* on which our active operations are performed, p. 201.

I. The external objective entities of the different classes.

II. Past mental operations of every class.

III. The natural signs by which these representatives are expressed.

CHAPTER I.

DIVISION AND DISCUSSION OF THE ACTIVE OPERATIONS OF THE SOUL.

All active operations are alike as it respects mere activity, but differ in regard to the end contemplated; in the operation performed; in the results of the action; and in the objects on which they terminate, p. 202.

SECTION I.

Of Inspection.

Inspection is that active operation in which the attention of the soul is directed to some entity, simple or composite; prospective, present, or retrospective, with a view to acquire some knowledge concerning it, p. 203.

The *specific object* of inspection, in *present entities*, may be,

I. To obtain more correct mental representatives of the properties of entities, p. 205.

II. To give more vividness to our mental representatives of them.

III. To ascertain their relations.

In *retrospective entities*, it may be,

I. To revive their representatives, p. 206.

II. To view their relations to each other.

Inspection embraces the voluntary operations of *Perception*, *Consciousness*, *Conception*, *Judgment*, *Recollection*, *Analytic Reasoning*, and *Conscience.*

The *Act of Memorizing* explained.

Analytic reasoning explained.

In all our reasonings we proceed on the implication of certain laws of human belief, which are admitted and acted on by all men.

Fundamental Laws of Human Belief.

1. That the testimony of our senses, clearly ascertained, is true.

2. That the testimony of conscience can be relied on.

3. That memory, as far as it is distinct, may be relied on.

4. The other operations of the mind, such as reasoning and judgment, may be relied on, with a certainty proportioned to the circumstances of the case.

5. That all men will naturally speak the truth, when they have no motive to practise deception.

6. That every act of consciousness presupposes a conscious being, the soul.—Case of Rev. Dr. Brown.

7. That every act of memory, or succession of acts of consciousness, implies our personal identity.

Other truths universally implied in reasoning.

8. That the laws of nature and known properties of entities will continue unchanged.

On the uniformity of these laws the enterprise of man and the business of life in general depend.

9. That different kinds of truth possess different kinds and degrees of evidence, producing different degrees of belief.

SECTION II.

Arrangement, p. 217.

Arrangement is that active operation of the soul by which we select some from among the mass, either of external entities themselves, or of our mental representatives of them, and place them, as wholes or units, in a particular order, with a view to a specific purpose.

The *purposes* of this arrangement, and the principles upon which it may be made, are various:

I. We may arrange them according to any one of the various relations of entities to each other; sameness, diversity, &c.

II. We may arrange them according to any principle of genus, species, &c.

III. We may arrange them according to the probative relation of entities to a given proposition, or to the human mind.

Here is included all syllogistic reasoning.

SECTION III.

Modification.

Modification is that active operation of the soul

by which we take some from among our mental representatives of real entities (rarely the objective entities themselves), and bring them into such forms or combinations as do not correspond to realities, p. 225.

This operation differs from the preceding; because,

I. The operations of Inspection and Arrangement are performed as frequently on objective entities themselves as on our mental representatives of them; whereas, that of Modification is conversant chiefly about our mental representatives.

II. The former two operations take our mental representatives of substantive entities as wholes or units, and leave them such throughout all the process of their influence; but Modification changes them from their natural state, and brings them into forms and combinations which do not actually correspond to real entities.

Modification embraces,

I. The process of *Abstraction* or *Generalization.*

Among the results of this are, (*a.*) Geometrical axioms; (*b.*) Metaphysical axioms; (*c.*) Mathematical truths; (*d.*) Moral general principles.

Objection to Kant's view of these truths, as knowledge *à priori.*

II. *Fictitious combinations of ideas.*

(*a.*) Fictitious simple entities: (*b.*) Fictitious composite entities or relations, imagination, fancy, wit, burlesque, painting, sculpture.

SECTION IV.

Mental Agency concerned in the production of Physical Action.

This embraces all voluntary control over the entire muscular system, by which alone motion is produced in any part of the body, p. 233.

The mode of this influence, of the action of mind on muscle, is inexplicable.

In all cases of voluntary physical action, we can distinguish the following mental processes:

I. The volition to exert the bodily organ.

II. The attention of the soul to that organ.

III. The inspection of the material on which the operation is to be performed.

IV. The active process of the mind conducting and regulating the physical action.

SECTION V.

Intellectual Intercourse.

This process consists in exciting in others the ideas which they themselves have already obtained from those entities on which we wish them to think, and exciting them in such order, and in such combinations, and with such adjective properties annexed, as we wish them to entertain, p. 235.

This process is carried on in different ways:

I. By *speaking*, or *expressing our ideas by articulate sounds.*

We do not, however, by speaking, excite in others identically the same ideas which we connect with our words, but such ideas as they formerly attached to the words which we utter. Every idea of a speaker is succeeded by the following operations before it accomplishes its design, p. 240:

(*a.*) The idea of the speaker himself.

(*b.*) The recollection of the idea of the sound formerly associated with that idea by the speaker.

(*c.*) His volition to articulate a similar sound.

(*d.*) The articulating action of his organs on the expiring breath, to produce a similar sound.

(*e.*) The hearer's idea of the sound produced by the speaker's voice.

(*f.*) The hearer's recollection of the similar sound which he himself had often made.

(*g.*) The recurrence of the idea which he formerly connected with the similar sound made by himself.

The structure of the human articulating organs is such, that all men naturally make certain elementary sounds; alphabetic sounds are, therefore, substantially the same in all languages, p. 241.

II. By *gestures* and *muscular action of the countenance*, p. 242. Pantomime.

III. By *written signs.*

(*a.*) Alphabetical letters; (*b.*) Arithmetical figures and signs; (*c.*) Musical notes.

SECTION VI.

Composition.

Composition is not a distinct active operation, but is complex, consisting of voluntary inspection and arrangement of ideas of entities, simple or composite, together with the act of expressing the ideas thus arranged, by signs, on paper, p. 243.

What are called new or original ideas are merely old relations, for the first time viewed by the mind.

SECTION VII.

Attention, p. 245.

Attention is likewise not a distinct operation; because,

I. We cannot conceive of it as acting by itself, but only in connexion with some other operation of the mind.

II. It does not give us any results of its action, distinct from those of the active operation with which it is combined.

III. It is common to all the active operations.

IV. It seems only to be a property of the active operation, conducted at the time.

Attention is *the energy of the soul exerted on some active operation.*

The causes which excite attention appear, in general, to be these:

I. A volition to bestow attention on the performance of some active operation.

II. The present interest or pleasure felt in the operation itself.

III. Some impression from without made through the bodily organs.

CHAPTER II.

THE MODE OF OCCURRENCE OF THE FIVE ACTIVE OPERATIONS.

Active Operations are either *Voluntary* or *Spontaneous*, p. 248.

SECTION I.

Of the Voluntary Occurrence of the Active Operation.

The active processes of the soul are *voluntary*, when undertaken from deliberate choice, p. 249.

Do we perform acts of choice ?

Yes ; the certainty of our performing such acts rests upon the same basis with the certainty of our other mental operations, such as knowledge and feeling.

What is the nature of acts of choice ?

I. All men agree that acts of choice differ from acts of necessity.

II. It is only for such actions that we accuse or excuse ourselves.

III. All men agree that only for their own acts of choice, and the consequences of them, can they really and justly be held responsible, either by God or man.

IV. Every reflecting man, who has attained mature development of mind, is conscious of the fact that he can and ought to regulate the voluntary actions of his life according to certain fixed rules and principles, p. 250.

But the soul is not left entirely free from bias in the performance of these acts of choice. There are two *constitutional inclinations* by which it is materially influenced.

I. The inclination to *Action in accordance with the fitness of things, moral, intellectual, and physical.* This inclines us naturally to speak the truth, and to do whatever is right. Crimes are the only exception to the observance of this constitutional inclination. This sense of obligation is universal. It embraces in it the impulsive part of

The Operations of Conscience.

The operations of conscience are complex, including a judicial, a sentient, and an impulsive ingredient.

Conscience, in its impulsive feature, is an original faculty. Each of its features is treated of in its appropriate part of this work.

The structure of all languages implies the existence and operations of conscience.

All men judge the authority of conscience to be supreme.

Conscience essential to our character as moral agents.

The influence of this constitutional inclination, like that of every other power of the soul, can be increased by obedience to its dictates and diminished by disobedience.

II. The inclination to *Well-being*, or the enjoyment of pleasure, present and ultimate, and the avoiding of pain. This embraces, 1. Love of Life: this is universal, and of great utility in its effects. On this principle is based the right of self-defence when unjustly assailed by personal violence.

The case the same in principle, whether the assailant be a serpent or ravenous beast, or a robber or murderer.

2. Love of esteem or power. Proper use of this principle. Its abuse.

3. Love of property or possession. Its use and abuse—avarice.

4. Love of novelty—curiosity.

5. Sensuality. 6. Love of Science. 7. Social Inclination, &c.

These inclinations are not faculties, nor mental operations, nor habits, but natural characteristics of the soul.

The first of these inclinations is evidently the more noble; but in the natural state of man the second preponderates.

These inclinations do not act irresistibly. The soul is secondly influenced by

External Entities.
1. Our own bodies, acting upon us through the bodily appetites.
2. All other entities in the universe, p. 264.

But these entities act not with irresistible force, else men would be compelled always to act virtuously, since God has made the inducements to virtue stronger than those to vice. Men can and do resist these motives.

Desires—their nature.

The native activity of the soul prompts us to action.

The constitutional inclinations of the soul determine the general character of the ends, or results, at which we aim.

Our knowledge presents to us the various entities with their different and relative properties, by active operations upon which the proposed end may be attained in various ways and in different degrees.

The different entities exert a motive power proportional to their relative adaptation to accomplish the end proposed; and, finally, in view of all these circumstances, the soul freely determines in its choice of the different means of attaining the desired end. Our definition therefore is,

The Will is *that power of the soul by which it* FREELY DETERMINES, *in view of motives, either now or hereafter, absolutely or conditionally, to perform or not to perform some one or more of the five active operations*, p. 270.

SECTION II.

Of the Spontaneous Occurrence of the Active Operations, p. 273.

There are two marks of difference between Voluntary and Spontaneous active operations.

I. The former are the result of volition in their commencement: the latter, not.

II. The former are carried on with much more attention and energy than the latter.

We are responsible to God for all our spontaneous actions.

I. *Spontaneous Inspection*, p. 278.

In the spontaneous inspection of entities or their

mental representatives, the mind is found to proceed in several uniform ways :

1. It seems to follow the relations of the entities which are the subjects of its inspection ; especially sameness, contrariety, contiguity, and causation.

2. It has a tendency to pursue the train of those entities, which have most frequently been the subjects of its voluntary attention.

3. It more readily recurs to those objects which have lately been the subjects of its attention.

4. It pursues more frequently those entities which excite the most pleasant feelings, and gratify the second constitutional inclination.

5. It is diverted from its spontaneous operations by the immediate action of some entities through the bodily organs.

6. It is interrupted by volition.

II. *Spontaneous Arrangement*, p. 281.

This operation is sometimes carried on spontaneously. Every figure of comparison consists of spontaneous arrangements according to the relation of similarity expressed in words.

III. *Spontaneous Modification*, p. 282.

This occurs very seldom, especially in persons of veracity.

IV. *Mental Process regulating our Physical Action*, p. 282.

This is very often exercised spontaneously. All habits of bodily action are spontaneous operations of this kind. But some actions apparently spontaneous are instinctive.

V. The Process of *Intellectual Intercourse*, p.

283, is sometimes carried on spontaneously in a revery; as is evident from our making articulate sounds, in the same spontaneous manner, to express our ideas.

PRAGMATIC VIEW, &c.

I. When a superabundance of animal and mental vigour has been accumulated during sleep, we make a transition from the sleeping to the active, conscious, waking state.

II. The moment we make the transition from the sleeping to the waking state, the mind begins to act, and the body, particularly the muscles and organs of sense, becomes subservient to the mind.

Its first action is generally spontaneous, but this soon gives way to,

III. The voluntary actions of physical agency; which are performed in accordance with the principles laid down in part iii., chap.. ii., sect. i.

IV Other voluntary operations of various kinds are undertaken; and the interval between them filled up by such as are spontaneous.

DREAMS.

Dreams are those spontaneous trains of mental operation which occur when sleep has in a great measure suspended that self-control through reason and volition, which we possess, and ordinarily exercise, when awake.

Dreams can have nothing ominous or prophetic in them, unless they are miraculous.

THE END.

Commendatory Letters—continued.

From Rev. D. M'CONAUGHY, *D.D., President of Washington College, Pa.*

I have read with much interest Dr. Schmucker's late work on mental science. It seems to me to exhibit an accurate and intelligible development of the phenomena of mind. They are all included in his divisions, and all are assigned to their proper classes. Those classes are entirely distinguishable and distinct. The objects which give rise to the various mental phenomena are well defined; and the resulting knowledge, feeling and action, are explained in a manner which is verified by the consciousness of every man who attentively reads the history of his own mind. Accustomed to terms and phrases which seem almost consecrated by their long association with psychological subjects, the new nomenclature strikes the reader as singular, but in import it is precise and significant. I congratulate the author upon having presented to the literary world a volume embracing so much useful information upon the constitution, laws, and operations of the mind, and I hope that its beneficial influence will be widely felt, and its merit be duly appreciated.

From Rev. S. BOYER, *A.M., Principal of the Academy in York, Pa.*

I concur in the opinion of Dr. M'Conaughy, believing the work of Dr. Schmucker to be a production of much merit, and well adapted not only for intelligent popular readers, but also for use as a text-book in colleges and academies.

Extract of a letter from Rev. M. CALDWELL, *Professor of Metaphysics and Political Economy in Dickinson College, Carlisle, Pa.*

I have examined and re-examined the work of Dr. Schmucker on Mental Philosophy, and, I must say, with increased satisfaction. I am pleased with the spirit in which the author has conducted his investigations, and doubt not but many of his original views will be adopted by future writers on the human mind. Notwithstanding the forbidding terminology adopted in the work, its truly philosophical character will cause it to be read with interest by every lover of mental science.

From the Rev. Dr. MORRIS, *of Baltimore.*

...It has long been known that the learned author contemplated the publication of his system of Psychology; and from the representations of its character by his pupils, to whom it has been taught for some years; it has been looked for with impatience. We are aware of his fondness for such investigations and his metaphysical acumen, and we had a right to expect a work of uncommon character and of an original cast—hence we have a new and original system. This work presents an admirable specimen of rigid analytical induction. It is all close, solid, massive argumentation. The lines of division are distinctly drawn—the whole subject is nicely dissected—each part is separately laid before you, and then, again, its connexion with the whole plainly demonstrated.

From the Methodist Quarterly Review.

...Designing the work, as the title intimates, for a text-book in colleges and academies, Dr. Schmucker has judiciously confined himself to a rigid outline of his system, leaving detailed illustration chiefly to the viva voce instructions of the teacher. This is a feature of the work which pleases us much. We are presented, as it were, with an anatomical skeleton, which shows us clearly the connexion and ramification of the operations of the mind; with a chart of our road, which may guide us safely as Ariadne's clew through the labyrinthine windings of the darksome way. Perhaps the most interesting and valuable portion of the volume is the third part: that treats of the active operations of the mind under five heads. inspection, arrangement, modification, mental direction of physical action, and the process of intellectual intercourse between different minds. We are convinced that those who have most deeply studied the constitution of the human mind will here find much matter for profitable reflection. We cannot conclude this review without a hearty recommendation of the work to the attention of instructers.

From the American Biblical Repository, in an editorial notice.

Dr. Schmucker, if we mistake not, has accomplished a valuable work by the clearness and simplicity of his division of the elements of this science. There is no affectation of novelty; but the author, having thoroughly studied the works of others, has carefully subjected every principle to the test of his

Commendatory Letters—continued.

own experience. The result is the suggestion of what he regards some important modifications and improvements in the arrangement and classification of the materials of the science; and which, as a system, may perhaps with some propriety be denominated *new*. This system has been constructed with great care and thoroughness. It is sufficiently condensed in the volume before us, and is stated and illustrated with unusual precision and clearness. It is in these respects well adapted for use as a text-book in academies and colleges. The difference between the principles of this system and those of others is only occasionally referred to, and the work is wholly free from that polemical aspect which has too mch affected most philosophical discussions. On the whole, we anticipate a favourable reception of this new system, as a concise, intelligible, and convenient class-book of mental science.

From the Lutheran Observer.

Dr. Schmucker's work bears the same relation to the present stage of mental science which was sustained by the immortal essay of Locke to the systems by which it was surrounded... The great incantation by which Locke wrought such wonders was not that he produced anything positively new, nor that his system advanced facts before unheard of; but that he remodelled, simplified, and stated with more correctness, and a reduction to truer *principles*, what had long been acknowledged as truth.... It is in these important particulars that we trace the resemblance between Locke's Essay on the Human Understanding and Dr. Schmucker's Psychology. The great (might I be allowed the expression), the transcendent merit of this Psychology, is its new division and its accurate definition. Completeness and order are the characteristics alike of the mind and writing of its author. . . To the Psychology, the cherished product of years of careful investigation, those qualities belong in an eminent degree, and moral evidence beneath his pen has assumed almost the simplicity of element, and clearness of mathematical demonstration.... In our opinion this work presents the clearest, most intelligible, and satisfactory view which has yet been furnished of the workings of the inner man.

From a review of the work in the New World.

...Casting away the trammels of authority, Dr. Schmucker has dared to be an original and independent thinker. Those who read the book will not fail to perceive that it is not the sole product of the study of the patriarchs of the science, but that its original features give the author a place alongside those patriarchs Locke, Reid, Stewart, and Brown Dr. Schmucker has given us a new analysis of the mental operations, by which their synthesis is illustrated and rendered more intelligible. The antagonism of his system to transcendentalism is decided. The friends of the German or transcendental school may naturally be expected to resist Dr Schmucker's publication, which, belonging to the school of Locke and Reid, was professedly and fairly constructed by inductive investigations.

From the Southern Literary Messenger of May, 1842.

...For purposes of education, we know of no book more available than a concise and well-arranged treatise on Psychology, or a system of Mental Philosophy founded on consciousness and common sense, by one of the able theological professors at the Gettysburg Institution. It is expressly designed for the use of academies and colleges, and we commend it to the attention of teachers and all interested in education.

From the Philadelphia Observer.

...It gives us pleasure to commend this work to the attention of the public. It contains the results of long continued thought and inquiries of a distinguished scholar and able writer on a science which is intimately connected with the progress of truth in almost every department of knowledge....We consider the work eminently worthy of the attention and study of ministers, students, and intelligent popular readers.

☞ In addition to the above, numerous notices, equally favourable, of Schmucker's Psychology, have been received from the most respectable sources, from some of which the publishers may hereafter present brief extracts.

Commendatory Letters—continued.

From Rev. Dr. AYDELOTT, *President of Woodward College, Cincinnati.*

An *original* work on the mind by a well-qualified writer cannot but be valuable and instructive. Should it even develop no new facts or views, still, as an independent witness, his testimony to what was before known must be important. But in both these points of view the Mental Philosophy of Dr. Schmucker is of much value. The section on Inspection or Perception (p. 293–313, 2d ed.), to give only one instance, certainly presents a novel view of the subject. It is also perfectly clear, though exceedingly condensed, and yet, we believe, contains more satisfactory information on the subject than can be found in any other writer.

It is scarcely necessary to add, that the results of Dr. Schmucker's observations and reflections always accord with the oracles of God, and thus furnish a species of evidence for Christianity peculiarly valuable in this inquiring age. The Bible and true philosophy will ever be found in perfect harmony. The poof of this, however, is *cumulative*, and it is the glory of modern science to have added so much to it. The work before us is here worthy of great praise. No Christian can rise from the study of it without being better prepared to give a reason for the hope that is in him, and, as we would hope, without an increase of that blessed charity which is the essence of holiness and aliment of happiness. I cannot, therefore, but regard the Psychology of Dr. S. as an important contribution to the text-books of colleges and other seminaries of learning.

From Rev. Dr. DICKINSON, *Professor of Sacred Rhetoric and Pastoral Theology in Theol. Sem. at Auburn, N. Y.*

I have just finished a somewhat careful examination of Dr. Schmucker's late treatise on the Philosophy of the Mind, and, I am happy to say, received decided impressions of its worth. There is ample evidence of original and patient investigation, and a thorough acquaintance with the general subject of mental science. In the nomenclature of the work there is a good deal of novelty; but the terms are all well-defined, the style throughout is chaste and clear, and the arrangement exceedingly lucid. Dr. Schmucker's classification of the mental phenomena has, I think, some important advantages; and I discern in it little that seems liable to objection. The work cannot fail to be read with interest and profit by any one devoted at all to metaphysical investigations. And I regard it as admirably adapted to elementary instruction in a vitally important branch of education, uniting, as it does, great condensation of matter with clearness and force of illustration.

From Rev. S. NORTH, LL.D., *President of Hamilton College, New-York.*

I have examined Dr. Schmucker's recent work on Mental Philosophy, and take great pleasure in saying that I think it in most respects well adapted to the important purpose for which it has been prepared. It is designed especially for use as a text-book in academies and colleges, and for this it appears to be admirably fitted, not only by the general correctness and soundness of its views, but by the concise, and clear, and comprehensive manner in which it exhibits the leading facts and principles pertaining to this important department of science. We deem it no inconsiderable merit, that while it exhibits a commendable familiarity with the writings of other philosophers, it is at the same time entirely free from a polemic and controversial spirit, and obviously imbodies the results of much original and independent thinking.

From Mr. N. C. BROOKS, A.M., *Principal of the High School, Baltimore.*

I have examined with much care Dr. Schmucker's System of Mental Philosophy, designed for the use of colleges and academies. I am much pleased with the arrangement of the matter, and with the clearness and precision of the language.

From the Providence R. I. Journal.

We have been much gratified by an attentive perusal of the Psychology of Dr. Schmucker, and have never met with any work on Mental Philosophy better adapted to the *general reader*. Books of this class are usually passed unnoticed, except by students and those who have a particular taste for them; but in the work before us the author seems to have *adapted his style and mode of reasoning to those whose minds are not generally turned to philosophical works*, as well as for colleges and academies.

www.ingramcontent.com/pod-product-compliance
Lightning Source LLC
LaVergne TN
LVHW020215110826
845151LV00003B/730

* 9 7 8 1 4 2 5 5 3 3 4 6 5 *